Teaching
the Child
Under Six

Third Edition

Also by James L. Hymes, Jr.

Editor

For Children

With Lucia Manley Hymes

Contents

Preface

My first work with children under six was in 1934. I was a research assistant in the nursery school of the Child Development Institute of Teachers College, Columbia University. My job: recording day after day the behavior of three- and four-year-olds as they played, worked, talked, fought. That was the beginning of an involvement with young children that has persisted for almost half a century.

In this long span of years I have participated in the three major national programs for young children. Beginning in 1936 I worked with the federally-financed, depression-born WPA Nursery Schools, our first big program of free public nursery education.

From 1943 to 1945, wartime, when our first nationwide federally supported child care effort was underway, I was director of the two Kaiser Child Service Centers in Portland, Oregon. Industry-supported, industry-based, these were the world's largest child care centers. Open 24 hours a day, 364 days a year, we reached a peak attendance of 1,005 children 18 months of age to 6 years. But it was not size alone that made the Kaiser centers special. They were that rarity—child care centers with a highly trained staff of teachers, aides, nutritionists, nurses, and social workers. The centers were also unusual in everlastingly reaching out for new ways to serve parents as well as children. We developed Home Service Food; infirmaries for mildly ill children; Special Service groups for youngsters who needed only an occasional day of emergency care; and school-age groups on weekends, holidays and during the summers.

Twenty years later, as a member of the National Planning Committee which developed the design for Head Start, I helped in the next massive effort to serve young children and their families.

Between these high points were other experiences. I was the director of a unique "co-op," a private experimental school for children two years of age through junior high. And Professor of Early Childhood Education, first at the State University of New York at New Paltz, then at George Peabody College for Teachers in Nashville and, lastly, at the University of Maryland where I also directed the University Nursery-Kindergarten.

This book, a new edition, is an outgrowth of this long involvement with young children. It is a very personal book. Throughout I present my point of view — one of great respect for children, of great respect for parents, of great respect for learning.

The book also reflects my deep concern about the state of our world, and the need for early childhood education to contribute to its betterment. Before my 1934 work in nursery education, my undergraduate major at Harvard College had been International Law and Relations. It may seem like a giant leap from one field to the other — from the study of world and domestic peace to the study of young children — but I came to see that the two fields have an intimate tie. Different as they may sound, both lead to the same end: better people, more decent living.

Since 1934, while lecturing, teaching, and traveling in every state, I have seen good programs for young children — and some not so good. Often, when a program failed young children and their parents, the failure seemed to me due to lack of a philosophy. I am persuaded that good teachers, first of all, must hold strong commitments and convictions from which their practices flow. By setting forth my own values, I hope this book stimulates teachers to think through their own beliefs.

Some of the schools that worried me seemed to fail for lack of skill and know-how. I hope, therefore, that teachers will find this book to be down-to-earth and practical. It does not try to spell out every classroom practice or to do all of a teacher's thinking so that teaching becomes simply a matter of remembering. It *does* try to indicate how one point of view translates into the specifics of a teacher's work.

This is a book for undergraduates, graduate students, and for teachers on the job to study. A lot of thought has gone into its organization to give it a clear focus on the many parts of a teacher's job: in the classroom, as a member of a profession, and, outside the classroom, as a child advocate. You can call the book a textbook. I hope it also proves to be a book that you will read with pleasure and with the feeling of being challenged and stirred.

Built into this book are two long-cherished dreams. The first: that the day would come, and soon, when all young children would have the chance to begin their schooling in a new "first grade." That *first* grade would be for three year olds. Fours would go to "second grade" and fives to "third grade." I have worked for many years for free public education that would be available to every child from age three on, for whatever length of day or week or year, and with whatever services, the child's needs or the family's needs required.

My second dream: that this extension of public education downward would be *good* education. No, not merely "good" — superb! Fitted beautifully to the young children who would be coming, and to our country's special style, and consistent with sound scholarship.

Through the years there has been a small gain in one of these directions. Public kindergartens have become much more available. However, this gain has been accompanied by a worrisome loss in quality. Our expanding kindergartens, in particular, but all of our programs for young

children—private nursery schools, Head Start, child care centers—have been buffeted (I think more so than in the past) by the old pressure to be "prep" schools—training centers getting children ready for "real" school at age six. Obviously no one benefits if we have more groups for young children, but the groups turn out to be geared to some older, different age.

This edition has added emphases that I hope will make a contribution in light of this present-day national scene in early education. It calls on all teachers of young children to take on the role of child advocate. Today it is not enough for any of us only to do a good job with our own children within our own classroom. The continuing shortage of programs plus the increasing threats to quality create a pressing need for teachers to be good friends to *all* young children, and to know how to act on their allegiance.

Secondly, and closely related, is a stronger emphasis on markedly improved communication between teachers of young children and two powerful sets of humans who can make or break a program: school administrators and parents.

A third emphasis is a more detailed discussion of how teachers of children under six can "teach the basics." The teaching of reading and the teaching of good behavior are deep concerns of parents and administrators. They must be deep concerns of teachers, too. It is very important that those who work with children under six be skilled in teaching the basics—*teaching them in ways that are appropriate to young children!* We must do these very important jobs effectively and competently. The only way we can meet those high standards is by being in tune with the nature of our children.

This edition, although expanded, still centers on three, four and five year olds and on their life in school. This specific focus is not meant to minimize the importance of the real "preschool" years: from birth to age three. Nor is it meant to minimize the importance of children's education within their homes by their basic teachers—their parents.

James L. Hymes, Jr.

Berkeley, California
Fall 1979

Teaching
the Child
Under Six

Third Edition

1

THE STATE OF
THE PROFESSION

Early group education occurs under many names. The most familiar ones: nursery school, kindergarten, child care center, and Head Start. But each has its variations.

There are cooperative nursery schools, private nonprofit nursery schools, private *for*-profit nursery schools. There are church-sponsored nursery schools and Montessori schools that cling to the name of their spiritual founder. There are nursery schools that exist primarily for training—not for training children but for training teachers, nurses, religious education workers, doctors, and social workers. There are nursery schools for preparental education in junior high schools, senior high schools, in community and senior colleges. And, of course, there are nursery schools for parent education.

Youngsters with handicaps are often included in these groups, but some nursery schools are specifically planned for children who are deaf or for those with speech difficulties, crippling conditions, or vision handicaps. Some nursery schools are for the mentally retarded or for those who have emotional problems. Hospitals sometimes maintain nursery schools for their convalescing children. A few nursery schools also exist primarily for research. The only nursery school we don't have—yet—is the free public nursery school, the school any three-year-old can go to just because the youngster is three.

We do have many free public kindergartens for five-year-olds. A few of our public kindergartens are part of a two-year program—they are designed specifically for four-year-olds as well as five-year-olds. Of course, many chil-

dren start to public kindergarten for five-year-olds when they are only four: 4.9, 4.10, 4.11, and sometimes younger. We have private kindergartens—private nonprofit, private *for*-profit. We also have half-day kindergartens, plus a few others that are in session for the standard school hours of nine to three—our rare full-day kindergarten groups.

Child care centers show the same variety. They may be called child care centers, day care centers, or by their oldest name: day nurseries. For that matter, child care centers sometimes are called nursery schools, sometimes kindergartens, sometimes play groups. And they often bear cute names like "The Kiddie Kollege of Kareful Kare." Churches sponsor child care centers. So do some labor unions and businesses and industries, some hospitals for their workers and some government agencies for their employees. Child care centers may receive public funds from a variety of federal, state and local sources, or they may be supported in part by charity. Some centers are run for profit by individuals. There is also the big business of day care: centers which are part of chains and others that are franchised operations. We have child care centers in the heart of our cities, in mountain factory towns, and out in the fields for the children of migrant agricultural workers. There are centers in department stores that care for children while mothers shop, and centers on shipboard and at resorts for use while parents play. There are centers where children may be dropped off for an hour or two, and centers where children come one day a week on "mother's day off."

We have early childhood groups primarily for children who have been hurt by poverty. Head Start, the best known of these, is sometimes like a nursery school serving three- and four-year-olds, sometimes like a kindergarten serving five-year-olds, sometimes like a child care center operating throughout the long day of a mother's working hours. Head Start groups often call themselves Child Development Centers. Other groups with other names also serve children from the same poverty background: Title I groups, whose funds come from Title I of the Elementary and Secondary Education Act; Title XX groups whose funds come from Title XX of the Social Security Act; and both California and New York have their own state-supported preschool programs for poverty children.

Most early childhood groups serve youngsters who are three, four, or five years old. However, we have long had nursery schools for two-year-olds, and many child care centers offer service not only for twos but also for toddlers and even infants. Child care centers may be hesitant about including children this young but often find themselves confronted by a reality: the parents are at work; the children need care; nothing else is available. Some groups, however, are specifically geared for these young ages; infancy and toddlerhood are their specialty. Among these are the Parent and Child Centers, a downward extension of Head Start, for parents and their children under age three who are living in poverty.

Confronting such a wide array of names, sponsorship, purposes, and sources of funding, one cannot help envying the simplicity in early education that is developing in Norway. The trend there is to use two names. These two cover all groups for children age three to seven. One is called the "half-a-day school for young children," the other, the "full-day school." These take care of

nursery school, kindergarten, child care centers, plus all the other variations we have, *and* include six-year-old children whom we place in first grade. The USSR has a similar simplicity. Two names cover all there is in Soviet preschool education: the *yacli,* or nursery, for children two months of age to three years; and the *detsky sad,* the kindergarten, for children aged three to seven.

If the array of names used in the United States is confusing, it does indicate one thing: The education of children under six is a wide-open field. It has not settled down. It is not cut and dried. Teaching the child under six is a lively and bubbling profession. Ever so much is going on.

The Basic Similarity of All Programs

One outcome of our variety of names is not helpful. The multiplicity of titles makes it sound as if each program were drastically different from all the others. This is a misconception. This should not be the case.

The names tempt you to draw a sharp line between nursery school and kindergarten, to make a distinction between child care and all other groups, to think of Head Start and other programs for poor children as a totally different breed of cat. Beware!

There *are* administrative and organizational differences between various groups, but none of these is very important so far as teaching children is concerned. Day care children, Head Start children, nursery school children, kindergarten children are . . . children. And they have one great bond in common: They are *young* children. The education of all of them ought to be basically the same. *Once a child is in a group the similarities should overwhelmingly outweigh the differences.* The name of the group should no longer matter.

If you were to visit a group in the middle of the morning, you ought not to be able to tell by looking at the equipment, the program, or the teaching methods: Is this a nursery school? A child care center? A Head Start class? Unless you are very skilled in judging children's ages, you ought not to be able to tell: Is this a nursery school? A kindergarten?

If you were to visit a program in the late afternoon, then you could make a good guess: This is probably a child care center. But you shouldn't be able to tell by looking at the teacher, the materials, or the activity. You would guess by looking at the clock. Child care centers are the only programs apt to be operating at that time.

The basic educational equipment, supplies, and materials should be the same—nursery school or kindergarten or child care center or Head Start. The space should be about the same. The adult-child ratio and the class size ought to be similar. The tone and the spirit of the group, the methods of teaching, and the content ought to be the same.

This basic similarity should carry over to the Sabbath. A large number of young children have their first experience in education outside the home in church schools. These are brief experiences, only a few hours one day a week. The content taught in these schools sometimes—not always—differs from the content of general education. Yet young children are still young children on the

Sabbath. The methods of teaching, the climate of the groups, class size, the adult-child ratio, the materials, and equipment all should be geared to the age of the child.

Church-sponsored religious education often finds itself free of the critical thinking and legal regulations that control general education. Churches have the leeway to do whatever they wish because they do it in the name of religion. For that very reason—because it is done in the name of religion—most want their early education to be the best. It is hoped that much in this book will help churches make their Sabbath experiences for young children exactly that—as good and as right for the age of the child as they can possibly be.

The Immediate Goal

Most important: Once a child is in the group the immediate goal of all the programs—nursery school and kindergarten, child care center and Head Start, even church school—should be the same. The name of the group should not make any difference.

These are *schools,* all of them. They are not "pre" schools. They are not "prep" schools or training centers to get children ready for some future year or grade or school. These are schools for *general* education, for a liberal education.

These are schools for the development of the whole child. Each one of them—nursery school, kindergarten, child care center, Head Start—helps children develop to the maximum their intellectual powers, their social powers, their emotional capacities, and their physical powers.

What is the goal of nursery school? The goal of kindergarten? Head Start? What will a child gain in a day care center? The common aim of all these groups is to help each child learn as much as he or she can in all areas of human experience and to do this in such a way that the youngster lives the years of three, four, and five in the richest, most satisfying, most constructive way possible. Once a child is enrolled, the one big job of all groups is *to teach* and to do so in such a way that each child is more glad to be alive during these early years.

Future Payoffs

Nursery schools, kindergartens, child care centers, and Head Start programs are schools for *now*. Their eyes are steadfastly on the present. But good early education almost always pays an extra dividend. It pays off in the future, too. This is the bonus.

Sound programs provide experiences in literature, music, and art; in the sciences; in mathematics; and in the social sciences. They provide experiences in health and in physical education. Children have the chance to gain in language; to expand their store of knowledge; to grow in curiosity, problem-

solving, and creativity; to stretch their attention spans. Youngsters have the chance to improve in coordination, balance, speed, grace, vigor, strength. They have the chance to widen their sense of trust in adults and to deepen their sense of joy in their age-mates. They have the chance to grow in independence, in self-direction, in self-control. Sound programs are thoughtfully oriented to our democratic values. In them, children have the chance to live in a little spot of American society operating at its best.

No guarantees come with all of this. Early education can only promise to help make the third, fourth, and fifth years of life good ones. It cannot insure without fail that any tomorrow will be successful. Nothing "fixes" a child for life, no matter what happens next. *But* exciting, pleasing early experiences are not sloughed off. They go with the child, on into first grade, on into the long life ahead.[1]

Exciting, pleasing early experiences have a special significance, too. What happens to a child in nursery school, kindergarten, the child care center, or Head Start are the *foundational* experiences. They are the initial confrontations with the child's own generation, with the wider society, with organized learning. These beginnings, the first impressions, have a unique, predisposing importance. The child who gets a good start in early education stands a better chance of doing well in later education. Modern experience confirms this, but the idea is old and a solid part of folk widsom: As the twig is bent . . . From little acorns . . . A stitch in time . . .

The child is lucky—we all are lucky—when good early education gives a youngster a strong start. Lucky the child who finds the first schooling rewarding. Lucky the child who is not a reluctant adventurer. Lucky the child who does not regret the present, longingly wishing for a time past. Moving onward and upward and outward is the story of life. Moving onward and upward and outward with *zest* and *joy* is the *good* life.

_____ **The Shortage of Programs**

Some teachers, many parents, and others in the general public think of early childhood education as a newcomer. The fact is that the group education of young children has roots far back in the past, with many years of practice and experimentation behind it.[2]

---

[1] For a discussion of some recent objective evidence on future payoffs, see pages 21–22.

[2] The firsthand story of some of the significant happenings in American early education is told in *Early Childhood Education Living History Interviews, Books 1, 2, 3* (published by Hacienda Press, distributed by the Southern California Association for the Education of Young Children, 6851 Lennox Ave., Van Nuys, CA 91405). These are transcripts of interviews I held with pioneer educators who were directly involved, from the start of our first nursery schools, through the Emergency Nursery Schools of the depression years, the World War II child care centers, and on to the beginning days of Head Start.

What could be called the first child care center was established in 1816, in New Lanark near Glasgow in Scotland by Robert Owen. The first group called a kindergarten was begun by Friedrich Froebel in 1837 in Blankenburg, Germany. The first nursery school was created by Margaret McMillan in 1911 in Deptford, near London, England.

The "old age" of programs in the United States for the young is equally impressive. What could be called child care centers existed in Boston in 1838; in New York City in 1854; in Troy, New York, in 1858; in Philadelphia in 1863. Our first private kindergarten was established in Watertown, Wisconsin, in 1855, and our first public kindergarten in St. Louis in 1873. Our first nursery schools date back to 1922. The Ruggles Street Nursery School in Boston (now a part of the Eliot-Pearson Department of Child Study of Tufts University), the nursery school of Merrill-Palmer Institute in Detroit, the Harriet Johnson Nursery School of Bank Street College of Education in New York City, and several others were established in that year or in the years immediately following.

The United States has had public kindergartens for more than one hundred years.

We have had nursery schools for more than half a century.

We have had child care centers the longest time of all, for more than one hundred and fifty years.

How well have we done in this long span of years?

Despite our experience, our wealth, and our alleged concern for children, we fall far short of providing the programs young boys and girls need. We call under-six children "preschoolers." They are "preschool" only because we do not have the schools for them. We don't have enough kindergartens. We don't have enough nursery schools. We don't have enough child care centers. We don't have enough compensatory education programs. *The most serious problem facing early education is that there simply is not enough of it.*

We Americans talk about *equal* educational opportunity. The fact is we practice great discrimination—we practice *age* discrimination.

We pay lip service to the importance of the early years but our deeds do not square with our words. Children under six are grossly under-served. There are many more *never-ins* than drop-outs. Far too many of our young children, never in school, live the third and fourth years of life, in particular, and large parts of the fifth year, underemployed, underchallenged, wasting their time, missing the chance to live up to their potential.

The picture is not all black. Some pleasing developments have taken place, especially since 1965 with the establishment of Head Start. The flurry of excitement that accompanied the beginning of that program raised America's consciousness about early education. Programs for young children gained what public relations experts would call a "good image."

One of the most impressive advances in early education was the passage in 1975 of PL 94-142, the Education for All Handicapped Children Act. This law requires state-by-state counting to identify handicapped children from birth to age twenty-one. It includes the specific requirement that states edu-

cate all handicapped children *beginning at age three!* And the law, of course, provides financial aid. Within two years, 196,287 handicapped three, four, and five-year-olds were receiving education under the law. Even more dramatic: 11,800 children from birth to age two were also being served. Within three years, by 1978, thirty-one states had made it mandatory for communities to provide education for preschool handicapped children, beginning from birth, some at age two, with still others beginning at ages three, four, or five.

Kindergartens

Kindergartens also gained greatly in the years following the birth of Head Start. In 1966 only 60% of our five-year-olds attended school. In 1978, 82% went to a public, private or church-sponsored pre-primary group, a spectacular leap ahead![3] In 1966 only twenty-five of our states provided aid for public kindergartens. In 1980 *all* states except Mississippi provided some aid. Another improvement: Each year since 1965 new states have joined the list of those making it mandatory for communities to provide kindergartens.

All this recent growth in programs for five-year-olds is impressive but it is hardly a basis for complacency. For one reason, there are jokers hidden in the kindergarten statistics which mislead. Forty-nine of the fifty states do provide state aid for kindergartens but several provide only enough to support pilot programs. Kindergartens are not yet an integral part of their whole public school system.

We also fool ourselves when we say that 82% of our five-year-olds go to school. Most of those children go only to a *half-day* school. We talk about kindergartens. We gloss over the fact that we really have only *half-day* kindergartens.

We have talked this way for so long that we have come to believe that kindergarten, by divine law, means a class that meets only two-and-a-half or three hours a day. We have forgotten that there was a time in the not-distant past when kindergartens were in operation for the regular school day, 9 A.M. to 3 P.M. Five-year-olds ate lunch at school. They napped. They worked and played in the afternoon, and they returned home with other school children. One teacher taught one group of kindergarten children, and that was her sole job.

The cutback to half-days came in the years following World War II. Americans gave birth to a great many children. We also began spending more of our wealth on pursuits other than education. Kindergartens were moved to the bargain basement: two groups for one teacher; one group in the morning and another in the afternoon. Two for the price of one, and half the school experience for each child. Realistically, we should cut in half that impressive figure of 82% of five-year-olds attending school.

---

[3] *Digest of Education Statistics, 1980.* Washington D.C.: National Center for Education Statistics.

To be sure, half a day of schooling may be exactly right for some individual five-year-olds. (If "schooling" means sitting, paper-and-pencil tasks, readiness assignments, keeping quiet and lining up, then even half a day may be too much.) We need to remember, however, that the half-day kindergarten did not develop because half a day of school was all that most five-year-olds could stand. The half-day kindergarten is essentially an economy measure. Today most states that provide state aid for kindergartens provide only half-aid. Five-year-olds receive only 50% of the support given to the education of children six and older.

There is reason to hope that this bargain-basement approach to kindergarten may lessen in the years ahead. The original reason for it, the flood of children entering school, has eased. The percentage of five-year-olds attending school increases year after year but the actual number of children has decreased. This falling-off of population, the result of our declining birth rate, could mean that five-year-olds might once again have the chance for a full day of schooling.

Full-day kindergartens would make it possible for those children who need only a half-day experience to attend that length of time. Other fives, for whom the full school day would be more appropriate, could attend from 9 A.M. to 3 P.M. Such leeway is uniquely possible at the kindergarten level because no state makes it *compulsory* for parents to send their five-year-olds to school. More and more states make it *mandatory for communities* to provide kindergartens, but kindergarten attendance is *voluntary*. The availability of full-day schooling would enable each child to have the amount of group living that would best enrich the fifth year of life.

Such a plan would be a boon for kindergarten teachers, too. Half a day of school may be exactly right for some individual children but two half-day groups is seldom right for any teacher. Two half-day kindergartens confront teachers with too many different boys and girls, too many parents, too much pressure and too little time. Half-day groups mean hectic days. Past experience shows there is no trick to creating a challenging, yet well-paced, relaxed full-day school for five-year-olds. Such a kindergarten would provide teachers with the opportunity to use better their teaching skills, and would result in immeasurably more satisfaction for them.

One other present-day reality dims any great jubilation over the fact that 82% of our five-year-olds go to kindergarten. In this instance the joker is hidden in the definition of "kindergarten." One can, of course, call any group of fives a kindergarten. A careful definition would be worded like this: *A kindergarten is a group of not more than twenty children about the age of five, taught by one teacher who has specifically trained to teach five-year-olds, and who is assisted by one aide, either paid or volunteer.*

If we hold to that definition of class size, and to that definition of the training required, and to that requirement of one aide, how many of our five-year-olds actually go to *kindergarten*? Certainly not 82%! Class sizes of more than thirty five-year-olds, with one teacher, and no aide, are common today. Ironically, the drop in birth rate too often has meant a rise in class size, as the

smaller child population has led to the closing out of some groups, thus squeezing the remaining numbers into others. The sad fact is that too many children attend what is a kindergarten in name only.

Nursery schools

In 1980 it was estimated that 34% of our three- and four-year-olds were in early childhood groups.[4] In 1967 the Census Bureau had estimated that only 14% of these ages were in classes. The gain is pleasing, but does 34% represent adequate progress for a movement now more than fifty years old?

In the 1920s, when nursery schools were first established, parents who enrolled their children were looked at askance, as if they were shirking their responsibilities. Today, sending one's child to nursery school, if one can afford it, is a status symbol. The name, "nursery school," is known and liked by the American public. But we have made almost no progress, after more than fifty years, in incorporating nursery schools as a part of public education, free and available to all.

We have inched in this direction. From 1927 to 1959 Wisconsin provided state aid for two-year kindergartens. This state aid did not help three-year-olds but during that period Wisconsin four-year-olds could go to a free public school. Pennsylvania today, on the record, provides state aid for two-year kindergartens, but there is little provision for four-year-olds to attend. California gives state support to parent participation nursery schools. It finances these schools, which do enroll three- and four-year-olds, through adult education. The recreation departments in a few communities—Washington, D.C. is one example—offer half-day groups for nursery age children, either free or at minimal cost. Many public kindergartens enroll children who are 4.9 or 4.10 or 4.11 at the start of school, but the program is seldom adjusted to their four-year-oldness, and the trend is toward raising the entrance age for kindergarten so children will be more ready for the formal experiences that lie in wait for them.

We have had the idea of nursery education for more than fifty years, but still only the lucky children of wealthy parents, of more conscientious parents, or the children whose families are poor enough to be eligible for a poverty program have the opportunity to take advantage of the idea. *Nursery education, where it exists, is overwhelmingly private education.*

Good private education is always costly. Many good private nursery schools, like our best private colleges, count on huge "endowments" to keep tuition charges within reasonable limits. College endowments are in cash, or in stocks, bonds, and other investments. The nursery school "endowment" is completely different. That "endowment" is the deep commitment of an owner who contributes time, energy, skill, and other resources, far beyond any hope of recompense, because of a belief in the importance of early education. Needless to say, such unusual commitment is not universal.

---

[4] *Digest of Education Statistics, 1980.* Washington, D.C.: National Center for Education Statistics.

The *cooperative* nursery school offers a way of bringing good private nursery education within the financial reach of more people. In a co-op, mothers and fathers participate in all aspects of the school. There is a trained teacher who is skilled in working both with children and with adults. But parents regularly take turns as assistant teachers and on all the other jobs needed to keep a school going well. Parents pay for their child's education with their services and sweat, as well as with some cash. The first co-op was established in 1923 in Cambridge, Massachusetts. The idea is an old, an honorable and an ingenious one with many virtues in addition to financial savings for parents.

Co-ops, however, do not fit everyone's life style. Full tuition in a good nursery school fits even fewer pocketbooks. The high cost of good private education explains why so few of our three-year-olds and four-year-olds are in groups. It is hard, indeed, to imagine any scheme for private education, with no public aid, ever serving large numbers of children in these ages and serving them well. More than half of all mothers of young children are at home, alone with their youngsters, trying to meet their children's needs as full-time parents. These mothers and their children need and deserve a helping hand. If they are ever to get it, if nursery education is not to stay the privilege of the few, some form of public support seems essential.

Head Start

The Head Start picture is hardly any brighter. In its first summer, 1965, Head Start got off to a brilliant beginning. Coming on as a new program, starting from base line zero, in that first summer Head Start served 562,000 young children in every corner of our land: in Eskimo villages, on Indian reservations, in our cities, in Appalachia, in the Virgin Islands and Puerto Rico and Guam and Samoa. This dramatic achievement—headline-making, the occasion for flying the Head Start flag in 2,500 communities by Presidential proclamation—focused national attention on young children.

The fanfare and warm acceptance by the country made it easy for Head Start to become a prolific mother. Head Start itself grew into a year-round program, not one available simply during the summer weeks. Some Head Start centers became child care programs, open all day. Parent and Child Centers, reaching down to children under age three and to their parents, were born. Follow Through, and, later, Project Developmental Continuity came into being, both efforts to carry a program like Head Start on into the primary years. Home Start, an experimental effort to help poor parents teach their own children within their own homes, was developed. Health Start was created, designed to bring the medical, dental, and other health services of Head Start to children who were not in a Head Start group.

The excitement about Head Start carried over to other programs for young children. Head Start stimulated the growth of private nursery schools. In particular, it gave sharp impetus to public kindergartens. Because it included at least 10% of preschool handicapped children, it fed in to the interest in PL 94–142. Its example led to the channeling into preschool groups of

major sums from Title I of the Elementary and Secondary Education Act. Head Start also spurred the development of California's state-supported Pre-school Program, and New York's Experimental Prekindergarten Program.

In addition, in the late 1960s, Head Start was a prominent contributor to the growing world wide recognition of the special value of early education for youngsters disadvantaged by poverty. In the United Kingdom the Plowden Report, a very influential 1967 government paper, gave strong support in that country to early education. Australia funneled money into preschool pro-grams for Aboriginal children and their parents. New Zealand gave financial aid to Maori Play Centres and to Maori Family Preschools. Israel provided free nursery schools for a large percentage of that country's disadvantaged, the children of so-called Oriental Jews in whose families the illiteracy rate was high. Sweden made a special effort to establish free nursery schools for the young children of the many immigrants who came to that country either to seek jobs or as refugees from eastern Europe.

Today, among Head Start's credits, is the simple fact that it is a survivor. Begun as a part of one Democratic President's now largely forgotten War on Poverty, Head Start has lasted through successive Republican and Demo-cratic administrations. Among its parents and staff the program is greatly loved. Sensitive to Head Start's grass-roots support, Congress has kept extend-ing the life of the program and has made small increases in the budget.

There is a bleak side to this picture, however. When Head Start was begun in 1965 it was estimated that 1,193,000 young children at each early year of life lived in poverty in the United States. Approximately 3,600,000 such youngsters were of Head Start age, the three-, four-, and five-year-olds. Our "massive" 1965 program reached about one-seventh of these children! And only for a quickie, condensed program of six to eight weeks duration! We can be glad but hardly gleeful over that beginning, and the present status offers no greater cause for joy. In 1979, 18,000 children were still in the condensed summer pro-gram; 369,000 were in the better but more expensive full-year program. These sound like impressive figures, but there is one thing wrong with them—the same difficulty as in 1965. Head Start still does not begin to reach all the children who could benefit from the program. In the glory days of its begin-nings Head Start served approximately 14% of all eligible youngsters. In 1979, fourteen years later, it served about 20%. The 1978 Annual Report of the Children's Defense Fund pointed out the gap in blunt words: "Over a million needy children and 1,000 eligible communities lack Head Start services."

Child Care Centers

Children in need of day care services fare even worse. The young boys and girls whose mothers cannot be at home with them are our most vulnerable chil-dren, and their numbers are growing.

More than seven million children under age six have mothers who work outside the home. In 1980 these mothers constituted 43% of all mothers of children under six. The trend toward the employment of women has continued

to go up and up and up. In 1976 the Chairman of the National Commission for Manpower Policy called the flood of women into jobs "the single most outstanding phenomenon of our century."

The need for child care — for *excellent* child care — is one of life's pressing new realities, yet our society is reluctant to face this fact.

We act as if every young child had a full-time mother at home, a loving and available mother always ready and able to do everything that a child needs. Or if we accept the fact that mother is not at home, we act as if someone else is there taking her place: grandmother; an aunt, a known and trusted and well-loved servant.

The fact is: Mother is not at home. Five and a half million mothers of children under six are out working. Grandmother, that aunt, that beloved and faithful retainer are not at home either. The chances are that they are also out in the labor force.

During World War II the federal government faced up to the reality of the working mother. Our country had what were called the Lanham Child Care Centers, which took their name from the sponsor of the legislation in the House of Representatives. At their peak in 1945 these 2,000 federally-supported Lanham Centers in all parts of the country served about 70,000 children under the age of six. Then the war ended and the program ended, even though many mothers remained in the labor force.

Since the end of World War II public support for child care has been spotty. One state, California, has provided state aid for children's centers all through the post-World War II years, although not enough to serve all the children of working mothers. New York City and Philadelphia have similarly provided local tax support through these years. Some of Head Start's money has gone into child care, as has some Title I money and especially funds from Title XX of the Social Security Act. Model Cities legislation was a source of some child care support; federal funds also made possible day care for a few thousand children of migrant families. All together, some sixty or more federal programs have at one time or another provided money (usually very little) for some day care.

In addition, the federal government has granted rather generous income tax credits for child care to working parents. These sizable reductions in income tax give parents more money with which to buy private child care. Spurred by the income tax credit and by the obvious need stemming from the mounting numbers of mothers working, many individuals have opened private child care centers, and businesses, operating chains of centers or franchising centers, have come in to the field. Unfortunately, while the need for child care is clear, the complexities of operating good centers are not as well known. Just as private nursery education faces almost insurmountable financial problems, private child care centers — open longer hours, needing larger staffs, serving poorer parents, involved in major food service — face even greater difficulties in offering good education. There are only two ways in which economies can be effected: increase the class size and pay the staff less. Too many private child care centers have to do both to survive.

The tragedy is that we know how to give young children excellent care when their parents are in the work force, but as a society we simply do not choose to do it.

The Need for Child Advocates

Some day this great, strong, wealthy, often-caring country of ours must make the pledge: *We will offer top-quality education for all young children. We will maintain excellent public programs for whatever duration of day or week or year the child's needs or the family's needs require.*

This commitment means good public nursery schools, enough at least for all our three- and four-year-olds.

It means good public kindergartens for all our five-year-olds.

It means our creating whatever supplementary and compensatory programs may be needed, enough for every young child who could benefit by them, available for sufficient duration, *and* topnotch in quality.

It means good public child care centers — this is an especially urgent need. We are far from accepting the notion that good child care should be available free to all, just as first grade or twelfth grade is. Yet our ultimate commitment has to be the same as our public school commitment — to provide whatever service a child or the family needs. We do not charge the fourth-grader extra if the youngster requires remedial reading help or speech therapy. We try to serve each child fully in terms of the child's needs. Until we build this attitude about child care we should at least make available enough public support so that public aid, plus parent payments on a sliding scale adjusted to income, are sufficient to guarantee the number of child care centers we need *and* all of high quality.

This happy day, when excellent early education will be a reality for all young children, will come sooner if all of us who care about young children think of ourselves as child advocates, friends of children who speak out. It is not enough for any of us just to do a good job with our own children within our particular classroom. A good teacher has an allegiance to *children* — to all of them. The shortage of programs creates a pressing need for everyone to present children's needs to friends, to neighbors, to labor and business and political figures, to church leaders and to professional workers, to the press and radio and TV, to all our citizens who ultimately choose how we will spend our wealth.[5]

Complicating Social Trends

Three social factors heighten this need for able presenters of the children's case. All three hold the threat that the shortages of programs will worsen unless the friends of children actively command the public's attention.

---

[5] There is a further discussion of still other jobs for child advocates on pages 172–80.

The declining birth rate is one new condition. In 1976, for the first time, the total number of three- and four-year-olds in groups dropped. In 1977, for the first time, the total number of five-year-olds in groups dropped. The *percentages* of young children in these groups increased, but the total *numbers* of children decreased.

Theoretically, the fact that fewer children are being born could free our country to concentrate its resources on its smaller child population and thereby do a better job with each youngster. The danger, however—the greater likelihood—is that the falling birth rate will switch America's attention from young children to young adults and to the older years where the numbers are greater and the political clout stronger.

The second hazard—it sounds very strange to call it a hazard!—is the otherwise fortunate absence of any national crisis which might sweep programs for young children along in its train. Historically the unpleasant fact is that early childhood education has made its greatest gains, not because America loved little children, but as a by-product of national emergencies.

Nursery schools received their first boost during the depression years of the 1930s when, primarily to put unemployed teachers and others to work, the federally-funded Emergency Nursery Schools were created. Child care centers first surged ahead during World War II when the federally-funded Lanham Centers were designed so mothers could work in shipyards, in airplane and munitions factories, and in other jobs geared to bringing America victory. Head Start was born as a result of the civil rights movement and of the War on Poverty.

It has taken a severe economic depression, a worldwide military conflict, and a socio-economic crisis to bring our programs for children to their present status. America, of course, today faces many severe problems, just as it has in the past. However, two concerns that rank very high in people's minds do not look the least bit promising for becoming the midwife to further gains for children. America is worried about inflation, and America is worried about government spending and government regulation. Certainly these two anxieties offer little hope for bold, new advances on children's behalf.

A loss of momentum is a third new complicating element. From 1945 to 1965, from the end of World War II to the start of the War on Poverty, early childhood education stood still. The enthusiasm that had gone in to the Emergency Nursery Schools and the Lanham Child Care Centers had seemingly spent itself. Early childhood education held its own, but for twenty years scored no marked gains. A comparable danger exists today. 1965 to 1980 was a period of high activity, filled with the excitement of Head Start's early days, with the steady advances in public kindergarten education, with the strides ahead for the preschool handicapped. But enthusiasm is running down. Unless friends of children can shake America out of complacency we may rest on a plateau, idling in neutral, stopping far short of serving all of our young children and their families.

_____ **The Arguments Against Under-Six Groups**

Friends of young children, child advocates, must be aware of the feelings and values of those who are unenthusiastic about extending early education.

Certain long-standing, deep-seated attitudes toward young children, toward homes, toward women make up one roadblock. Despite much talk about the importance of the early years, many adults—especially those not living with children—still think of boys and girls under six as little babies tied to their mother's apron strings. Age six stays pegged in the public's mind as the time when children become ready to learn. A large part of the populace still completely underestimates the maturity of three-, four-, and five-year-olds.

The low quality of commercial television for young children is a symbol of this low esteem. TV aims almost exclusively at amusement. It treats young children as if they were prethinking, prefeeling tots to be titillated. TV obviously does not look on under-six children as real people with ideas, taste, awareness of and interest in the world around them. This point of view coincides with our national unwillingness to take young children seriously.

The difficulty is compounded by a tendency to overrate the home. Many blithely assume that good homes can meet all the needs of young children. Worse yet, they mistakenly assume that all homes are good. They close their eyes to the changes in home life. They forget that millions of young children are cooped up in city apartments, that millions live in unchallenging suburban areas, that millions of farm children live lonely lives. They do not face up to the fact that almost one-half of the mothers of children under six are in the labor force and not at home at all. A "dream" picture—mother and her young child playing together, talking together, whiling away the happy hours together—clouds the view of reality.

The obstacles are reinforced by the negative attitudes toward women that permeate our society. Mothers who are at home who seek nursery schools so they can have some time alone—for rest, recreation, shopping, a hobby, reading, catching up on housework, for anything—need great inner strength to claim time for themselves without feeling guilty. Providing a group for a child for the sake of the mother is seen by society as a luxury not worthy of the expenditure of public money.

Mothers who seek more intellectual, social and physical stimulation for their children than they can provide at home are still sometimes made to feel they are dumping their youngsters. The assumption still prevails that a woman is supposed to be strong enough, smart enough, and devoted enough to take care of all the needs of her young children.

This glorification of woman into Superwoman especially hurts the mother who is in the labor force. It is up to her to take care of her own children. If she chooses to work—no matter that most working mothers have no choice!—then she herself has to solve the problem of child care. Angry,

punitive feelings are at the bottom of some of this unwillingness to extend a helping hand. There are still those who believe that mother ought to be at home and, if she isn't, any trouble she has serves her right.

Strange fears also enter the picture. Some think the availability of child care facilities will make it too easy for women to work. These people are not sufficiently alarmed by how much the absence of good day care complicates the lot of women who have always worked and who *must* work. Nor do they realize how much the absence of good care harms children. Not enough of us let ourselves dream of good child care centers complete with skilled counseling staffs. Such a staff could help mothers think through whether they should work. Such a staff could help those mothers who do work to decide whether group day care is the best solution for their particular children. And if group day care is the answer, such centers would allow mothers to work with peace of mind, knowing their children are well cared for during their absence.

The Demand for Proof-Positive

A second roadblock to the expansion of early education is the insistence on hard evidence that good early schooling pays off. There is much modern-sounding talk about CBR, the cost-benefit ratio, the requirement that any proposed program produce tangible results equal to or greater than the expense. As the relative newcomer, early education is often held very rigorously to this requirement. Fourth grade seldom has to prove that it pays for itself, but a four-year-old group is expected to.

Unfortunately almost no tests are available to measure some of the most significant gains both children and parents make when a youngster is in a good group. This difficulty is not confined to early education. Many of life's experiences do not lend themselves to statistical measurement. For example, a husband and wife vacation together. They are stimulated by new sights and by meeting enjoyable new friends. They explore fascinating foods. They are provoked by customs new to them. They hear unusual sounds and smell odors that are intriguing. Then they return home rested and full of memories. Statistical evidence will never be available that measures their state on the return home, or that proves that this couple will live longer, earn more, stay married to each other longer, vote more wisely or drive more carefully as a result of their vacation. Since this kind of proof is not forthcoming, was their money wasted on the trip? Should they have stayed at home?

Or think of a man who changes his job. He switches from boring companions and unexciting activity to a new position in which he works with humans he enjoys and confronts tasks that stir him with their challenge. Is there only one significant question: How much money is the man now making? Is he getting more cash or less? The monetary reward can be counted. The other rewards cannot. Does only the measurable reward matter?

Unfortunately, some adults are impressed only by scores on tests that show immediate gains. The tests may measure quite unimportant items, but

the demand persists: Prove beyond a shadow of a doubt! People mean by this that they want only hard, statistical evidence on tangible outcomes right here and now. Don't bother them with talk about proof of future payoffs, such as those discussed on page 21. At times one wishes that children attending good groups would immediately turn blue, and those not able to attend a group would conveniently and quickly turn green!

The demand for quantitatively measurable proof creates pressure on kindergartens, Head Start, child care centers, and even on nursery schools to distort their programs by concentrating on the few areas where tests exist and where scores can be counted. Sadly, the results even from narrow and distorted programs may not be convincing enough to the statistics-lovers to support the effort to get the children's programs that we must some day have.

Our Economic Situation and Our Priorities

A third roadblock to needed early education is what we think of as "our economic plight." We are the world's richest country. We have the wealth to do anything and everything that young children's needs require. But we feel poor. We never seem to have enough money for the expansion of education or for other needed social services.

Under-six education scrambles, in a race with all other levels of education, for the remnants of funds in the public purse. It vies with the growth of higher education, with the expansion of junior and community colleges, with the pressing needs of elementary and secondary education. This competition is heartbreaking because it profits a young child very little to be lucky enough to have excellent early education only to move on into mediocre, meager upper education. And it profits none of us if a child has excellent elementary, secondary and collegiate schooling that is built on a weak and shallow foundation in the early years. Supporters of early education want good schools for children when they are young _and_ they want good schools for children as they grow older. When programs compete against one another, the child is crushed in the middle.

Early education also competes for funds with pressing needs in many other fields. We have pitifully few child guidance clinics, for example. Every teacher of young children knows how difficult it is to get professional help for a youngster in psychological trouble. Our jails the country over are in miserable shape. We do too little to help our alcoholics and our drug addicts. We do not begin to spend the money we should to make the days of our aging citizens bearable, to say nothing of making them enjoyable. We continue to suffer from diseases because we are niggardly in financing research to uncover cures or forms of protection. Countless humans endure countless days of pain and distress because we do not spend the funds to deliver medical services to everyone in need of them. There is hunger in America. There is extensive malnutrition. Our humanitarian and our educational efforts lag far behind our needs.

One statistic—of particular interest to those who care about the young child—symbolizes the terrible disparity between our wealth and our social behavior. America ranks thirteenth among the nations of the world in infant mortality.[6]

Our problem is not that we lack the money to do better. It is not that we lack the knowledge. Instead, we seem to lack the will to do better.

We spend a tremendous share of our resources paying for past wars and on our never-ending preparation for future wars. We spend a tremendous share of our resources on private pleasures. We feel put-upon by demands made for the public good. We are content to let many resources escape taxation. The result is a self-induced sense of poverty. But we are not poor—we have a poor order of priorities.

The Arguments in Favor of Under-Six Groups _____

Child advocates must help other persons to know the basic understandings about under-six children that have been streaming in since the beginning of the twentieth century.

We must help people to see that young children—from cradle days onward—need stimulation. Their full growth requires that young boys and girls have sights to see, sounds to hear, surfaces to touch, odors to smell, tastes to taste.

We must help people realize that young children—from crawling days onward—need opportunities for venturing and exploring. Their healthy growth is based on their having chances for the development of independence.

We must help people know that young children are highly social. From two years or so onward, they are joyously eager to talk to and play with humans their own age. From birth on, they are dependent on loving adults who will nurture them.

We must help people to appreciate the fact that young children have ideas of their own. They are young but they can think. They are young but they plan. They organize.

The task is to take the psychological understandings which have long been known professionally and to make them the possession of parents and citizens generally. You can sum up these understandings very succinctly:

---

[6] Our Bicentennial celebration triggered several publications assessing the current state of children and their families. Among the best: *America's Children 1976 — A Bicentennial Assessment,* a chart and fact book by the Coalition for Children and Youth, 815 15th Street N.W., Washington, D.C. 20005; *Toward a National Policy for Children and Families* (Washington: National Academy of Sciences); *All Our Children: The American Family Under Pressure,* by Kenneth Keniston and others, a report of the Carnegie Council on Children (New York: Harcourt, Brace, Jovanovich, 1977).

Every age under six—the infant, the toddler, the two, three, four, five—has needs, powers, feelings, purposes. The task is to help more people share this insight.

The Impact of Social Forces

Simultaneously, child advocates must help parents and citizens appreciate more fully how our whole way of living is changing, and how the changes have complicated the task of rearing children. Today's life-styles have made it harder than ever for even the most fortunate family—alone, unaided, with only its own resources—to provide all that the good growth of the young child requires. Those parents who are harried by poverty, those exhausted from full-time jobs, those troubled by their own illnesses or by the care of other dependents in the family, and those hampered by inadequate housing find their child-rearing task mountainous.

Obviously the 5.5 million mothers of young children who are not at home, who are in the labor force, desperately need help. For them, a good early childhood group is not simply a desirable supplement to family life—it is an essential.

But all of today's families need help. The number of homes with only one or two children has increased. The smaller family unit complicates the task of providing companionship. The work of the family within today's apartment or small suburban house or even the rural home has been greatly simplified. Challenge, involvement, participation, and firsthand experiences for a young child are all harder to provide. The automobile, a child-killer, has invaded every neighborhood. With today's mobility, few of us truly live in "neighborhoods"—we live among strangers. Many young children, especially those who live in high-rise apartments, can only go out to play when someone is free to supervise them. Independence for a child is harder to stimulate. The young child is cooped up at home and, with the child in almost every single living room, there is a new intruder: TV, feeding in scenes of violence, encouraging passivity, confusing with its commercials, stealing time by its allure.

Home and family life make essential contributions to a child's development. But industrialization, urbanization, suburbanization, mechanization, mobility, and other social forces create great problems for the family today. It is no simple, easy job to provide the growth ingredients a child needs: stimulation, space and freedom, companionship, raw materials for the expression of ideas, tolerance of youngsters' noise and mess. Wise homes reach out, whenever they can, to early childhood centers to supplement their own efforts to promote their children's well-being. Searching for a good group is the act of a conscientious, caring parent—not of someone ducking the responsibilities of parenthood.

Good groups for young children are increasingly being recognized as a help to parents, too. The care of young children is exhausting, demanding, con-

Confined within the home, young children often rely on T.V. for stimulation.

fining. Mothers especially have always needed some time away from their young to refresh and refuel themselves. Today this need is felt more keenly. Mothers at home today are well-educated. They are more open to the world at large and to its ideas. They seek more strenuously to satisfy their own adult needs, while not neglecting the needs of their children. A good children's group, for part of the day, can be a godsend.

Today's parents are also in very unusual need of help in better understanding their youngsters. More women and some men, too, are single parents working at the awesome task of making decisions about child behavior on their own. Even two-parent families often find themselves in new communities, cut off from relatives and from familiar, stable neighborhoods which once helped to set standards for behavior. This isolation is especially difficult at a time when values and life-styles are changing so rapidly. Many parents, divorced and now remarried, are mothers and fathers of combined families, always a complicated role. A good children's group, especially one led by a teacher sympathetic to grownups as well as to children, can become a stabilizing factor in today's family life, and a welcome source of insight into child behavior.

Early childhood education offers quite special qualities of timeliness and relevance to today's society. At its best, it serves both children and adults well. It works for all of us as a source of strength in our communities. Small wonder it has grown as much as it has. Great wonder it has not grown even more.

Value Received

Entrenched attitudes are not easily changed by simple exposure to facts, but there is evidence that money invested in early education pays off. Child advocates must be sure this news gets around.

Much of the evidence is *subjective.* This is not the evidence preferred by those who are impressed only by scores on tests — the show of hands means nothing to them. But overwhelming subjective evidence deserves respect.

One such kind of dramatic and incontrovertible evidence abounds: The "consumers" approve of early education. Young children have been known to cry on holidays because they could not go to school! This whole-hearted "Yes" vote should carry great weight at a time when much of upper education is plagued by drop-outs, and when so many older students show their discontent with schooling by the snide slogan: TGIF — Thank God It's Friday.

Parents overwhelmingly also give their "Yes' votes to early learning groups. Through the years they have seen with their own eyes a child who goes to school and who comes home from school. Parents say almost unanimously: "School (nursery school, Head Start, the child care center, kindergarten) has been good." These parents have not given tests to their children. They have a better source of evidence: They have *lived* with them.

No magic is involved in this almost universal child-and-parent approbation of early education. A good school respects children. A good school pleasurably challenges them. A good school gives youngsters a chance to use their powers. A good school fills children's days with humans they enjoy. A good school makes children happy they are alive and helps them to live with more zest. Children and their parents, understandably, have voted "Aye" for all these advantages.

Objective evidence on the value of early education is not completely lacking. One impressive report published in 1978 could go far to satisfy some of the demand for proof-positive. A follow-up was made on 3,000 low-income children who had first been studied in early intervention programs in the 1960s. At that time the children were three months to five years of age. At the time of the follow-up they ranged from nine to nineteen years. Twelve investigators who had studied the children separately in different parts of the country pooled their initial data and designed the common follow-up research.

This longitudinal effort uncovered some surprising "sleeper effects," results not available in the 1960s but apparent as the follow-up study got direct measures of the children's actual school performance in the 1970s. Among the conclusions: "Early education programs significantly reduced the number of children assigned to special education classes. . . . Early education programs significantly reduced the number of children retained in

grade. . . . Early education significantly increased scores on fourth grade mathematics achievement, with a suggestive trend toward increased scores on fourth grade reading tests. . . . Low-income children who attended pre-schools surpassed their controls on intelligence test scores. . . . Children who attended preschool were more likely than control children to give achievement-related reasons for being proud of themselves."

The report concludes: "These are striking findings and worthy of careful consideration. . . . Currently the public appears to be disillusioned with large-scale social legislation and spending. We ask the public and policy-makers to notice the strength of these findings and to reconsider their commit-ment to the nation's children, especially low-income children, by continuing to invest in preschool education."[7]

One of the longitudinal studies took the unusual step of translating chil-dren's gains into dollars and cents. Its conclusion: "What is good for children also appears to be of benefit to taxpayers." This study showed that money in-vested in a year of excellent compensatory preschool education was more than paid back because the children required less costly special education and institutional care through the years, were more likely to finish school, more likely to find good jobs and to avoid welfare rolls.[8]

All the investigators recognize that further analysis of their data is needed, as well as further research. They think they have reason to believe, however, that the longitudinal evidence will continue to show that preschool experiences can make a lasting difference in the lives of low-income children. Certainly it is no great leap or wild act of faith to believe: Good preschool edu-cation can make a lasting difference in the lives of *all* children.

Some International Comparisons

America is a proud country. We like to think of ourselves as the leader of the free world. We are a competitive people who take delight in being rated first and in having the best and having the most.

It may be a healthy jolt for us to realize how far behind our friends we are in providing early education. Possibly child advocates can use shame—"We are not even second best!"—to prod our country into doing more for young children.

People should know, for example, that the United Kingdom has had free and compulsory education for its five-year-olds since 1872. Israel has provided free and compulsory education for its five-year-olds since 1949, the year

---

[7] *Lasting Effects After Preschool,* a Summary Report of the Consortium for Longitudi-nal Studies, by Irving Lazar and Richard B. Darlington. Washington D.C.: U.S. Gov-ernment Printing Office, 1978. DHEW Publication No. (OHDS) 79–30178.

[8] *An Economic Analysis of the Ypsilanti Perry Preschool Project,* by C.V. Weber, P.W. Foster and D.P. Weikart. Ypsilanti, Mich.: Monographs of the High Scope Educa-tional Research Foundation, No. 5, 1978.

following the birth of that country. A report from Israel says with stunning simplicity: "The latest study shows that 51,500 five-year-olds are in public kindergartens — and that is the total number of our five-year-olds. All of our five-year-olds go to kindergarten — they are required to by law."[9]

Japan is following a plan that will make groups available for all of its four-year-olds by 1981.

The United Kingdom in 1972 set the goal of having free schools for every one of its four-year-olds by 1982.

The Netherlands in 1974 had 89% of its four-year-olds and 97% of its five-year-olds in school, and provided 100% financing for all preschools, private as well as public.

The Australian government gives a subsidy for new buildings, new equipment, and for one-third of a teacher's salary to private schools for three- and four-year-olds. We would call these groups "nursery schools"; Australians call them "preschool kindergartens."

New Zealand does even more. The New Zealand government pays the teacher's full salary in what we call "nursery schools." It pays retirement for the teachers and gives subsidies for new buildings and for new equipment. Parents pay a fee in these schools but the fee is small because of the government's help.

In Norway, Denmark, and Sweden, parents also pay a fee both for the "half-a-day schools" for children three to seven, and for what we would call "child care centers," their "full-day schools" for children the same ages. However, in all three countries the national governments and the local communities subsidize the groups, covering up to 70% to 80% of the cost. The result: The fee paid by parents is small.

It ought to trouble America, the world's wealthiest country, to hear of a 1972 report from India: "Social justice demands attention to the preschool child because the first five years are crucial for all forms of development. Investment in human resource development at a later stage may well prove a waste, if the foundations are neglected."

This report from India indicates an awareness of the early years that is not so apparent in the United States. Whether a country where poverty is the all-pervasive fact of life will ever be able to implement fully its awareness of the significance of the early years is a question. But in America we face prior questions: How persuaded are we of the importance of these years? Do we care enough to spend the money that good programs for young children cost? Child advocates, friends of young children, must help America face up to the choices we have made, and to the possibilities for children that we neglect.

---

[9] All the information for these international comparisons comes from a series of taped interviews with national leaders in early childhood education. The interviews are available on tape cassettes in the album *Early Childhood Education International,* edited by James L. Hymes, Jr. (Arlington, Virginia: Childhood Resources, 1973).

Pushy Programs ━━━━━━━━━━━━━━━━━━━━━━━━━━━━━

We need more programs for young children. Just as urgently we need to improve the quality of our existing programs. It would be ironic, it would be tragic, if we succeeded in bringing more programs into existence only to have more children spending their days in settings blind to their needs.

Too many of our existing classrooms suffer from one or the other of two great prevailing weaknesses: They are either too pushy, or they are too passive.

Vast numbers of young children's groups have one overriding goal: to get the children ready for first grade. This pushy goal is unworthy. It is hurtful.

This goal has had the most distorting impact on five-year-olds. It causes kindergarten to be merely the handmaiden of first grade. First grade sets the standards; it sets the style. Eyes must be on it. Kindergarten teachers cannot look at their own children and plan for their present needs as five-year-olds.

We say there ought not to be a sharp break between kindergarten and first grade. First graders, after all, are only three months older than they were in June at the end of their five-year-old program. Many first grades, in fact, include large numbers of five-year-olds, children who are 5.10 or 5.9 or even younger. We speak of "articulation" between kindergarten and first grade. We are careful in our terminology to talk of K through Six or K through Eight. We speak of the need to make the transition from a five-year-old program to a first-grade program slow, gradual, and imperceptible. And we have done it—but how we have done it! More and more kindergartens are now like bad first grades, but first grades are in no way like good kindergartens!

The undesirable aspects of first grade often seep down most quickly. Get-them-ready-for-first-grade kindergartens stress "socialization." But too often they equate pre-first-grade socialization with conformity. The main goal is to produce a child who will fit in and not cause any trouble. Walking in line, walking on tiptoes, using "our indoor voices," raising one's hand—these are the overly prized social skills.

Pre-first-grade socialization too often is equated with obedience. The main goal is to produce a child who will do what teacher says to do (and, in the process, begin to learn to do what anyone "in authority" says: boss, corporal, leader . . .). The basis for morality is watching the other fellow. The ultimate reason for doing or not doing something is that "WE" do or don't do it: "WE don't throw sand" . . . "WE don't shout" . . . "WE wait our turn."

Pre-first-grade socialization too often is equated with erasing individuality. The fully socialized five-year-old is an in-member of the group. The child finishes work when the group finishes . . . comes to every Story Time . . . is musical because it is Music Time and arty because it is Art Time . . . turns on imagination and creativity because it is time to act out *Little Red Riding Hood* or *Billy Goats Gruff.*

The picture is no more cheering on the academic side. Mechanical procedures are imported: Show-and-Tell . . . workbooks . . . coloring . . . Good-Morning songs . . . dreary nose-counting attendance-taking . . . too much

teacher-talk while shushed children sit in a circle. The dullest content is borrowed: A heavy-handed harping on up, down, left, right . . . even a fussing with
phonics. It sometimes seems as if those parts of first grade least right for six-
year-olds are the ones most apt to be imposed on five-year-olds.

So much that is wrong for children under six is done in the name of
Reading Readiness. "Readiness" is talked about as if it were a distinct and
scholarly field of study, like physics, history or literature, a field especially
designed for kindergarten children. If this were true, it would be a sad mistake
because the content of this so-called field is dishwatery and anti-intellectual.
Many of its methods—contrived sets of paper-and-pencil puzzles—are drab
and artificial. Good kindergartens teach reading to their children, as much as
the children are ready to learn. They teach reading in lively, functional ways
that their five-year-olds are ready for. They stay far away from the made-up
readiness gimmicks.

Kindergarten must get rid of the pressure of preparing children for first
grade. First grades can find their own good goals and their own good ways of
proceeding in light of the children who enter first grade. Kindergarten has *its*
legitimate job to do.

The "Dribble-down Disease"

The awe and dread of first grade is beginning to stain the nursery school whose
job is increasingly seen as getting children ready for kindergarten.

Some day care centers, worried about first grade, deny their own educational significance—they send their five-year-olds away from their own program in the morning so that the children can be sure to get the readiness program of a public school kindergarten. Other day care centers mimic what they
think a kindergarten ought to do. They give their five-year-olds lessons in learning the alphabet, learning the colors, learning to count to ten.

The impending onslaught of first grade can have an especially corrosive
effect on Head Start and Title I programs. The corrosion goes on despite the
clear and sound official position of Head Start. Head Start is deeply concerned with later school success, but it recognizes that many human qualities
feed into success: a child's self-confidence, trust in adults, motivation to learn,
background of success, ease with age-mates. Head Start calls its groups Child
Development Centers. It envisages them as centers for the whole child—for
physical, social, emotional, and intellectual development—and as centers for
the family from which that child comes and for the neighborhood in which
that family has its roots.

In the official Head Start view, a child's success in first grade and in the
long life ahead is not dependent on the forced mastery of a few tiny readiness
tricks. Head Start is concerned with its children living their Head Start year
vigorously and healthfully in ways that are right for them at that time.

There is many a slip twixt the cup and the lip, however. Some compensatory programs zero in on readiness activities with a fervor even fiercer than

that of the frightened kindergarten. The shortage of skilled teachers of young children is one reason for this excess of zeal. The quantity and promotion of readiness materials is another reason. The terrible time-panic that can engulf Head Start and other compensatory programs is another grave source of pressure.

No professional in early education ever thought that the short weeks of Summer Head Start could work miracles in making up for all the deprivations that four or five years of poverty living had caused. Even the longer period of year-round Head Start, thus far the privilege of relatively few poor children, cannot in itself compensate for three or four times that span of earlier deprivation. Youngsters who have been hurt by the bleakness and isolation of poverty need a long stretch of years, all organized with the special interests and capacities and enthusiasms of these particular children in mind. But when first grade is seen as the end of time, Head Start teachers lose all freedom to plan for their children during this fourth or fifth year of their lives.

This kowtowing to first grade—in kindergarten, in Head Start, in nursery school, in day care—is an insult to first grade teachers. They need no one to soften up the children for them or to break the children in. Good first grade teachers can do their job. They have the same job every teacher faces: to work with the children who come. The hegemony of first grade is equally an insult to teachers of children under six. We are professionals and we have our work cut out for us—to teach the children who come to us, the children who are now three, four, or five.

Developmental Theory

This "dribble-down disease" is an old one. The education of children under six is not the only level to suffer from it. High schools have long paid a price because they must get their youngsters ready for college. The junior high school feels it has to get its boys and girls ready for high school. Fifth and sixth grades know the cold shadow of junior high school. Even the first grade teacher has her eye on second grade and imposes its standards on her six-year-olds.

Developmental theory describes an upward-moving process. Children carry much of their infancy with them into toddlerhood; they carry much of their toddler nature on into years three, four, and five; many of their under-six characteristics stay with them as they move on into later childhood. Developmental theory envisages an emerging self, slowly opening up, expanding, tentatively reaching out into new and higher forms of behavior. Incorrect educational practice is the reverse, a downward-moving process. Tomorrow's schooling shapes today's.

An effort to break this top-heavy power structure was made in the late 1930s. The Commission on the Relation of School and College of the Progressive Education Association worked out arrangements so that the graduates of thirty high schools could be admitted to college on their prin-

cipals' recommendations rather than on the basis of having followed a rigid college preparatory program. The thirty schools were free to develop curricula tuned to the needs of their high school youth on the premise that college in its turn could take care of itself.[10]

The thirty high schools, free agents by agreement, did not all take equal advantage of their release from existing academic pressure. Some schools did experiment freely, however. The results were exactly as developmental theory would lead one to expect. The more that high schools developed programs which were "right" at that time for their adolescents, the better those students succeeded in college. The same will hold true for under-six education: The more fully we meet the needs of our children — *now*, when they are with us, as threes, fours, or five-year-olds — the more effectively the children will meet whatever demands are put on them in their tomorrows.

Psychiatric experience provides strong support for this confidence. Those who crumple under life's later demands — the pressures of marriage, the pressures of war, the pressures of independent existence — do so usually because their earlier life experiences were unsatisfactory. Good early living is no sure guarantee of strength and stability as life moves along. Later trauma can be so overpowering that, no matter how supportive early childhood was, humans find themselves confronted by more than they can stand. But good early experiences do strengthen us; they do not weaken us. Unsatisfactory experiences weaken the human; they do not prepare us.

Cognitive Development

The long-standing exploitation of early education in order to get children ready for first grade received reinforcement from a post-World War II anxiety. America developed a frightened sense that there is so much to know and so little time to learn it. This harried feeling was triggered by Russia's shocking initial lead in space achievements, and was set off again by China's unexpected advances in nuclear know-how. America built a picture in its mind of its "enemies" driving their children, working their children, making their children smarter than ours. Nervously, tensely, America looked askance at its young and worried for fear they might not be up to snuff.

This was the period that spawned the campaign to "teach your baby to read," beginning at twelve months of age. Equally symbolic of the anxiety, and more important, is the much-praised television program, *Sesame Street.* In 1980, almost 90 percent of our three-, four-, and five-year-olds watched *Sesame Street,* making it by all odds the largest early childhood "school."

There can be argument over how much good *Sesame Street* does young children — whether its rote learning is destructive or constructive; whether its irrelevant learnings stimulate curiosity or contribute to killing it off; whether being manipulated by quick-moving wizardry energizes or enervates young

---

[10] Adventure in American Education (New York: Harper & Row, 1942, five volumes).

children in the long run. Some critics have attacked *Sesame Street's* "oral ag-gression" on the young; others have had kind words for the program.

There can be no argument over how much good *Sesame Street* does for adults. Its overriding tone is reassuring to adult America's anxiety, even if the program is not in tune with young America's needs. *Sesame Street teaches!* It teaches the alphabet. It teaches numbers from one to ten, and then it teaches them from ten to twenty. It teaches the numbers backwards. It teaches and teaches, minute after minute, and it moves so quickly that it squeezes a full sixty seconds of teaching out of every minute.

Sesame Street is doubly reassuring to adults because it teaches the old *familiar* alphabet and those good old *familiar* numbers. Some part of America's anxiety stems from the shock of seeing fast-moving developments everywhere we turn. Heart transplants . . . men on the moon . . . supersonic travel . . . instantaneous telecasts from Peking via satellite . . . magical com-puters . . . birth control and fertility pills . . . all under the cloud of a bomb that could end life on this planet. The new happenings often come with a dreadful mien; they always come with an unsettling impact. These are times when we all, unconsciously to be sure, yearn for the security, the stability, the safety of what we have known. Teaching little children little facts — the letters, the col-ors, the numbers, sizes, shapes — makes many an adult feel safer. In addition, such teaching provides that great mental health response to anxiety — at least we are doing *something!* *Sesame Street's* feverish activity is typical of much that is called "cognitive development." The fact that babies and toddlers and two-year-olds can see the program is added balm. Early childhood education makes sense for some adults just so long as it says: "Here we come, ready or not; you can't start too early to learn, learn, learn."

Since fear of Russian superiority is at the root of some of this pressure, it is interesting to note that Russia does not put the heat on its young children. In the Soviet Union, the formal, structured teaching of reading does not begin un-til first grade, and first grade does not begin until age seven. There are some people in the Soviet Union who would like to push formal reading instruction down to age six and even to younger ages, but these efforts are being resisted. One Soviet educator argues against this pressure in words that should give pause to up-tight Americans: "Teaching reading to five and six-year-olds would take away their childhood"![11]

Children's Many Needs

Cognitive development is a basic and legitimate concern in the education of children under six. The bright new spotlight on it can be a useful prod to those schools that err by having programs that are too passive. In many programs, however, cognitive development has become the sole concern.

---

[11] Quoted by Susan Jacoby in her report on preschool education in the Soviet Union in *Early Childhood Education International,* edited by James L. Hymes, Jr. (Arling-ton, Virginia: Childhood Resources, 1973).

This concentration is an ironic development at a time when even the most anxious adults know that our pressing problems — and the pressing problems young children will have to face as they grow up — are not basically problems of fact or problems of knowledge. Our experiences today make it abundantly clear that we need children with healthier feelings and with sounder social sensitivities fully as much as we need better-informed children. Today's education makes a major error when it concentrates on knowledge alone.

In recent years, we have seen churches bombed, school buses burned, and whole areas of our cities destroyed by fire because some of us fear and hate some of our neighbors.

Sick and driven individuals have assassinated some of our country's finest men. Barricaded on a university tower, on a hotel roof, attacking from countless less dramatic settings, disturbed men and women have lashed out. They were not responding to the people they hurt and killed as humans; they were responding only to their own inner torment. We have so much to learn about handling our emotions and about healing emotional hurts.

Young people by the tens of thousands have felt so alienated from their homes, their schools, and their communities that they have fled — either as physical runaways or as refugees into drugs.

These are the problems that truly worry America: How can we live with ourselves? How can we live with our feelings? How can we live with each other? We have called ourselves a "sick society," a "violent society," a society of escapists.

Every mother and father of a young child has known moments of stark fear contemplating what life might be like for the child — and what their child might be like — as the youngster moves into adolescence and adulthood. Every mother and father has known moments of despair as the day's news unfolded its tales of brutality, of hostility. In these times, to describe as "ironic" the concentration on cognitive development alone is not strong enough. To concentrate singlemindedly on one goal and one goal alone is myopic.

Out-Of-Date Approaches

The error is compounded when cognitive development is equated with the old readiness devices, with constant talking *at* children, with artificial lessons unrelated to children's living. It is unfortunate that some of the newest ideas in the recent surge for cognitive development are identical with the approaches in the oldest workbooks: "The goal of this exercise is to teach the names of the shapes (circle, square, triangle, rectangle) . . . to teach the colors (red, blue, green, yellow, black, brown) . . . to teach concepts (under, on top of, over, beside, small, larger) . . . to teach counting (1, 2, 3, 4)." The battle cry is new but the result is old: We bring the dreary parts of first grade down into younger children's lives.

Children under six must use their minds, and they want to. They must learn, and they want to. But the challenge to good education is to find the con-

tent and the methods of teaching that fit young children. Then their minds will really stretch. Youngsters are not necessarily thinking their best because they are sitting their straightest. The particular challenge is to find the ways of teaching that are most apt to encourage children to go on with learning. There is so much to learn today, more than the pushiest program can ever cram into children no matter how early it starts. Our concern has to be to develop a love of learning. Because of the knowledge explosion, children will have to continue learning, on their own, all through their lives.

Passive Programs

Passive programs are almost as hurtful as pushy ones. Passive programs are monuments to missed teaching opportunities.

For years in the past, most day care centers had programs that were too passive. Too many still do even today. The goal of old-time day care was simply to provide custodial care—to take children, to keep them safe, to return them whole to parents at the end of the day, in one piece and undamaged.

The millions of mothers of young children who are on jobs today or who cannot care for their children at home because of illness or some other reason can understand this simple goal. The pressures on these mothers are such that, if need be, they will gladly settle for someone who will keep their child out of harm's way. They are willing, often desperate, to buy even such a program if they can afford it.

There is nothing wrong with the word "care." The education of young children is the education of dependent children, of active children, the education of youngsters with little impulse control and little understanding of potential dangers. Children under six, more than any other age, are prone to accidental death and injury. *Good* care is a legitimate concern of every group: nursery school, kindergarten, Head Start, and day care. Every good teacher in every good program, no matter what its name, owes it to a parent to say: "I will be responsible . . . I, the teacher, am here; you, the parent, are not . . . I will do whatever needs doing, just as you would if you could; you can rest assured."

We can meet well this minimum standard: comforting young children, as a good parent would, when they need comfort; listening as a good parent would; being thrilled with achievement, as a good parent would; feeding when a child is hungry; letting the sleepy child sleep; individualizing and personalizing, as a good parent would. *Good* care—nurturing, protecting—is so rock-bottom a goal that we often forget to spell it out and sometimes forget to provide it.

Custodial Care

Custodial care is something different, however, A custodial care center is like a parking lot. Presumably, children come back in the same condition in which

they were left: no dented fenders, no paint scraped, no changes for the worse, and none for the better, either. Nurses in sterile white caps and uniforms often were in charge of early day care centers. Their job was to keep children from doing anything, because doing something might lead to trouble. Today, the nurses have disappeared; in their place are minimally trained staffs. Custodial care demands little in equipment, materials, or supplies. Only one big expenditure seems legitimate: a television set. It keeps the children quiet.

The goal is narrow. The goal is unrealistic.

Young children share a characteristic with all ages: *They learn from everything and they learn all the time.* They learn from what we set out to teach them; they learn also when no one thinks a lesson is being taught. There are direct learnings *and* there are incidental learnings. Children never come, stay, and go untouched by an experience, with no change for the worse and none for the better.

In custodial care, the unsuspected side effects can be disastrous. No one sets out to teach it, but there is the danger that children will learn passivity: Don't show initiative; they will yell at you . . . Don't be curious; it gets you into trouble . . . Don't ask questions; no one listens.

No one sets out to teach it, but there is the danger that children will learn conformity: Don't get out of line or you'll get in trouble. There is the danger that they will learn not to trust adults and not to trust themselves. Children dropped at a custodial care center, herded at a custodial care center, ignored at a custodial care center may learn ways of rebellion or ways of escape.

Custodial care centers often deny that they are teaching anything. They do this to avoid having to meet standards for staff, equipment, space, programs that are set for schools. Many state departments of education are foolishly reluctant to license day care centers. They say, "These are not schools" and gladly relinquish the job of supervision to the department of health or welfare. The words—"We are not teaching anything" and "These are not schools"—do not alter the facts. They simply give custodial centers the freedom to be bad schools.

The inescapable fact is that every day care center, whether it knows it or not, *is* a school. The choice is never between custodial care and education. The choice is between unplanned and planned education, between conscious and unconscious education, between bad education and good education.

Most parents who today turn to day care centers are driven to them by sheer economic necessity. They must work or their family situation is so strained that they have no alternative. It is tragic when such already distressed families are forced to turn to centers which achieve only custodial care.

This fate is a common one for working mothers and their children. A 1972 investigation showed that 35 percent of the day care centers run for profit were essentially custodial. They provided at best "fair" care, in the limited sense of meeting physical needs but doing very little, if anything, to meet other basic needs. Fifty percent of the centers run for profit rendered *less* than custodial care! They gave poor care; in some cases, very poor indeed. This investigation rated nonprofit centers as being somewhat better. Fifty percent of

these were described as providing custodial care, but only 10 percent were rated as poor—an improvement, but hardly an earth-shaking one.[12]

A significant number of today's mothers choose to work; they do not have to work for compelling economic reasons. Many work for the sake of their child. They want more income for future education, or for a nicer home, or for more comforts. It is ironic as well as tragic when these parents are forced to turn to custodial care centers. Most ease their consciences by blithely assuming that if no one is teaching, the child isn't learning. Many would be dismayed to know some of the learnings children drink in "when no one is teaching."

It is easy to leap to an unrealistic "solution": Make every mother stay at home! The better solution is to provide public day care centers. With adequate tax support, day care centers can have trained staffs, good equipment and a sound curriculum. They need not have passive programs. With the resources to buy good teaching, their programs can be good.

"Play" Schools

Nursery schools traditionally have been scornful of custodial care. Many, however, have their own brand of passive program. Such nursery schools frequently have good play equipment; they may well have ample space; they usually give the youngsters considerable freedom. But once the teacher has set the stage, she has done her good deed for the day. She turns the children loose, injecting herself only rarely to prevent accidents or when there is a bad quarrel. These nursery schools shun television sets. Their big money is apt to go, just as wastefully, into swings or a merry-go-round.

The passivity of some nursery schools stems in part from inadequate goals. These schools think only of socialization. Their one big concern is to help children learn to live together, to get along together, to share, and to cooperate. Their concept of good socialization is apt to be more wholesome than the confining and stereotyped aims of those kindergartens that focus on pre-first-grade socialization. But the isolated concentration on any *single* goal—social development in the nursery school, cognitive development in the kindergarten—underestimates children's capacity to learn, misjudges the realities of life, and always narrows a program needlessly.

Promoting sound social development is a worthy educational goal—it is *one* worthy goal. But good schools are schools for the development of the *whole child.* They seek to help children develop their social powers *and* their intellectual, emotional, and physical powers.

Three- and four-year-olds have not been hurt as much in passive nursery schools as have those children caught in custodial care centers, but they have

---

[12] *Windows on Day Care,* by Mary Dublin Keyserling, ed. (New York: National Council of Jewish Women, 1972).

not learned as much as they comfortably, readily could. The children usually are active. They learn a little from their use of materials. They learn a little from their age-mates. But their learnings are apt to be haphazard and spotty, with little of the learning individualized. Chances to count, measure, and compare slip by. Opportunities to enrich vocabulary go unnoticed. Opportunities to provoke thinking about cause and effect are ignored. Factual misunderstandings are not heard by the teacher and not clarified. The teacher is on the sidelines. No adult is close enough to what the children are doing to take advantage of the teaching opportunities.

Even in the top-prized area of social learning, the teacher stays aloof except during crises. The materials and equipment do all of the teaching; the adult looks on, usually from a distance. The children teach each other; the adult looks on, usually from a distance. Sound learnings about ways of living together may emerge, or individuals may as easily learn to give in, to go along, or sometimes just to give up. The teacher is simply the safety supervisor, not the skilled yet unobtrusive leader who sensitively knows when to step in to reinforce sound learnings and to clarify and to avert miseducative happenings.

The passivity of these schools stems also from their overeagerness to let the child have fun. They escalate *play* from its rightful position as one of the prized methods of good education to an end in itself. These are "play-play-play" schools, not schools which wisely use play as one solid means of helping children to learn. They have one standard that justifies any activity, no matter what: "The children love it!"

This measuring rod—"The children love it!"—is a kindly standard, a gentle one. "Play-play-play" schools can take pride in their sensitive concern for the feeling tone of a child's daily life. Regrettably, many other schools do not care enough whether children are happy, whether they are pleased with what they are doing. This is most unfortunate. A school's job is to give children life, not to rob them of it. Early education must value highly each child's happiness; it must never lose a deep concern for bringing joy to children's days. But the educational challenge is to bring this about through maximum learning.

"The children love it!" can justify an excursion (not a carefully planned field experience) to the ice cream plant—"They always give the youngsters a popsicle at the end." It can justify an over-exciting, confusing, wearying trip to the county fair, or to the circus, or to see a parade. It can justify taking no trips at all and never varying the equipment indoors or out-of-doors—the children seem to be playing happily enough.

Youngsters must love what they are doing. Their "love"—their rapt attention, their voluntary self-selection—is the surest indicator of their readiness to learn and the best guarantee of retention of learning. But *what the children are doing* has to be an educator's first concern. Young children are our newcomers. They are wide open. The most amazing array of novelties will please them. They can have fun watching a movie cartoon. They even take a bemused sort of pleasure in a story they do not understand. Most can go on day after day contentedly enough "just playing" out their home experiences

and what they see on TV, never receiving new stimulus or challenge from their school. They can "love" (or like or be willing enough, if nothing better is available) to go down a slide they have gone down a thousand times before. But this is not enough.

A good school is not a parking lot, a custodial care center. Neither is it an amusement park, a "play-play-play" school.

Young children need ample chance to play. They need the chance to play at school throughout all the early childhood years. But they need the chance to play in response to provocative stimulation. They must be playing out—sorting out, trying out—in response to a rich stream of mind and body and feeling-stretching experiences flowing in to them. Good programs carefully, consciously confront children with the most significant experiences available. Then, consciously, sensitively, teachers help children learn all they can from these experiences. Youngsters love this, too. Children have their deepest, truest "fun" when they function at their best.

Passivity in many nursery schools stems from inadequate goals. It stems from confusion of method and goal. It stems from poor implementation of method. But all these causes of passivity usually have their root in that persistent devil—lack of money! School days have lift and bounce when teachers plan the right experiences for their youngsters and give children whatever help is needed. Good planning demands active, not passive teachers—teachers skilled in opening up new choices, new challenges. It demands careful, continuous planning, not the same old thing day after day. It requires a personalized program, not one that turns children loose.

These fine teaching skills cost money. Like private colleges, no nursery school can operate well on tuition income alone. Few parents are wealthy enough to pay all the costs of good education. Until there is tax support for public nursery schools, nursery education is in danger of becoming a part-time job for part-time people with partial training. Too many children who go now to private nursery schools will continue to receive partial, passive early education.

Top-Quality Education Under Six

Many lucky youngsters get off to a good start. Despite the problems facing early education, there are outstanding nursery schools and day care centers. There are superb kindergartens. Many Head Start and Title I programs are excellent. The teachers in these good programs look to sound theory as the basis for their curriculum. They deliberately build their programs on their best knowledge of why they are teaching, whom they are teaching, what they are teaching, and how they are teaching.[13]

---

[13] When the singular pronoun is called for, the teacher of the child under six is referred to in this book as "she." Statistically, "she" is a logical choice, although it is unfair to the small but growing number of male early childhood teachers. And it is misleading if "she" seems to imply that only women can teach young children. Unfortunately, the English language has its limitations and the lack of a bisexual singular pronoun is one of them.

Teachers in these good programs keep their goals utterly clear. They aim to help their children *learn,* and to do it in such a way that the youngsters live their years of three, four, and five in the richest, most satisfying, most constructive way possible.

Teachers in these good programs are child-centered. They know what young children are like. Young children are different from older youngsters—they are not the same, simply cut down in size. These teachers' awareness of the special qualities of the very young colors everything that happens in their classrooms. Their keen, sensitive understanding of child development is a prime factor in making the third, fourth, and fifth years of life as pleasing and as productive as they can possibly be.

Teachers in these good programs are society-centered. They know and love our country, the best of its past and present. They hold bright hopes and conscious dreams for our future. These teachers' sense of democratic values colors everything that happens in their classrooms. All of their relationships, everything they do, the whole life of their rooms is consistent with the finest qualities of our society—the values we hold dear and want to preserve, the values we want to nurture and help expand. These teachers know that young children are our future, but they know, too, that the future is not tomorrow—the future is now. The way young children live and learn today becomes the way they will live and learn tomorrow.

Teachers in these good programs are subject-matter-centered. They know academic content and they know sound ways of teaching it to young children. Good classrooms for the very young teach the sciences and mathematics; they teach the social sciences; they teach the humanities; they teach health and physical education, as all schools of general education must. These good teachers are skilled in adapting these fields of learning to young children. Their methods are not unusual ones. Like teachers at all levels of education, they, too, use lectures and discussions, tutoring, and face-to-face instruction, laboratory and workshop sessions, buzz sessions, and committee work, first-hand investigation, independent study, all kinds of audiovisual and other learning aids. But they use these standard methods in the right proportion for the young children they teach. They use them wisely in ways that fit the age and fit our democratic society.

Teachers in these good programs have the tools they need to do their job. They have the right class size and the right ratio of adults to children. They have the space they need, and the equipment. They have the professional freedom to do what they know should be done. Sometimes they have had to argue, cajole, and fight on behalf of their classrooms and their children but they know: If school is school is school—the same school for everyone regardless of age—it never is a good school for the very young. These teachers have what it takes, in spirit and in material stuff, to tailor-make their classrooms to fit the children who come to them.

2

A CHILD-CENTERED PROGRAM

Young children are a special breed. Children under six are different from the eight-year-olds and twelve-year-olds and sixteen-year-olds that our schools have served so long. They are so different that it is useful to think of early education as a kind of "special education."

Three-, four-, and five-year-olds are exceptional children. They are not mentally retarded or physically handicapped or emotionally disturbed, but they have their own kind of exceptionality that marks them off and demands special approaches: These children are *young.*

Some people think that Head Start children are the ones who are exceptional—that poor children are the different ones. People who hold this opinion set Head Start youngsters apart from all other young children. They envisage a program for them that is different from all other programs for the very young.

It is not accurate to draw a line between Head Start children and other young children. All young children—the children of the poor, the children of the rich—have a typical style and a typical swing in common. These qualities stem from the children's age and developmental status. They flow from the children's human nature. These qualities are not drastically changed by family income, geographic location, or other external factors. They come with being young and all young children share them—Head Start youngsters, nursery, kindergarten, and day care children.

Individual boys and girls, because of family background or personal traits, may show some of these special qualities to a greater or lesser extent. Groups— Head Start youngsters, children of affluence—may exhibit some of them in a more accentuated or diminished fashion. Slight age-level differences show themselves as the children move from age three to four to five. The variations are minor, however. The special style and the special swing of the young are deep-rooted, pervasive characteristics, and they stamp all children in the entire age range.

The right distinction is between *all* young children and all older young-sters. The line of distinction usually is drawn at age six, but it should not be. Six-year-olds have a great deal in common with children under six. Sixes share all the qualities that go with being young that are described in the following pages; they are involved in the same basic growth tasks that children under six face. The real dividing line between early childhood and middle childhood is not between the fifth year and the sixth year—it is closer to when children are about seven or eight, moving on toward nine. Building the barrier at age six has no psychological basis. It has come about only from the historic-economic-political fact that the age of six is when we provide schools for all.

The Style and Swing of the Young

In at least a dozen specific ways—other specialists might list more—young children flow differently from their older brothers and sisters. They have their own ways of operating. Some of these qualities of being young can be ir-ritating for adults to live with. Some are difficult qualities for the usual school to take into account. But young children are made this way—this is their nature. The capacity and the willingness to live with these qualities make the crucial distinction between a good classroom for young children and one that does not fit the age.

Young Children Are Not Good Sitters

Give them time and some day they will stay seated. Give them five or ten years. Then they will love to lounge and loaf, to stretch out, to stay put and take it easy. At this special point in their development, however, three-, four- and five-year-olds are people on the go. They can sit. They will sit briefly, at the table for juice; briefly, sprawled on the floor for a story; briefly, hunched on their chairs working a puzzle. But sitting is not the young child's natural, com-fortable position. It is not the pose the young child often chooses or stays in for a long period.

Energy is popping inside these boys and girls. And the world around them always seems unusually alluring. These are active children, seldom still, seldom in a chair. They would make very bad office workers; they make a very bad audience. They feel almost all of the time what older children feel some of the time: "Please don't tie me down. Please don't fence me in."

Young children need room. They need two classrooms. They need ample space *indoors* for one classroom; they need even more generous space *outside* reserved for their very own outdoor classroom. The standard space has been thirty-five square feet per child indoors, but this is minimal, really too little.

Forty-five to fifty square feet of open, usable space per child is more nearly right. Out-of-doors, the accepted standard of 200 square feet per child seems to be adequate. How to provide this needed fenced outdoor classroom is a great challenge to urban schools with no playground—sites where many Head Start programs and day care centers are located. Roof tops may have to be converted for use as outdoor classrooms. Or, at the least, "outdoor" equipment must be made available at times indoors so that young children have the chance they are so eager for to perfect their body skills.

Indoors and out, young children need room for an eight-ring circus, not a mere three-ring one. The space is important because every classroom activity must offer an opportunity for action. These boys and girls cannot simply sit, listen, watch, and still be true to their nature. The good classroom does not operate on the premise that a child must sit down in order to learn. The good teacher has the know-how to teach active children significant learnings even though the youngsters are on the move much of the time. Any school that urgently needs to save money should not buy chairs or certainly not one for every child. Chairs ought to be the least used pieces of equipment in early education.

Young Children Are Not Good at Keeping Quiet

Young children can and do keep quiet—for brief and exceptional periods of time. They are quiet when they are asleep. They are quiet some of the time when their mouths are full of food. They are quiet when someone talks to them personally, face-to-face. They are quiet through some but seldom all of a story.

Young children can be quiet, but at this point in life, silence is not golden. Young children enjoy noise for its own sake, and the activity that means the most to them makes noise. Their moving about makes noise. They speak out what comes into their minds, and they want to talk with their friends.

Young children are subject, as we all are, to the fatigue of overstimulation and to the tension of confusion. Pandemonium will get them down. But the sounds of a laboratory or of a workshop, the happy sounds of friends, and sounds of work do not bother them. Good order in a young child's classroom—good working conditions—differs from the order and quiet of a library or a church or from that of the book-centered classroom.

Young children need freedom to talk as they play and work. They are the ones—not the teacher—who do most of the talking in a good classroom. The size of their groups must be right so that the natural noise of busy people does not mount simply because there are too many humans in the room. Their rooms must be situated—or acoustically treated—so that hammering and laughter, drums and a piano, blocks falling and children's conversations do not become crises for a whole school. A good classroom for young children need not be so quiet that you can hear a pin drop before a child can learn.

Young Children Are Shy

Children under six are not yet "hale fellows well met." They love people and are fascinated by them, but they love people best in small doses. Masses overwhelm the young child.

Young children are at their best in a class of ten, twelve, fifteen, or twenty children depending on their age. This is not small class size for them. For them, this is *full* class size, up to the brim and almost overflowing. These children are just beginning, gingerly and tentatively, to thread their way into the wider world. These are shrinking violets, so easily stamped back by crowds into an uncomfortable sense of their own littleness.

Even right class size has to be broken down into still smaller subgroups, into safe personal clusters. Then young children really blossom out. Face-to-face with their teacher they can be at ease. Face-to-face with one other child—or with two or three or four—they can be talkative and good listeners, comfortable and responsive. If children have to spend much time in the group as a whole, even a class of right size can seem like Times Square on New Year's Eve. That is why young children need a teacher who is not under a compulsion to keep the whole group together around her. A good teacher has to be mobile and move around as much as the children do.

Young children need a room with nooks where they can be by themselves at times, alone with a book or puzzle or game. They need a room that is large enough so that, most of the day, they can work with two or three or four other children. Children under six are not yet "joiners," not yet ready to shout, "Hail, hail, the gang's all here." They get along beautifully if you let them make their own definition of *gang*: a small, intimate group.

Young Children Are Highly Egocentric

At some point far in the future, if their growth has been healthy, young children will think in terms of a team, a mate, a family, a nation, a world. Now, they are in the early springtime of this life-long development. They are aware of *themselves*. Their one clear point of reference is an intensely personal one.

Their keenest interest lies in themselves. This self-centeredness shows in their greetings: "I have new shoes." . . . "I have a new belt." Their truly precious self is in every train of thought and pops out in interruptions of story and discussion and conversation: "I have a puppy." . . . "I went to the hospital once." All their understanding ties back to themselves: "My daddy shaves." . . . "My mommy works." . . . "My uncle is visiting us." . . . "I saw a policeman." On every issue, the vote is the same: The "I's" have it!

Not so long ago, these children were not even aware they existed as separate individuals, persons apart. Now they are overwhelmed by this awareness and expect the whole world to be equally amazed. "Old hands"—more certain of who they are and what they are like, more accepting of their limita-

tions, clearer on their powers—can relax. These "new hands" are full of themselves. They want to make choices. They have strong preferences. They love to take the initiative, to have an idea and carry it out themselves. Eventually, these children will be able, if their life goes right, to follow the commandment, *Love thy neighbor as thyself.* Right now, they are taking the first step: Children under six are learning to love themselves.

Their teacher must take the time to listen to each child and, most important, be willing to praise and to puff up each youngster. Our adult attitude is so important. Good teachers believe that, given healthy growth, a strong social sense will develop in children in good time. But now is the time for a sense of *personal* worth. It is all too easy, in the name of morality, to suppress this budding individuality. We must be glad to see each child blossom.

In one way, the young child's egocentricity ought to make us glad. For it gives us a good approach to curriculum. As long as the child sees himself or herself in the picture, we can be sure interest and enthusiasm will run high in the classroom.

Young Children Want to Feel Proud, Big, and Important

Success matters very much to the under-six age group. These children want so desperately to be able to hold their heads high.

They sound exceedingly boastful: "I can count to five." . . . "I can tie my shoes." . . . "I know how old I am. Do you want to see?" . . . "I fell and I didn't even cry." Young children maintain their own "public relations" offices. They are continuously concerned with getting their names and their skills and knowledge and powers into the "headlines." But we mustn't be misled by this drumbeating. The self-glorification is as much for the children's benefit as for ours—they can't quite believe their own importance.

For all their braggadocio, these are still very incompetent children. A hundred times a day their smallness, their ignorance, their limited capacities bring them face to face with an irritating, frustrating fact: They are still little shavers; they still cannot do very much. Inescapably, they are confronted with things they can't reach, things they can't lift, things they can't carry, things they can't see but want to see.

Success tastes sweet because it comes too seldom to young children. No wonder they beat the drums to celebrate: "I can write my name. Do you want to see me?" . . . "I can hop on one foot. Watch!" . . . "I can climb all the way up to the top!" The rumble of the drums makes achievement seem like an every-minute event. The child wishes it were; in reality, success is rare.

Added man-made failure really hurts young children. No one needs to contrive lessons for these youngsters so that they learn how to lose—they are losers too much of the time as it is. No one has to put them in their place—they know all too well the little place they are in. No one has to cut them down to

size—their size is painfully small. At this stage in their development we are wise not to build competition into our classrooms, or games, or races, or contests with winners and losers. It matters too much to each child to come in first.

A good classroom offers many ways in which many children can know glory. It must not have a program which prizes only certain kinds of abilities, a track where the race is only to the swift. It must have many jobs that youngsters can do, many responsibilities they can carry, the widest variety of burdens and challenges within the capacities of the widest variety of children. Each day, each child must go home with head held higher.

Young Children Have Their Private Dream World

Boys and girls under six perform many realistic, honest-to-goodness jobs. They learn many down-to-earth facts and build many practical skills. It is up to us to plan the environment so that they know objective success often during a day. But young children also have a kind of personal insurance policy. They live a large part of their time in a private dream world, one they themselves plan, manage, and control beautifully. In their dream world, things always work out as they should. In their dream world, each child can be as strong and powerful and masterful as ego demands. Each child is guaranteed all the sympathy, support, love, and tenderness that any loser could ask.

This dream world is young children's private world of play and pretend. They create it through their own imagination. Make-believe serves many developmental purposes. It is the arena for much of the young child's early thinking, planning, and organizing. Intellectual processes go on in play that are foundational to all the clear reasoning of which the child will be capable later. Make-believe is the avenue to much of the young child's early understanding. Children sort out impressions and try out ideas that are basic to later realistic comprehension. This private world sometimes is a quiet, solitary world. More often, it is a noisy, busy, crowded place where language grows, social skills develop, and perseverance and attention spans enlarge. But always underneath, while these other purposes are being served, make-believe is also the young child's private haven.

Older, more confident people have less need of dream worlds. Only rarely do they turn to imaginary conversations, their brief flights of daydreaming, their Walter Mitty moments. Young children, on the other hand, unsure and open to hurt, have a continuous need for settings where they themselves can make the rules—"This must be our garage and this must be our car"; and where they can control the outcomes—"This must be my birthday and you must bring me a present"; and where they are the masters—"I must be the doctor and you must be sick."

At the under-six age, reality—accuracy, the facts, what actually goes on, how things really work—must not dominate the day. Teachers must know how to encourage fantasy, how to stimulate a child's own spontaneous make-believe world. Play is so important developmentally. We must make sure that going to school does not rob the child of opportunities to pretend.

Young Children Are Very Tender

Young children need to know they are loved. Every human, even the strongest among us, shares this hunger. But young children are dependent in the extreme. They are the newcomers to our earth. The aliens. The strangers. They are feeling their way, just getting the hang of things. So much is strange, incomprehensible. They must be able to turn with full faith to the old-timers, to the people who know their way around.

Older children have developed resources within themselves. In contrast, the young child's pillars of support are parents and teachers. When these supports seem angry or cold or aloof or disinterested or busy, young children have nothing. They are left alone, which is more than they can bear. Young children want to grow in their own strength, but they have to grow from a position of safety. They need big people whom they can trust.

These are affectionate youngsters. They are demonstrative at times. Wordy assurances of love from adults do not always fill the bill. Young children come to us for a kiss or a squeeze, the physical proof that all is well. They seek sympathy, the playful pat, the gentle arm, the friendly hand. Their classroom cannot be an impersonal standoffish place.

Most of all, it cannot be a harsh, angry, dissatisfied classroom—young children count too deeply on our goodwill. They scare easily—a tough tone, a sharp reprimand, an exasperated glance, a peeved scowl will do it. Little signs of rejection—you don't have to hit young children to hurt them—cut deeply. Sometimes their response fools us. In their panic when they feel they are not loved, young children often behave badly. If they are to be at their best, their classroom must be suffused with gentleness and warmth.

Young Children Are Beginners

Their classroom must be infused with patience and tolerance, too. Young children are life's amateurs. They make all kinds of mistakes, as any fumbling beginner must. Give young children a kitten and they squeeze it too hard. Let them touch a baby and they touch it too roughly. They spill their juice. They knock over blocks. They run where people should walk. They make noise where older people are quiet. When they first try to write their names, they often write backwards. They punch, pinch, and grab at times even though they "know" they should not. Young children are mistake-prone youngsters.

They make errors partly because their coordination is still uncertain. They err partly because their emotions are so strong. They err because life's big lessons simply take a long time to learn, and young children are still inexperienced and uninformed. They "know" a little about these lessons but they haven't mastered them—and they forget.

The patience we need in living with young children comes more easily if we remember: *They have time!* They have years stretching ahead of them. The chances are great indeed that today's young children will finish high school.

Start them in school at three and they have fifteen years of formal schooling ahead. The chances are good, too, that today's young children will go on to college—they probably have seventeen to nineteen years or more of formal schooling ahead. By the time they reach young adulthood, graduate, specialized, or technical training will be even more common than it is today. Today's young children may well have twenty or more years of schooling ahead. More and more of them will live to age ninety. They will live in a time where there will be better and easier means of informal schooling and of independent study. The child in nursery school today may well have eighty-seven years of learning stretching out ahead.

Time is not running out for young children. Time is just beginning. Because of this, the young child's classroom, more than that of children at any other grade level, ought to be free of cram sessions. More than any other, it should be tension-free. It ought to be calamity-free and crisis-free. Mistakes must be corrected and the right ways must be learned, but there should be no feeling of panic that one has to stuff these beginners quickly with social, physical, emotional, or intellectual learnings.

Young children have the time but they need the time. Intellectually, they cannot incorporate learnings into themselves with words said once, words said quickly. They need more than a once-over-lightly approach. Emotionally, they cannot stand the pace of acceleration and pressure. Their classroom must run on slow time. After all, these are the children who at home and at school beg to hear the same story over and over again. It is the adult, not the child, who is in a hurry to move on, thinking, "Oh, no! Not the same one again!"

Young Children Are Hungry for Stimulation

Their pace is slow. They repeat themselves. They are not bored easily by what can seem to quick-moving, quick-thinking adults like "the same old thing." But young children are not blasé. They want to learn. They are curious. They carry within them—they have since they were born—a sharp hunger for stimulation.

When they were crib-bound babies, their minds were not idle. As infants, these children used their eyes as their first investigators—roaming, peering, probing. Their fingers have been tools for learning ever since they learned to make hands and eyes work together. Just as soon as those exploring hands could carry objects to the mouth, youngsters as infants began to use lips and tongue to find out about the world. They tasted and sucked more weird things than parents care to remember. Once language developed, these same children began a steady, wearying stream of questions.

Young children are slow learners—they like to take their time. But these are not reluctant scholars. They are the most eager age ever to walk into a school. In school, they continue to want to see, to touch and handle and use, to taste, and to sniff. Words alone seldom satisfy the deep-rooted curiosity of this age. Call young children cynics. Call them skeptics. Say they all come from Missouri. They prefer not to take anyone's word or to take much on faith. They want to test things out for themselves.

It is this drive for stimulation, this hunger to find out, that alerts middle-class, conscientious parents that their child needs more than home alone can provide: "I can't keep up with him." . . . "She's always getting into things." Once children are in nursery school or kindergarten (or day care or Head Start), the group must not tone down, dull, or deaden this curiosity. Because children are in a group, it must be easier, not harder, to confront them with objects, people and events for their eyes, ears, nose, mouth, and fingers to explore.

The young child's two classrooms — indoors and outdoors — must be rich in variety, rich in newness, rich in challenge. They must be open classrooms: Open-shelved, with youngsters free to explore the feast before their eyes, and open-doored, with youngsters more able to explore the world outside their schoolroom because they are in school. "Going to" school need not mean "staying in" school. To satisfy this eager age, school cannot mean a period of confinement and containment; it must mean a chance for the child to engage in wider exploration.

Young Children are Earthy, Practical, Concrete-Minded

Young children learn from words, of course. They have been talked with and at in their homes. In all schools — inevitably, necessarily — they will still be talked with and at. But words alone — symbols, substitutes for the real thing — are not yet their best means of learning. Words, in fact, can fool them: They think they understand. Words can fool us too: We think they understand.

Today's children are often good talkers. They give the impression of being smart, but some of their smartness is simply their "line." The TV they have seen and the talk they have overheard give them a veneer. They can become good parakeets, but understanding is their goal. It ought to be our goal, too.

Young children are starting from scratch. It sounds harsh to say, "They are ignorant," but they do know so little. They must first pile up the specifics, pile up the incidents, pile up the situations so they can have a solid base of things they do understand. Not until then do they have something concrete to which they can relate new ideas as they come along. Not until then can they use symbols with a clearer, truer sense of knowing what they stand for.

A good classroom for young children is not in a hurry to skip over the real, the actual. It must be glad to begin at the beginning. People always say that experience is the best teacher. It certainly is the foundational teacher. And because of that, it is the ideal teacher for the very young. These youngsters can make the greatest sense out of what they have had the chance, at firsthand, to see and do and explore.

Young Children Are Acquiescent

Young children — new to the world, new to school — are not yet in a position to be critics. They must take things as they come. They must assume that

whatever happens is the natural order of events. This acquiescence is part of young children's armor against trauma and tragedy. It is part of their protection against the many disasters that say to older people: "Something is wrong!" Young children make only the simple assumption: "This must be the way things are."

This naiveté is compounded by young children's dependence on adult goodwill. They stand ready to go along with whatever adults seem to want. They stand poised, trying to figure out what is wanted. Young boys and girls are almost at the mercy of adults — it is so important to children to please. This is a hazardous position for boys and girls whose developmental need is to be pleased with themselves.

This combination of newness and dependence means that it is easy to take advantage of young children. With only a little force, with only a little sweetness, teachers can make young children jump through hoops for them. Teachers in good classrooms must bend over backwards not to manipulate youngsters. They must be strong adults who are not afraid to be adults when a child needs from them the strength that only an adult can have. But these strong adults must also be humble adults who are uncommonly honest with themselves. They must constantly ask themselves about the activities in their room: "Whose idea was it?" "Whom does it please?"

Older children are more apt to fight back when they are exploited or pushed around. Young children do, too, occasionally — they are not acquiescent all the time. They have their moments of rebellion, but they are more apt to try to play the game by the rules.

The teacher looks and sees willing faces. She must be uncommonly honest in assessment. Do these expressions signify mere lukewarm going-along or children's wholehearted desire? Young children's easy acquiescence can make it difficult to tell.

A wise classroom teacher offers many choices. She counts a lot on self-selection, on children freely "voting" for what they will do, with whom they will do it, and how long they will continue to do it. The "votes" are not by written or spoken ballots but by behavior. In a climate of freedom, in a setting of many worthwhile possibilities, what children choose to do is apt to stem from deeper, more significant strands than simple acquiescence. Children's self-selection is the teacher's best insurance policy against inadvertently imposing, intruding, and over-controlling.

Young Children Are Illiterate

A few children begin to learn to read as early as age three. A few more begin around four. A larger handful begin when they are five. Yet even the most advanced, most precocious of these early readers are still in the dog-paddling stage. They are a far cry away from getting from the printed page the rich flood of stimulation all children need.

And these early readers are the exception. The overwhelmingly largest number of children under six are not yet even dog-paddling. They are not yet

hanging on to the side of the pool practicing their kick. Actually they are not yet in the water! Even those who can read a little—and certainly all the rest who cannot and who could not care less—are illiterate. This is an obvious characteristic of young children and, sometimes, the most frustrating of all.

People worry if children don't read at an early age today, but most of this worry is needless. The chance to read surrounds young children—words on the TV screen, labels and signs in every store and on every product; billboards and street markers and highway signs; words in books, newspapers, comics, letters, notes, calendars. . . . Furthermore, reading is a skill that brings young children many sweet-tasting delicacies: mastery, power, control. Once children have this mastery, they become extra-lucky. The world of the far-away is opened to them. The world of the gone-by is opened to them. They are no longer tied to the small world of their own experience. Reading is such an attractive, appealing "product," available everywhere a child turns. It requires no hard sell. There is no need to push it, anxiously and nervously.

Nor is there any argument at all against helping young children move toward this fabulous power, helping each one of them move as fast as the child can comfortably go. Youngsters themselves will want to leave their illiteracy behind them, just as they want to leave their dependency behind, just as they want to leave their ignorance behind. But each child must set his or her own pace. The urge to read blossoms in different children at different times. A strong argument can be made against forcing all children to begin at the same time. This hurts too many youngsters, and it spoils reading for too many.

There is a strong argument, too, against saying that reading is the *only* way of becoming smart at an early age—you have to learn to read first and then you can be taught other things. A good classroom can be geared to illiterates. It capitalizes on what children *can* do: They can see, they can hear, they can ask, they can touch, they can talk. . . . It makes the most of the powers the children *do* have to teach them no end of worthwhile learnings, before they learn to read *and* as they learn to read. This is the kind of classroom young children need.

Individual Differences

Young children are marked by one other special quality which must be mentioned: There are great individual differences among them. This characteristic is not "special" because it marks young children off from older boys and girls, but it is extra-special because it is so important. Provision for diversity is imperative in good early education, just as it is in all good education.

During the under-six years, children are in the process of taking many giant developmental strides. These are years of transition and of great movement in many fundamental growth areas. Young children are moving from dependence toward independence. From clumsy coordination to finer skills. From body talk to verbal communication. From a strong reliance on outer control to a developing inner control. From imagination toward reality. From exclusive personal awareness to growing social concern. From the here-and-now

to wider intellectual awareness. From illiteracy to a deepening interest in symbols.

The young children who make up a classroom can be at many different places along these various paths of growth. And individual children can be at different places on different days. The overall growth process is steady but unstable—children can spurt ahead, they can slide back, they can stay seemingly still for periods. A good teacher seeks to know exactly where each child stands on these many paths and to gear the classroom to where each child is.

It is so easy to lump children. We tend to put them in a pile, put a label on the pile, and then we forget ever to look again at the people in the pile.

Head Start boys and girls, in particular, face this danger. They face it doubly today. Some teachers mistakenly assume that these children are different from all other children. Then they mistakenly assume that everyone is alike within the Head Start pile. We label the youngsters "culturally disadvantaged" . . . "economically underprivileged" . . . "children of the poor." Once we put the label on we find it harder to see that *these are all individuals.* Each has his or her own history. Each has his or her own personal family. The label blinds us. We see the tag but we cannot see the child.

Some youngsters in Head Start reveal an unusually deep need for affection. Poverty living has robbed them of adults who might have had the time and the spirit to give the tender care that all young children need. These youngsters are starved for love. *Some* children in Head Start are. Many may be. But not all. Other youngsters who live in poverty come from warm and loving homes. They have a strong inner sense of security, much sturdier than that of some economically advantaged children. Homes of the wealthy can be houses full of things but empty of people who take the time to show their love.

Some Head Start children may seem wild. They may act as if they have never known discipline. Poverty often takes adults out of the home, leaving the children free to roam. But some children who have grown up in poverty have experienced severe, overly strict, almost repressive discipline. And some, of course, have experienced the reasonable limits that young children thrive on.

Some boys and girls who have grown up in poverty have more language handicaps than do many other young children. Some of them, that is; not necessarily all. Some may be more distractible. Some may be less interested in books. Some may be more independent. Some may have well-developed body skills. Some may seem less curious and some may already be persuaded that they cannot succeed. The key word is *some!* Labels can usefully alert us to the probabilities, but we must not confuse probability with certainty. Our eyes must stay on each child, not on the tag.

Unless we specifically guard against it, the Head Start label can make us think: "All these children are stupid—if you are poor, you must be stupid." Scores on initial tests given by strange people in strange settings in a strange form of their language, often confirm the stereotype. Once we build a fixed opinion, there is the danger that children will, in fact, live down to it. We have to remind ourselves constantly: There are some retarded children in Head

Start groups; there are many more of good average ability; there are some who have superior innate power. The label must not make us prejudge.

But Head Start children are not the only ones with labels. We label other children and put them in piles too: "Immature" children, only children, high-IQ children. We even build generalities about boys and girls—their sex becomes a label. Putting children in categories so we can talk about them is hard to stop, but to teach children well, we have to zero in. The essence of knowing children is knowing each child well.

Tailoring a Program to Fit

A good teacher has a series of sharp, individual, portraits etched in her mind. She is leery of group pictures. Then this personal information must be put to work. Knowing individuals is not an academic exercise; it provides the data for tailoring a program to fit each and every child.

Teachers of young children must use every approach to bring each youngster to life as a distinct person. Visiting youngsters at home and seeing them in their own setting has to become standard operating procedure. We have to work to reduce class size and teacher load so such visits become easily possible. There must be time for personal walks and talks with individual children. Finding time to observe each child carefully at school—how a child stands and talks, what a child does and with whom, a youngster's speed and style—must become a built-in part of each teaching day. Youngsters should not always be seen en masse.

A teacher needs to learn as much about a child's earlier development as parents, the child's doctor, and any previous teachers can report. A teacher needs to know as much about each child's present status as every kind of test— physical examinations, mental tests, achievement tests, emotional and social inventories—can reveal. She needs to know a child's whole day, whole week, and whole month and year—not only the hours of the school day, but the full day and weekends, too.

There ought to be no impersonal, one-way report cards in under-six education. Parents and teachers need to talk together. They need to talk before school opens and to talk often once school is under way. Conferences ought to be the established form of reporting. There should be no hesitancy about closing school for children, if need be, so parents can come to school. Communication between parents and teachers is an essential, not a luxury, in under-six education.

A good classroom cannot be tailored to fit "almost all" the youngsters—it must be right for everyone. A good test of this custom-approach is our attitude at the start of school. "Almost all" young children will feel at home in school in a short time, especially if the start is gentle and patient. Young children should never come trooping in all at once on opening day, strangers to each other, strangers to the teacher. Nursery schools, kindergar-

Parents and teachers must communicate.

tens, Head Start need many "opening days." Children ought to come in small groups so they won't feel lost in the crowd. The hours at the start ought to be shorter than usual so that the separation from home is gradual. Mothers should be encouraged to stay, when their child needs them or when they need their child. Treated sensitively, warmly, "almost all" young children will take this crucial separation from home in their stride.

But there is no reason why a Billy who needs his mother for two or three weeks or for a month cannot have her in school with him, if she is free to stay. There is no reason why a Grace who loves school for two hours, and then worries during the last half-hour, cannot go home early, if transportation is no problem. There is no reason why a security blanket or favorite doll cannot come to school with the child who needs it to help the youngster feel safe.

There are countless other "tests" of our commitment to individual differences, once the program is fully underway. A good kindergarten—a good nursery school, day care program, or Head Start—must be geared for the Sue who is entranced with reading, as well as for all others who show minimal signs of interest. Sue has to be able to hear tens of stories, while the others may be content with one at "official" story time. Sue has to be able to dictate her own stories, one after the other, as many as her strong drive demands. Her dramatic play must be embellished with signs, labels, and all kinds of appropriate writing. This won't hurt the others playing with Sue, but it will make her life more meaningful. She must be able to play countless matching games—pair-

ing objects, letters, or words as her reading ability dictates. There must be a typewriter and printing sets in Sue's classroom for her to turn to whenever she wishes. Whatever her taste and ability, she must have books without stint to read on her own: primers and easy-to-read trade books, books of her own-dictated stories. And, of course, she must have all the teacher-help she needs as she reads, whenever she needs it. Class size and staffing must make this personalized approach possible. No Sue should ever have to slow down because she is in a group; nor should anyone else have to speed up because Sue is in the group.

Some of today's children know a great deal more than young children of the past. Their parents have spent hours with them, answering their questions, reading stories to them, and taking them on trips. For many of them, the family automobile has been a "school," taking them places that yesterday's children never saw. These youngsters have been in on family conversations, not shut out and set apart. Almost all of them have been exposed to a variety of television programming.

Children with a solid store of information must not become bored in nursery school, kindergarten, or day care. They need the chance to pursue activities in depth so the program becomes as challenging to them as it is to the child who has a more meager background. A daily program is not an election which the majority wins. Majority and minority have equal rights. No one can be short-changed.

Rules must be adjusted to the child who needs clear limits, to the child who needs elbowroom, and to the many who need only a few reasonable regulations. We must make every effort to adjust schedules to the child enamored of climbing, to the one bitten by the tricycle bug, and to the child who could paint until the cows come home. Stronger interest, greater gift, special need, slower speed must not set the pace for all. Neither must these personal qualities be lost in the shuffle as the price a child pays for being in a group.

Who Gets Ready—Child or School?

Can we have good schools for young children with this baker's dozen of special qualities?

Some communities say: "No. The children are too young. They are 'immature.'" These schools keep raising their entrance age—a child must be fully five years of age by the start of kindergarten.

The fact is, however, that most three-year-olds, almost all four-year-olds, and the very largest number of five-year-olds are mature enough, developmentally ready, to go . . . *somewhere*. These are young children but they feel independent. They want to venture out. They have reached a point where they need to be with people their own age. They want to go places and do things.

Young children do not usually end up in a group because their mothers have pushed them out. The children are reaching out. They are propelled by the same hunger for stimulation that sends the freshman eagerly off to col-

lege. The drive for companionship, for challenge, does not begin at age six or eighteen. It shows clearly in most children around age three. Often by then, certainly at age four, almost always at age five, young children are ready for school . . . . *if* the school can be ready for them.

Raising the school entrance age is a backward approach. It has been well demonstrated that there is no great trick to running a good school even for two-year-olds! Exclusion policies are appropriate only if a school conceives of its first grade as a fixed package which you have to buy "as is." Such schools contend that the child must be ready for school; the school cannot get ready for the child. But this is an attitude of stubborn, unnecessary rigidity.

Still other schools know all the characteristics of young children and say: "Ah ha! Come! Young children are active . . . noisy . . . shy . . . egocentric . . . boastful . . . illiterate . . . We will change all that." These schools are dying to get their hands on at least some of the youngsters. But they don't want three- or four-year-olds—they are too young. And they don't want anything to do with day care—that is not their business. But five-year-olds! Especially poverty children whose homes and communities have not taught them all they should know!

Such schools do not feel "anti-child." They are persuaded that what they do is for the child's own good. Their rationale is that the youngsters have only this summer or this year, this brief time, in which to make up the gaps necessary to survive first grade. Once they get ready to read and learn the ropes, then they will have it made. The children will be honestly proud . . . They can be legitimately boastful . . . Their egos will be stronger . . . Success will breed success.

This doctrine is dangerous.

The qualities that come with being young are not imperfections or flaws. They are not minor irritants to be brushed aside lightly. Early childhood is a marked and definable stage in development, with basic growth tasks that must be achieved at this time. We are naive if we assume that we can ignore what children are like, manipulating and managing and forcing them, and still get off scot-free.

No one knows for sure what the price is of stopping young children's play, of curbing their initiative and spontaneity, of deadening their energy, of blocking their social exploration. But unless we want to assume that young children's style and swing are God's mistake, we must recognize that we are playing with fire when we skip the years of three, four, and five to hurry children into being age six.

The doctrine is immoral and unethical, too.

Every child has a right to his or her fifth year of life, fourth year, third year. He or she has a right to live each year with joy and self-fulfillment. No one should ever claim the power to make children mortgage their today for the sake of tomorrow. Individuals can do this with their own lives. They often do, in pursuing technical, professional, or specialized education. But in general education—liberal education, humane education—the moral imperative stands clear: *Today counts.* Today becomes tomorrow but today is here. And important. And worthy.

Come as You Are

First grade need not be a black cloud that darkens all the days that precede it. Nor must children's essential nature be exploited in order to make intellectual gains, social gains, emotional gains, or physical gains.

We need say only one thing to young children: Come as you are! Come with your age-level characteristics. Come with those qualities that make you a unique and special person. Schools can have the flexibility, imagination, and sensitivity to be ready for the children who come.

There is nothing daring about this. Schools now do it for many age levels. School is no one thing. It need not be one set thing. True, if you say "school," images come to everyone's mind. One is apt to picture desks, books, chalkboard, teacher up front talking, children sitting, children quiet, reading, writing, raising their hands. . . . But these are partial pictures. Some parts of some schools are like this. But, in truth, schools are many things. They can have—they do have— the equipment, the supplies, the space, the class size, the administrative arrangements to fit the people who come to them.

Schools are playing fields, gymnasiums, and stadiums. Schools are classes of one and classes of five, classes of ten, and classes of several hundred. Schools are farms, camps, planes, stoves, and refrigerators. They are test tubes, Bunsen burners, laboratory benches. Schools are lathes and print shops, lumber yards and metal shops. Schools have indoor classrooms; schools also have cow barns, hothouses, geologic diggings. Schools are typewriters, adding machines, computers, automobiles. Schools are studios. Not everyone who comes to school comes to sit, read, listen, and be quiet.

Children come with their special needs: mental retardation, cardiac conditions. . . . They come with their special interests: home economics, agriculture, business education . . . . They come with their particular age-level demands: sports, dramatics, graduate seminars. . . . Good schools for older age levels are tailor-made to fit the students who come. Schools can be tailor-made to fit young children, too.

It is time for communities and for school people to take pride in creating the special adaptations that make school distinctively right, uniquely geared, beautifully fit for the three-, four-, and five-year-olds who come.

Three-, four-, and five-year olds deserve a child-centered program, not a first-grade-centered one. They need a program planned for their age, not a "pre" school which is a lackey of "regular" school. Three-, four-, and five-year-olds— nursery school, kindergarten, day care, Head Start—deserve a school that welcomes them for their own sake: Come as you are!

The DEW Line

In one legitimate way, under-six education can be the lackey of over-six education. Rightly, without distortion of its own program, under-six education can be the public schools' DEW Line, the Distant Early Warning System. It

can—consciously, deliberately—be the screening device to spot children early who have special problems so that these youngsters can early begin to get the help they need.

Early education has a unique opportunity to serve this purpose. As good a chance will not come again. Because of the young child's dependency, the teacher has a golden opportunity to know parents. Because of the nature of a good program, the teacher has a golden opportunity to know children. Because of the age of the youngsters, the teacher has the golden opportunity to get beneath the surface. Young children are in motion more than older youngsters. They have not yet learned the disguises, how to cover up and hide their real selves. They are not yet quite civilized. When they are angry, they show it. When they are pleased, they show it. The teacher of young children can get data easily that soon become hidden from other teachers.

One of the great gaps in public health is that children are not seen regularly by trained and objective eyes when they are young. Large numbers of children of the poor never see a physician after they are born. More fortunate youngsters receive good medical care prenatally, at the time of birth, and for the few months immediately following. Then for the long span of years from early infancy until school entrance, often as late as age six, even these youngsters are viewed only through their parents' subjective and untrained eyes. The doctor is called in emergencies. Too often, he then sees only the sickness and not the child. In these long years of gap, physical and psychological problems can develop, grow in size, and become harder to correct the longer they remain unnoticed.

While some conscientious parents worry needlessly about their children, far too many do not worry enough. They live in hope. They are fully ready to believe that a child's slowness in talking or his great distractibility or his tempestuous temper or his bad coordination are characteristic of all children. Their wish is father to the thought: "He'll outgrow it." Children do outgrow their normal, healthy, age-level characteristics. They do not outgrow their problems; these only become worse with the passing of time.

Our whole society pays a staggering price when we do not identify early and help early those people who are in trouble. We know the price tag for police protection, for jails, for mental hospitals. We have no way of getting at the cost in wasted talent and wasted energy of people well enough to stay out of institutions, but not well enough to function at their best. Millions needlessly sell themselves short. They carry prejudice and suspicion inside of themselves. They are angrier at life than they need be, more hostile than they need be, more compelled to be "anti" than they need be.

The American Academy of Pediatrics recognized the importance of early objective intervention years ago when it gave its blessing to the fledgling nursery school movement. The Academy saw the nursery school as a device necessitating a complete physical examination before entrance. It wanted some means of bringing the seemingly well child back in touch with a doctor to be sure the child was really well. Early intervention is even more needed today and on an expanded scale. It must reach all of our young children and with a

wider concept of health, including mental as well as physical health. It must show a concern for how children feel about themselves and others, and how they relate to life around them. Early education can and should do this job.

Careful, complete physical examinations ought to be a "must" for all programs of early education, but they *also* should lead to any remedial treatment needed.

Early Screening, Early Help

Careful, complete observational records by teachers ought to be a "must" for all programs of early education. These records should be passed on religiously to the next teacher. They should flow from the private nursery school or day care center to the kindergarten without fail. They should go from Head Start to the kindergarten, from the kindergarten to first grade as a matter of firm, fixed policy. Sometimes, the next teacher does not want to see the records—she "wants to make up her own mind." It is up to her to be an isolationist if she must, or to make wise use of the information available. But the responsibility of early education is clear: We must pass on every understanding we have about our children.

Good teachers of young children strive hard for good discipline. With some youngsters who are badly hurt emotionally, however, success cannot be measured by whether a teacher can quickly make them behave well. The task is to help them feel well and be well, and this may take many years to accomplish. With such hurt youngsters, the right measure of success is not: Did you make them toe the mark? The right measure is whether the under-six teacher began to understand them and whether she passed on her understandings to the teacher who followed. To help children with severe unmet needs, we have to work as a team, one year building on the progress of the year before.

The insights passed on, of course, need not be confined to warnings of possible trouble. The largest number will relate to healthy youngsters and to good ways of working with them: Joe has a keen interest in motors . . . Frankie is a delightfully verbal child with an extensive vocabulary . . . Beth has beautiful coordination . . . Tim is a highly social boy with truly winning ways. Youngsters have many gifts that stay hidden unless there is a setting where the gifts can reveal themselves.

Too soon the stage narrows. The children sit; the children read. Gifts of only one particular kind—academic brilliance—get the spotlight. Children possess— and the world needs—a wide array of talent. We must not lose sight of the gifts of humor, of imagination and creativity, of doggedness and perseverance; the gifts of strength, of organizational ability; of sympathy, of bravery and courage. As easily and as legitimately as it can be the warning system that sends out early alerts, under-six education can also be the talent show that uncovers many stars.

A SOCIETY-
CENTERED PROGRAM

Young children are a special breed. So, too, are Americans. A school for young Americans ought to have a distinctively democratic flavor. It should have a way of doing things that marks it off from a school for young Chinese, Russian, or Spanish children. American youngsters living their third, fourth, and fifth years of life ought to breathe in the air of America. They should know our life, the best of what our country is now, the best that our country can be.

Young Americans

Schools are not only for the individual's benefit. Schools are for the benefit of us all. They are society's protection. They are our national insurance policy, the preserver of our common good, so that—educated—we don't slide back, so that—educated—we keep moving ahead.

It is easy to forget that man is made and is being constantly remade. Society is being remade constantly, too. Nothing—neither peace nor pain, neither prosperity nor poverty, neither pride nor prejudice—is guaranteed to last. Nothing inevitably persists—neither the desirable nor the hateful. No country, not even powerful America, ever "has it made," its bright future assured.

Change is evidenced throughout world history. We know of the fall of the Roman Empire, the ending of the power of the Greek city states, the waning of the once-great dominance of Egypt, China, Babylon, Turkey, the Incas. A variety of cultures is evidenced through anthropology. We have read of cultures where women dominate, where cannibalism is approved, where goods are owned communally. We have read of societies where to die is glorious, where this life matters not at all except as a painful brief passage through which to travel.

57

The human is an assorted being. He has the potential to believe and to behave in the most amazing ways.

In modern times there has been rich evidence of people's chameleon capacities. Germany turned hateful and hurtful, cruel, callous and uncaring. And then turned again — the same people — into industrious, friendly, cheerful, rational human beings. The cowed behavior of Southern blacks changed to the magnificent courage of leaders for civil rights. A warring Japan — the invader of Manchuria, the pillager of China, the bomber of Pearl Harbor — wrote the renunciation of war into its constitution. Italy has changed; India has changed; China has changed. Attitudes and responses, for years seemingly so frozen, are changing in the entire bloc of European communist countries: Yugoslavia, Rumania, Poland, Hungary, Czechoslovakia. . . .

People can be passive, or they can take their fate into their own hands.

People can be conformist and servilely obedient, or they can be questioning and individualistic.

People can be hostile or helpful, competitive or cooperative. They can be wedded to due process of law, or true believers when a leader proclaims: "L'état, c'est moi."

Some still say, "You can't change human nature." They continue to mouth racial, religious, and national stereotypes, fixed concepts about people: "People will always be the same." The evidence is all the other way. People can be different, for better or for worse. They can sink so low, rise so high. No country is the chosen of God, the favorite of fate, the blessed of blood and genes. People are malleable. They are made and shaped by their environment and by what happens to them. The kind of human who results — the kind of society that is built — all depends. . . .

It depends on a variety of things. On trauma, like Hiroshima. On leadership: An FDR, a Churchill, a Hitler. It depends on climate, on land, on resources. On the religion that holds sway. On the organization of family life. On communication — press, radio, TV, magazines, books, pamphlets, posters — and on whether the people have the chance to get facts. It depends on the form of government. On the heritage from the past that people carry in their minds and memories.

And, it all depends on the schools.

Schools are people factories. All schools are. Nursery schools, kindergartens, day care centers, Head Start centers . . . and all elementary and secondary schools and colleges. There are no differences here. We all aim at the same target: the human. We make people. People are our product.

School is the means; people are the ends. Science, mathematics, the social sciences, and the humanities are the stuff through which we work; people are the ends. Puzzles, climbing apparatus, microscopes, blocks, show-and-tell, easels, trips: all are means, our tools. People are the ends.

A teacher of young children is not a baby-sitter, to keep children safe. She is not a jester to keep young children smiling. She is not a technician, to build little skills or little bits of knowledge in little parts of the human. A teacher of young children is more than the nurturer of maximum individual growth. A

teacher helps to make society. She must know children. She must know the fields of human knowledge and wise ways of teaching them. But she must have a vision, too. She must have a dream of the good society, of the best, the most decent, and the most constructive ways in which the human can function.

The Sources of a Dream

The sources of this vision are manifold. All of the social sciences — history, political theory, sociology, psychology, anthropology — can contribute. All of the humanities — philosophy and ethics in particular, literature, the study of religions and of art and of music — play a part. A good teacher must be immersed in more than child development. Child development can give us a sense of a child's good life now. We need, too, a balancing sense of the good society, now and for the future.

Biography can be a fount of inspiration. The lives of those we admire can spur our thinking: prominent political figures or less well-known people of courage . . . movers and makers of the past or of the present . . . great Americans or world leaders . . . those we admire or those who help us set our standards by their depravity.

The landmark political documents of human advance can feed into our dreams; proud political acts can shape our aspirations. Philosophical and ethical and religous sources can stir our hopes. The songs of our country and of the world, poetry, the great novels, and works of music and art — all can help us know more clearly what a good life ought to be.

Thoughtful introspection is still another source. Each of us has had personal experiences that we treasure. We have known at firsthand a quality of human relationship that we want to see duplicated more and more in the future. And each of us has seen the mean, the petty, the destructive that we want to help wipe out.

The sources of our dreams are many. The possible answers are many. The answers are always subjective and highly personal.

Disagreement is bound to exist. No one can presume to say, "This is *the* answer." But everyone who teaches is dutybound to say, "This is *my* answer . . . . These are the precious qualities I think make up the best of our country today . . . . These are *my* dreams for an even better land tomorrow."

People Who Use Their Heads

What kind of people do we want our schools to help build, now and for the future? Certainly boys and girls, men and women, of many qualities. But high among them: *People who use their heads.*

We need thinkers. Knowledgeable people with savvy. Skilled people with know-how.

This is our American of the past, the citizen we need for tomorrow. Our country has no party line we all follow blindly, no Great White Father who tells us what to do, no Big Brother who does our thinking for us. We believe in the open marketplace of ideas. Ours is the land of the free press, the land of freedom of speech and freedom of assembly. Politically, we count on rational people—people who have facts at their fingertips, who believe in getting new facts, who make up their minds on the basis of fact.

Our people, however, "vote" in more than political elections. We vote all the time. We vote in labor and business management elections. We "vote" on what to buy and how to worship, on where to live and how to travel, on the work we do and how we play, on who our friends will be. Ours is an open society, a mobile society. We place faith in the good sense and intelligence of the people.

Force does not decide our issues for us—neither the big issues of national life nor the day-by-day issues of personal life. Unbridled emotion should not decide for us. Propaganda, brainwashing, the big lies and the little lies cannot be the basis for our decisions. The dramatic word on Harvard University's crest—*Veritas*, Truth—is a good motto for nursery schools and kindergartens, for day care centers and for Head Start, too. In a country of the people, by the people, for the people, information and know-how have a special importance.

Children should never go to a school that convinces them of how stupid they are. That is un-American. We want every youngster to come home from school every day with head held higher, proud as punch, feeling smarter. Our best way of doing this is to provide classrooms with the widest variety of worthwhile activities. We have to "trap" children in a classroom where no matter which way they turn there is something significant to do that challenges thinking—where there is no escape.

Children learn what baby ducks are called or what stamp to put on a letter—they are more knowledgeable. Or they learn who treats sick animals or where bread comes from or when the ground is right for planting. They learn how to use a ruler or a magnifying glass—they are more competent. Or how to rollerskate, how to dial a telephone, tie a bow, or how to open a door with a key. They learn why snow melts when they bring it into the classroom—they are more rational. Or why blocks topple or why chicks take twenty-one days to hatch.

We need a comprehensive approach, with paths to thinking open to all. We must avoid focusing too early, too narrowly on some one royal road to knowledge and competence.

Motivation Is the Key

We need people who know and who want to know more. We need people who are skilled and who seek more skills. We need people who think and who enjoy the exercise.

In our schools, the question of motivation has top priority. Our stake is not in any specific learning as such. We need children who like to learn and

who will go on learning. On the other hand, we have to be leery when they learn in school solely because someone makes them . . . and then they have "had it." For us, the key questions are: Why does the child learn? Whose idea was it in the first place?

There are three broad kinds of motivation. All of them work. Each has its place. Every teacher uses all three to some extent in the course of a day. But the three are not equal. They work in different ways and each carries a different chain of consequences.

First, is *inherent* motivation. Children do what they do because they love doing it—nothing could be nicer. The activity itself is its own reward.

Second, is *necessary* or *inevitable* motivation. Children do what they do because life gives them no alternative—it is the only way they can reach something else that they prize. The children are not in love with what they are doing. If they were, you would call it "inherent motivation." They are in love with the end product of their activity but there is no way of skipping the in-between step. It is not the teacher who says they must do it—life says so. That is the way the ball bounces. If they want the pudding to taste right, they have to measure the ingredients carefully; if they want the board to fit, they have to measure carefully—there is no other way out.

Third, is *imposed* motivation. Here another human being is the only motivating force. Some real-life person is the reason why children do what they do. That person will hurt them if they don't and will be nice if they do. The motivation is all personal. The *reason why* is not in the activity itself nor in the long-range goal. A paymaster gives the reward or docks the pay. Keep an eye on that paymaster. Please the teacher—she is the motivator.

For the future we want, inherent motivation obviously wins hands down. When children love what they are doing, when they do it of their own accord, the chances are they will work their hardest, learn quickest, and remember longest. The whole learning process will become a part of them.

The chances for these good outcomes are just as promising with necessary or inevitable motivation.

But imposed motivation is a real pig in a poke. It is by all odds the trickiest. No one can be sure how it will work out. Children may work hard or they may do just as little as they can get away with. They may stick at what they are doing or they may daydream, giggle, roughhouse, or "goof off." The only way you can be sure of results is to watch them very carefully. You have to keep after them and keep them on their toes. Learning is not their main goal—pleasing teacher or avoiding her displeasure is. A teacher has to be right on hand, alert every minute.

Even then you can't be sure. You have to stand ready to increase your prizes or double your displeasure. The external force—"That's good work, Billy. You get a star" (or a raisin, a cookie, my frown, or the back of my hand)—is the motivation. You must adjust constantly to be sure the pressure stays on.

Children may remember what they learn under imposed motivation, but you cannot bet on it. The skills or facts or concepts to be learned are side issues. Pleasing the teacher or avoiding displeasure is the main business at hand. The learnings may stick. They may even last a long time. Children may be persuaded

that some Big Brother is always watching them so they become afraid ever to let down. But external, imposed motivation can work as easily the other way. It is a toss-up. "No one is around. Why should I?" . . . "No one will see me. Why should I?" . . . "It was all her idea, not mine. Now she isn't here. Why should I?" The fewest guarantees come with imposed motivation.

The great trap of imposed motivation is that it is so frighteningly easy to use. A teacher hardly has to think—she simply has to be bigger. In the upper school, the grade book, the pop quiz, and the threat of being retained are ever present. The teacher has the upper hand, and the children know it. Woe to our future when this is the reason why children learn. But the danger is even greater with younger children. The teacher has the upper hand, and even *she* may not know it. The youngsters are eager to go along, so accepting. Their eyes are constantly on her. Every teacher of young children exerts more external force than she realizes.

Some teachers know the power they possess and they rationalize their use of it. There is the great temptation to think that young children need someone big to tell them, someone big to show them, someone big to make them. Unfortunately, no rationalization changes the way the odds work out. Use imposed motivation and no one can tell what the chances are. The child may remember or may not. The child may continue learning or may not. The child may enjoy the process or may not.

A wise school does well to play the game the safest, surest way. It strives for inherent motivation or for that reasonable facsimile thereof, necessary or inevitable motivation. It does not make this choice for romantic reasons, or to be "nice" to little children. Nor does it deny that life is full of many things we all have to do, whether we like them or not. The reliance on sound motivation is hardheaded realism. Learning is too important a business to take a chance on it. There is much for children to learn today and there will be even more for them to learn tomorrow. We have to use the safest motivation just as much as we can. It is the only sure way of producing people who use their heads, who like to use their heads, who learn because learning is their own idea.

Any nursery school, kindergarten, day care, or Head Start program fails its children—and all of us—if its youngsters end the day on a plateau having learned nothing new. They fail their children—and all of us—if the youngsters end the day feeling deflated, having learned that they cannot do what is expected. They fail their children—and all of us—if the youngsters end the day having learned many skills, facts, and concepts but always under imposed motivation with its ever-present risk: "Learning is for the birds . . . We have had it!"

People Who Are Rugged Individualists ━━━━━━━━━━━

What kind of people do we want our schools to help build? *Rugged individualists* ought to be a prized target.

Our schools should be committed distinctively to nurturing initiative, imagination, drive. They ought to be wedded to the development of resourcefulness, independence, and ingenuity.

Ours has been a "can-do" land: "The difficult we do immediately, the impossible takes a little longer." Proudly, we have proclaimed, "You can't keep a good man down." We are a nation of men and women with creativity and guts.

This spirit has brought us our high standard of living and our material comforts. We joke about Horatio Alger but Horatio has innumerable real-life counterparts—people who had an idea, who took a chance, who moved ahead. Through all the years, people have tried to dream up a better mousetrap so the world would beat a path to their door. The "mousetrap" has turned out to be a cotton gin, an elevator, automobile, computer, harvester, typewriter, refrigerator, pen. . . .

Our entire life, not only our economic life, bears this adventuresome stamp. Our land was settled by "can-do" people who conquered a rock-bound coast. We are the people who crossed the Great Divide, who dammed the raging Tennessee, who built the Panama Canal, who accomplished the Berlin Airlift, who built those thousands of Liberty Ships for World War II, who landed on the moon. "They" said "it" couldn't be done, so Americans—smart, yes, but ingenious and inventive more so—found a way to do it.

Fortunately, the Jonas Salks are in our tradition as much as the Daniel Boones. Our better world of tomorrow will not come through the production of more goods and chattels alone. The future lies in the imaginative solution to basic problems of living: taming the city, farming the sea, finding more drinking water, developing new energy sources, purifying the air, conquering crippling and killing diseases, controlling the weather, building greater sensitivity in human relationships. Yesterday's Americans did not wait for "George" to do it. Tomorrow's Americans must be activists, too. We need a continuing flow of innovators, of originators of creative humans.

All the components of creativity are far from being known. But at least three elements of free-floating thinking stand out. These three—*curiosity, ego-strength, absorption*—ought to be among our most prized targets.

Curiosity

Our schools must foster the probing, wondering mind. They must be schools full of surprises, full of mystery. We must do our best to nurture the openness of people, their sense of awareness, their responsiveness to the life around them. Schools that promote curiosity search out the eye-catching picture, never settling for stereotyped reproductions of ordinary everyday life: mother, father, a kitten, a glass of milk, "cute" baby chicks. They seek arresting displays, not content with the staid and mundane that no child ever notices. We must keep feeding into our classrooms new pieces of equipment, new juxtapositions of the novel and the familiar so that school life never becomes old hat. We must weed out the drab, all the dull routines of education: the boring sit-in-a-circle

attendance-taking every morning, the monotony of everlasting Show-and-Tell. We should have no stake in classrooms where one day is dismally like every other, all drearily the same.

Our goal should be to get children to use one form of sentence structure more and more: *the question*. "What is that?" . . . "What is it for?" . . . "What can you do with it?" . . . "Where did it come from?" . . . "What is it made of?" . . . "Why does it work that way?" These must be our children's refrains. And the answers must come, not through our words alone, but through children using their fingers, noses, their eyes and ears, the tips of their tongues to taste. Questions must also be the teacher's main stock in trade: "What do you think?" . . . "What is your guess?" . . . "How can you find out?" The American school must be a school for excited discovery.

Ego-Strength

We need to nurture uniqueness and independence just as strongly. Ours must be schools for ego-strength—the child's ego, not the teacher's. "You can do it!" should be the teacher's consistent, over-and-over steady slogan: "You can hang up your own coat." . . . "You can pour your own juice." . . . "You can climb to the top." . . . "You can figure it out."

We have no stake in schools where children learn to color within the lines. No stake in pushing for unnecessary conformity, no stake in children's submerging themselves in the group, no stake in everlasting lessons in obediently following directions: "Draw a line . . . " "Make a mark . . . " "Circle the one. . . . " The youngster whose ways are different ought to excite our attention, not our angry determination to make the boy or girl fit in.

We want our youngsters to learn to take a chance, to go out on a limb. We want them to try—and not suffer too-painful penalties if their way is not our way. Fortunately, early education is blessed with time-tested equipment and supplies that are "mistake-free." Many commonly used materials are designed purposefully so there is no one specific right or wrong way to proceed. A child cannot go wrong with easel or finger painting—there is no possible way to make a "mistake." There is no right or wrong way in dramatic play, whether in the housekeeping corner, or on the jungle gym, on tricycles, in blockbuilding, or wherever play takes place. There is no "wrong" way with clay or collage or sand or water activity. There are only right ways, hundreds of right ways, each child's way. An American school should glory in these open-ended opportunities. Let the cultures that prize uniformity, conformity, and passivity stock their schools with supplies and equipment designed to make children hew to a line.

The distinctive characteristic of play is that the rules are all in the child's mind. Play builds the kind of free-and-easy, try-it-out, do-it-yourself character that our future needs. We must become more self-conscious and more explicit in our praise and reinforcement as children use unstructured play materials: "That's good. You used your own ideas." . . . "That's good. You did it your way." . . . "That's good. You thought it out yourself."

Painting can be "mistake-free" play.

Children's play has never been well understood by many adults; it is, dangerously, under attack more now than in the past. There is pressure to cut out dramatic play or to treat it as dramatics—a performance. The child is assigned a role: "Be Little Red Riding Hood" or "Be one of the Three Little Pigs." The child becomes an actor, not a creator.

There is pressure to turn painting into a time for lessons: "Draw a turkey and make it look the way a turkey should" . . . "Draw a tree and color it green." . . . "Draw a house and put all the windows in." Finger paint, sand, and water play are skimped—they are too messy. Clay is tolerated, but too often the goal is for the child to make an ash tray for Mother's Day.

Puzzles enjoy prestige today, as do form boards and peg boards—there is a right and wrong way of using them. Games are the outdoor rage: London Bridge, Statues, Follow the Leader . . . The rules for the games don't originate with the children; the youngsters simply follow established rules. Achievement is becoming our number one goal: "Do you know your colors?" . . . "Can you say the alphabet?" . . . "Do you know some finger plays?" We must beware lest we end up with the wrong kind of achievement. In the push for a finished puzzle, we don't want to lose a confident human who has the capacity to come through with something novel. That human, boy or girl, could be our proudest achievement.

Absorption

America needs schools for absorption, as well as schools for curiosity and ego-strength. We should want our children to throw themselves into what they are doing, to lose themselves in what they are doing, to be so involved that they become oblivious to much that is around them. We cannot avoid all interrup-

tions of intense, personal drive. Of course, we will always need to say, "It's time for our trip." . . . "It's time to go home." But we must be wary of unnecessarily interrupting the enthusiast. We want to nurture the passion that young children bring to their personal choices. As much as we can, we must guard against cutting off the child who is lost in work: "It's time to clean up now." . . . "It's time for everyone to come to music." . . . "It's time for everyone to hear a story."

We are not after the all-around hack-of-all-trades. There is no point in saying: "You painted yesterday. Work with clay today." . . . "You have been at the workbench for two days now. You have to try something else before you can go back." True, there are dangers if fear or lack of skill holds a child in some uncomfortable rut, but there are no dangers if a youngster freely chooses and persists because the activity is important to him or to her. This is the kind of personal conviction we should cherish.

If we can make our classrooms provocative of curiosity, appreciative of uniqueness, respectful of passion and devotion and drive, we will do our children a favor — and we do a favor for the future, too.

People With a Heart

What kind of people do we want our schools to help build? Certainly we want *people with a heart.*

We seek the decent human being. Compassionate. Generous. Kind. Sympathetic. Friendly. Helpful. Cooperative. America needs people who care, people who are utterly repelled by cruelty, meanness, and the petty, hurtful ways of life.

Our religions have been saying to us through the years — *Do unto others as you would have them do unto you.* We have moved slowly but steadily toward this end in our domestic political life. Our freeing the slaves, child labor laws, minimum wage laws, and laws governing working hours; social security, unemployment insurance, welfare and old age assistance, Medicare, our civil rights legislation — all have been steps along the way.

Internationally we have been a nation with a helping hand. We have been at our best developing the Marshall Plan and in our continuing efforts at foreign aid, in the Peace Corps, in our contributions to UNICEF, as well as the other humanitarian programs of the United Nations today. We have caused our share of suffering, but suffering repels us. When we are true to ourselves, we try to make amends.

A strand in our living — one we should want to nurture — puts us on the side of the underdog. So strong a country, one so lucky in escaping man-made and natural disasters, could easily choose to live in isolation. We could enjoy our blessings and let the devil take the hindmost. Instead we have given generously, as individuals and as a nation, to flood relief and fire relief; to hur-

ricane, earthquake, and tornado relief; to famine relief. We have been aware, we must become more aware that no man is an island . . . all men are brothers. Our basic position was stated at the time of our country's founding—an unusual statement in public affairs: All men have the right to life, liberty, *and the pursuit of happiness.* Americans look on life as being good to live, not a travail to suffer through in pain, sorrow, and despair.

An American can be touched; an American can be reached. Our schools must help keep our people that way.

Today's young children are headed toward an increasingly interdependent world. The speed of transportation, the ease of communication, the interlacing of economies, the ever-present threat of universal destruction make this world one shrinking planet, one tight family of man. For children's self-protection, the capacity to care for others must be nurtured—for people we know, for people we have never seen; for people like us, for people very different; for people near at hand and for those far out of sight. This sense of caring must be nurtured just as much for children's self-fulfillment, so that they can grow into the deepest potential of their humanity.

The Lessons of Friendliness and Helpfulness

Children learn to care by experiencing good care. They come to know the blessings of gentleness, of sympathy, of patience and kindness, of support and backing first through the way in which they themselves are treated. This is a reason why young children need teachers who have the personal touch. They need a teacher who will come to see them when they are at home because of illness. They need a teacher who sometimes will call them up at the end of the day—a person-to-person call directly to the child—simply to say "hello" or to praise for something done well.

Not all children are so lucky as to experience these blessings in school. Although few teachers set out to be mean to youngsters many manage to be very, very busy, and many more build beautiful rationalizations. Either way children still feel rebuffed. We think our heart is in the right place when we say that we don't want children to be cry-babies or mama's babies, or to think they can get their way by whimpering. Many a youngster looking for a helping hand gets a cold shoulder instead: "Don't come running to me with every little hurt." We can succeed in teaching children that they cannot count on people—they are not around when you need them or they won't help you anyway. It is much better for all of us when we truly succeed in teaching that people do care.

Children learn to care by seeing others treated well. They need to learn that people matter most of all. Many youngsters escape being the object of petty meanness themselves, but they see others bear the brunt: "We've had just about enough out of you." . . . "If you want to cry, cry in the corner but don't bother the rest of us." Children hear sarcasm when they should hear sen-

sitivity. They see others shamed when they should see others helped. They see children picked on who should be picked up. They see boys and girls isolated who need most of all to be included. American youngsters need to live with the Good Samaritan. Many do, of course. More must, if we are to produce gentle people.

But too many children learn that the thing to do is to ignore the less fortunate or to take advantage of them: "We can't wait all day for Johnny." It is too easy for classrooms to have a scapegoat, to spotlight the unpopular minorities, the children whom it is legitimate and safe to pick on. Children hear others labeled: Slowpoke . . . Bully . . . Show-off . . . Cry baby. . . . These are the people we don't need to care about. But the victims are not the only ones hurt—the other children are also hurt by learning a little callousness.

Suffusing a classroom with sensitivity so that each child experiences it and sees all others experience it, too, is a challenge that must be met at every point in a day. Sensitivity cannot be the focus only in some "social studies" time when we talk about the policeman who is our friend and the fireman who is our helper. The lessons of friendliness and helpfulness must emerge from playtime and worktime, from toileting and juice time, from music and science, indoors and out, from the routines and the transitions. The teacher's personal relationships with each and every child must be the best possible exemplification of good nature and good nurture.

Children's relationships with each other are also of first-rate importance. A child must come to feel that people make life go better. At this early stage in social growth a youngster can easily come to think: "People are a problem." . . . "You always have to stop for people, you always have to wait for them, you never can do what you want to because of people." The group—society—can seem like a hindrance: "People are not a joy, they are a nuisance."

This negative outcome is more likely whenever children are forced into a society that is larger than they can cope with. Young children easily like people if there are not too many of them. They do beautifully any time they can operate on a face-to-face, one-to-one basis. They do beautifully any time they can work in small groups of two, three, or four. But jump this social beginner into a larger crowd and strain sets in. Schools concerned about children learning to care for others must be very cautious about all the mass meeting times: Show-and-Tell, planning times, story time, music time, evaluation time. We must be skeptical about the coliseum gatherings of young children: the all-school assemblies, the field days, the all-school movies. Our society can gain nothing by teaching children to exist side-by-side but in isolation.

We must be especially on guard against competition in young children's groups. It is tempting to pit children one against the other: "The girls are quiet. We're waiting for the boys." . . . "Billy is standing up nice and straight and quiet, but we're waiting for the rest of you." Competition works for some ends at some ages, but competition cannot work to teach young children that we must live together.

_____ **People Who Are Free**

What kind of people do we want our schools to help build? *A free people.* An American school ought to be especially full of the joys of liberty, the joys of openness, the joys of movement, and the joys of choice and fluidity.

Ours is the land of liberty. The desire for freedom led the first settlers to our shore. It brought our country its waves of later immigration. It was the motive behind our westward migration. Freedom was the rallying cry of our first revolution and remains the cry of our continuing revolutions: "Freedom now!" for labor, for women, for racial minorities. Freedom was the first demand following our revolution and was buttressed in our Bill of Rights. It continues as a concern today as our courts defend the concept of due process of law. We know freedom in our religious life, and we have woven it into the whole fabric of our social life. Americans do not kowtow to titled power, to moneyed power, to traditional power. We should have no fear of police power, no fear of the state itself.

Ours is the land of the free. It will continue to be, if our schools are freedom-full today.

No young child ought to go to school to learn to feel afraid. For children in the early years, freedom has an at-ease air. It does not agree with standing in line, standing at attention. Freedom has an informal, casual air. It becomes polluted by groups moving *en masse.* Freedom has an air of jollity, a happy buzz. The lid is not clamped down by force or sweetness. Freedom has an openness in human relationships. No inner or outer censor curbs every thought and action.

In a freedom-full school, choice is respected, choice is encouraged. Children choose their friends — playmates and workmates are not assigned. Children choose their work — it is not forced on them. They have freedom of movement. A child can stay with easel, book, workbench, or puzzle, even though all the others work on something else. In a free setting, a child feels safe to be a minority — not guilty, tense, offbeat, or oddball because of not going along with the crowd.

One tipoff on the extent of freedom is how young children regard their teacher. A teacher is authority, but free people are not afraid of authority. Nor do they stand aloof from authority, keeping a cool, calculating, suspicious distance — a you-go-your-way-and-I'll-go-my-way kind of distance.

Youngsters are close to their teacher — they love her — in a freedom-full school. They think she is the most wonderful person in the whole world. She could win a popularity contest with them any time, not because she lets them get away with murder but because she is understanding. She is firm when she has to be, a critic when she has to be, but she is gentle, too. She stops children when she has to, but she never undercuts a child. Most of all, a teacher is around when the children need her: sympathetic, supporting, interested, boosting, helpful. Youngsters know they can count on her. She is on the child's

side and the child knows it, just as in a free society the state and government are on the side of the people.

In a freedom-full school, painful punishments are out. Yelling at children is out. Shaming of children, embarrassing them, is out.

License and anarchy are out, too. A good school cannot be a school for a life in the jungle or for a dog-eat-dog society.

Ours is a land of liberty, but it is a land of law. We do not want a policeman at every corner, but we do want a conscience in every heart. A good school works for excellent discipline, but its methods fit the discipline of free people.

There are rules, but the rules are right for the age. They fit the style and swing of the young. They demand enough of children, but they do not ask more than under-six youngsters can do.

There are rules, but the rules are not arbitrary. Children are helped to understand why the rules have to be, what the logic behind them is, what good they serve. A teacher of young children is everlastingly making a case for decency and for appropriate behavior.

There are rules, but there are no cruel and inhuman punishments for violating those rules. Slapping children, pinching children, yanking children, tying them into their chairs, using dunce caps and "bad chairs"—these forms of punishment should never happen. Nor should the yell across the room, the furious scowl, the threatening tone. Our young children should grow up unhurt by law enforcement, undamaged physically or psychologically, no matter what their "crime."

When a law is broken, a teacher must cope with the immediate situation: comforting the victim, managing any property damage one way or another, restraining the aggressor if need be, so the trouble ends for the moment. All the while that this goes on, the teacher's thinking process has begun. *Why?* Why did the child do it? A good teacher has to be a detective, not to find the culprit but to find the cause. The goal is not simply to control a child, to make a youngster good in school. Teachers committed to freedom want children who will be good all through life, because the children want to be. Teachers seek to build children who know the right thing to do, who feel good about it, and who willingly act that way. Building such healthy, decent people takes the best thinking of a wise and sensitive teacher, of a patient and persistent teacher.[1]

Other Prized Qualities

What kind of people do we want our schools to help build? There could be five, six, seven, eight and still more ideals in any one person's dream.

---

[1] For a fuller discussion of discipline see Chapter 6, "Teaching the Basics: Good Behavior."

Some might say: *We need people with a sense of humor.* Certainly our country should prize gaiety, laughter, the lifting light touch. Life should never be sullen, sodden, soggy, a plodding existence. Our days should sparkle.

Some might say: *Aesthetes.* We should work to develop a keen appreciation of beauty in our people: the beauty in nature, in man-made products, beauty in human relationships. Ours ought to be a land where good taste pervades, where people live in cultivated high style.

Some might say: *People with vitality and vigor.* Our boys and girls should build grace, nimbleness, strength. They should be housed in bodies that are a joy to live in, a joy for others to see. Today's young children will live a long time, and they should live their lengthened span in glowing health.

Some might say we need *men and women of courage*—the brave physically, and those who will dare to stand up for their convictions.

Some: *Men and women who take pride in their work.*

Some: *Leaders who are skilled in getting the best out of others.*

People Who Thrive on Differences

Some will seek to build *humans who thrive on differences.* In the past, our country has been a place where all peoples came together. In our children's future the wide world itself will be exactly that. Children can be taught to feel that differences make life exciting, alluring, rich. They can be helped to build a positive taste for variety: in skin color and customs, in interests and abilities, in variety in sights, and sounds and smells.

This is a challenge of the gravest import. All of our young children—the children of the majority, the children of our minorities—stand in danger unless our country makes quicker progress in resolving racial, religious, ethnic, and class antagonisms. Schools alone cannot solve these problems, but schools must play a large part. And there are some special considerations that relate to schools for the young.

One is the fact that young children are aware of differences. Early childhood is not an "age of innocence" during which the questions of skin color, religion, and national origin never rise. Young children know something about these facts of life. As early as age three, they begin to express feelings about them.

Second is the fact that young children, more easily than the rest of us, can learn to accept differences. They can play and work happily with age-mates of varying backgrounds. It is important that we use this special openness of the early childhood years to start building the best possible interpersonal and intergroup relationships.

A third fact is that heterogeneity benefits children. Of course, if the spread of differences is more than a teacher can manage, children are hurt. Or if class size is expanded in order to achieve a spread of differences, children are hurt. But under reasonable conditions, young children, the social beginners, gain when everyone is not alike. They gain from mixed sex groups, boys and girls

together. They gain when children with physical differences—blind children, crippled children, youngsters with a hearing loss—are grouped with so-called normal children. They gain when groups are not segregated rigidly by IQ scores. They gain from good mixed age groups. Young children gain—it is a positive benefit at the right time in their lives—when their groups are "mixed," just as America is "mixed" and as their world of the future will be "mixed." They gain when, from the start, they grow up with boys and girls of differing skin colors, differing ethnic backgrounds, and differing economic levels.

A few children in private nursery schools, church nursery schools, and cooperative nursery schools are lucky. Their parents reach out and deliberately bring into their schools the differences that can make school a vital experience for all.

A few Head Start children are also lucky. From its beginning, Head Start has faced the dilemma of homogeneity. By law, this is an economically segregated program, designed specifically for poor children. A Head Start group might have an excellent staff, excellent equipment, and excellent space, but one significant educational force could easily have been left out: *heterogeneity.* When children all come from the same background, they learn less from each other. Fortunately, from the beginning, Head Start has been allowed to enroll 10 to 15 percent of its children from nonpoverty families, although this is only small leeway and is an opportunity not widely pursued. Fortunately, too, Head Start has consistently reached out to include preschool handicapped children.

Making Inner-City Groups Topnotch

Given the patterns of living that have developed in our cities and suburbs, it is not easy to create the perfect school setting where young children can have the experiences that will lead them into the pleasures of differences. In spite of the improvisations that will come along, large numbers of children are sure to continue going to schools for look-alikes. This homogeneity seems likely to remain the rule, especially in our inner cities. As long as it persists, there is one thing we could do: We could fund our inner-city early childhood groups bountifully. We could set out to make *them,* in particular, excellent learning centers—even though they do remain economically or racially homogeneous for a time.

The idea is not unheard of. Our wealthiest suburbs do this. So do our most expensive private nursery schools. And Head Start moves a little in this direction. Its appropriate class size and ample staffing give Head Start groups the chance to be good, although the shortage of skilled teachers and of skilled supervision, the uncertainties of financing, and other obstacles unfortunately make many a Head Start group less than topnotch.

From excellent inner-city groups more children could move into the wider society with healthy personalities, the outgrowth of topnotch early experiences. With healthy personalities, these children would welcome differences rather than feel threatened by them. This is no minor issue. Our children's well-being, our country's well-being, hinge on our learning to live together.

Thinking and Planning Together

The kind of people our schools help to build *depends* . . .

It depends on teachers who will dream and then translate their dreams into reality within their classrooms. Such teachers don't wait. They build the good society *now* . . . immediately . . . within the four walls of their rooms. They work consistently so that, from the beginning, children live the good life, love the good life, and carry it with them in their bloodstream into tomorrow. The good society is not in the future—it starts today.

Teachers, of course, must mesh their dreams with parents' dreams. We must think and plan together. This is especially imperative in the under-six age range where half-day sessions of school are so common. The half-day impact is only a tiny impact unless what happens at school is reinforced, extended, and deepened at home. One must pick up where the other leaves off, and both must move in the same direction.

Impact almost vanishes when home and school work at cross purposes. Too many children are caught in a cross fire. One of their "schools" teaches conformity; the other works for creativity. One prizes blind obedience, while the other seeks to foster critical thinking. One says, "Turn the other cheek;" the other urges, "Stand up for your rights." One deprecates a given behavior as tattling; the other rewards the same behavior as social awareness and involvement. One relies on force; the other on reason. A child caught in such a tangle of values all too often is indecisive and uncommitted. Home learnings and school learnings have fought each other.

We have to end the separation of home and school. Too much is at stake to let this foolish lack of communication persist. The left hand must know what the right hand is doing; the two hands must work together.

Head Start has taken a strong stand on the need for parents and teachers to work together, hand in glove. It recognizes that the corrosive effects of poverty can only be undone through a twenty-four-hour-a-day attack. The need is no less pressing in nursery school, kindergarten, or the day care center. The prod of poverty is missing, but the problem is the same. Children do not get a fair deal—and our whole society suffers—unless school and home consciously strive together to build the human we both want.

We must get together in markedly better ways than we do.

At present, too much time in our group meetings is wasted on unimportant business details. Too much time goes to fringe matters. Too much time is spent on generalities, far from the central issue of how these three-, four-, and five-year-olds should spend their life now. Too often in our home-school relations we simply go through the motions. Too many meetings merely let parents "chalk one up"—they have been "good" parents and have dutifully gone to a meeting. Too many meetings merely let teachers sigh in relief—they have been "good" teachers and have met with parents. But nothing is accomplished, and no one has any expectations of accomplishment.

It is time for a change.

Teachers of young children should meet in their own rooms with their children's own parents: no outside speakers, no froufrou, no folderol.

These room meetings must center on the crucial questions that these immediate co-workers face. As a prize example, nothing could be more crucial than discussions of the kind of person we want to build. What are the qualities we prize? What do we want to emerge from our joint efforts? What kind of a human are we after? And what are the appropriate ways of achieving our goal?

There are bound to be differences at first. The quick answer, the partial answer, the short-term answer is appealing: someone who minds, someone who is polite. . . . But we have to keep on meeting, keep on talking, and keep hammering away—one meeting once a month may not do the trick.

We are planning for young Americans. Barring personal or national tragedy, these boys and girls will live well past the year 2000. The will live in a century when man will be even more master of the environment. What kind of humans do we want our boys and girls to be? And what kind of environment do we want them to build? These questions cannot be postponed for the agenda of college parents and teachers, or for the high school team. The future human and the future society are built, in part, by the way boys and girls live in the nursery school, the kindergarten, the day care center, and Head Start. Parents and teachers of young children need to think through their answers now.

A SUBJECT-MATTER
CENTERED PROGRAM

Many people say: "Schools should teach the three Rs." There is no question about it. Schools must. Nursery schools must. Kindergartens, day care centers, Head Start . . . all schools must.

There is no conflict between this concern and the goal of under-six education to help children live their third, fourth, and fifth years at the peak of their powers. There is no conflict between it and the goals of a democratic school to develop rugged individualists, free humans, boys and girls who will use their heads, and have a heart.

The term *the Three Rs* is, of course, only shorthand — a quickie way of saying "human knowledge." We use this shorthand primarily in elementary education. Colleges have their own way of grouping knowledge, a much broader and more comprehensive label. Colleges teach the liberal arts. They teach the humanities, mathematics and the sciences, the social sciences, health and physical education.

Nursery schools must teach the liberal arts, too. And so must kindergartens, day care centers, and Head Start.

Subject Matter in the School

The job of any school for general education is to teach all the subject matters. Other institutions — libraries, museums, hospitals, recreation centers, neighborhood centers — work through their particular areas of speciality. Subject matter is the school's bailiwick. We have to teach subject matter — there is nothing else for us to work through.

You can use the shorthand symbol for knowledge: the Three Rs. You can use the broader heading: the liberal arts. You can start with *A* and go down the

list to Z and specify each subject matter. A school—nursery school, kindergarten, day care, Head Start, elementary, secondary, general college—must teach them all:

Anthropology	English	Mathematics
Arithmetic	Foreign Languages	Music
Art	Geology	Philosophy
Astronomy	Government & Politics	Physics
Biology	Home Economics	Psychology
Chemistry	Health	Reading
Civics	History	Sociology
Economics	Literature	Zoology

The teacher of young children cannot be simply child-centered. She must be child-centered, society-centered, *and* tuned in on culture, and on knowledge. She must be a broadly educated, well-informed person. Her "professional" training is not simply the pedagogical preparation that helps her to understand children and the techniques of teaching them. Her own liberal arts background is a fundamental part of her professional training. When you teach young children, you teach with all you know—and with all you can find out—about all fields of study.

For years there has been a common assumption: "Anyone can teach young children. All a nursery school or kindergarten teacher needs to know is how to mix the paints." This misconception is spreading today as the field expands. The result is that many teachers are being hired whose own cultural backgrounds are limited. High school graduates and those with one or two years of college study suddenly become "teachers."

Even before today's expansion, not all nursery-kindergarten teachers were "brains," in the academic sense of the word. Many had intuitive psychological understandings that made them skilled in human relationships and sensitive to children. Some of today's "new teachers" are equally gifted in empathy. Some understand children's poverty backgrounds well; some speak the language of the poor. These are great teacher strengths. But young children will suffer if early education always has to choose: Be sensitive *or* be smart . . . Be kind *or* be informed . . . Be gentle *or* be wise.

Smart teachers, bright teachers, informed teachers, cultured teachers are needed by young children, every bit as much as older youngsters need them. The good teaching of young children requires a rounded background, rich in psychological insights, rich in democratic awareness, *and* equally rich in cultural attainment. Facts, concepts, and skills must be taught. They must be taught starting at age three, not postponed.

The Ways of Teaching Differ

The crux lies in how subject matter is taught. To say that subject matter is the business of under-six education does not mean that the nursery school, kindergarten, day care center, or Head Start program will look and sound the

same as the upper grades. Although the same fields of study are taught, *the ways of teaching are different*. This is a fundamental difference.

Not that the methods of teaching young children are new or radical or revolutionary or unheard-of. They are all methods used with older students, too. But some of the methods command a higher priority in under-six education than in the grades. And some of the old, standard methods are used sparingly with young children. *The heart of the difference is in balance and in proportion.* This shifting of weight can make the good under-six class seem deceptively offbeat to anyone who only understands the education of older children. It can seem as if subject matter is not being taught. The subject matter *is* there, even though the difference in the balance and proportion of teaching methods may appear to hide it.

The teacher of young children lectures at times to the class—but seldom and briefly.

She holds recitation periods and question-and-answer sessions—but these are rare.

She leads all-group discussions—but infrequently.

The most widely used of all talking-teaching techniques are face-to-face, person-to-person lessons. This is tutoring, under-six style.

The teacher of young children, however, does not talk a great deal. Her relatively few words carry great weight, when she uses them properly. But the under-six teacher relies more heavily on other teaching methods.

She encourages youngsters to work alone. This is independent study and it has high priority.

The teacher emphasizes committee work, too. This is a standard teaching technique at all age levels, but a high-priority method with young children. Under-six "committees" are exceedingly informal and short-lived. They have a changing membership, self-chosen. The members seldom sit down to meet; rather they are working committees. But a major part of a teacher's skill lies in making it possible for young children to learn from each other.

The teacher also uses books, movies, slides, filmstrips, and tape recorders to some extent, as well as bulletin boards, pictures, and other kinds of audiovisual aids.

The strongest emphasis in under-six education, however, is the laboratory approach. Or call it field study. The teacher's biggest job is to take children where the action is or to bring the action to them. She tries continually to confront the youngsters with experiences, with events. She looks for significant situations in which the children can become actively involved. The teacher of young children seeks *happenings*.

A *happening* is always a verb. When the children are baking, buying, cooking, playing, painting, digging, washing, making, or selling—this is a *happening*. Science is not a happening. Mathematics is not a happening. Nor are the units found so often in kindergartens and in some nursery schools—the seasons, transportation, the home, the farm ... These are all nouns. Young children need verbs. Events. Action.

Small wonder some people think anyone can teach young children. A good teacher of the young does not look like a "teacher." You seldom find her in front of the class—she is in the middle of the action. The children don't sit

all day—they are up and around, busy and involved, doing things. The teacher does not rely heavily on books, textbooks, or workbooks. She concentrates on experiences in which the youngsters can participate. *Happenings* come first—they are basic.

Subject-Matter Labels

The teacher teaches subject matter but the subject-matter labels are primarily in her mind. They do not show on the outside. The teacher thinks in terms of mathematics, science, reading . . . the children cook, plant, or build a house. Inside her mind the teacher pinpoints the facts, concepts, and skills that lie embedded in the experiences. But the daily program only shows, and the children can only tell about, the *happening:* They are digging a garden; they are feeding the birds; they are going to the shoe repair shop. An alert teacher can pull the subject-matter learnings out of any significant activity, but the activity has to be going on in the first place for her to do her job.

Keeping subject-matter labels in the background, while putting the focus on experience is not a drastic step. We must not let these labels awe us. They are for the teacher's convenience. The labels are all man-made; we have thought them up ourselves and we keep changing them from time to time. Today we speak of the language arts in the elementary school. You seldom find that label used in high schools or colleges. At those levels, we speak of speech, creative writing, literature, or composition. Civics is a common label in junior and senior high school. The same subject matter is called government and politics in college. The elementary school teaches social studies. Colleges label each of the specifics: history, government, economics, sociology, anthropology. . . .

Through the years, once-popular headings have disappeared. Theology was once a central field in general education; today it is a part of professional training. We add new subject-matter labels as the years go along. Once there was only the label *biology.* Now there are many subdivisions: anatomy, taxonomy, cytology, embryology, ecology, histology, paleontology, teratology . . . .

The labels are simply administrative devices. They did not come from heaven and they do not exist in reality. No real-life event ever is limited to one label or one subject matter. Life comes in big bundles, with the contents all mixed up. Experiences never can be neatly compartmentalized.

A group of four-year-olds takes a trip to a farm to learn where milk comes from. If you make the teacher put one label on the experience, she will probably call it science. Or if that is too general, biology. Or if not specific enough, animal biology. But what about the conversation in connection with the trip: before, during, and after? That should be called the language arts. The stories before and after the trip are literature. The singing—"Old MacDonald Had a Farm" is fated to be sung!—must be called music. Rules for conduct are developed. This is what civics, government, and politics are all about. The teacher recalls what happened the last time the group took a trip: "You remember how we all crowded around and some people could not see." The

lessons of the past are usually labeled history. A child misbehaves; the teacher's response is a lesson in psychology. Someone counts the children to be sure no one is left at the farm: arithmetic. The trip costs money; that is when the four-year-olds take a brief course in economics. The cow is probably pretty, even if the farmer and the highway are not. The presence of beauty and the absence of it are matters of aesthetics. When the teacher soothes a disappointed child—"Things don't always work out the way we want"—the lesson is one in philosophy. And if, on such a trip, the children drink some milk, that experience is labeled nutrition. Yet the whole trip was labeled Science!

The best place for labels is in the teacher's mind. Knowing the organization of knowledge helps her to focus on what there is for her to teach. But the children do not have to sit down to learn subject matter. They do not have to keep quiet to learn subject matter. They do not have to stay together as a whole group to learn subject matter. They do not have to read subject matter out of a book. And the label does not have to show.

Stimulus

Under-six and over-six education share the same general flow and pattern of instruction—there is no difference here. The first job of all schools is to confront children with abundant stimulation. We must provide yeast, a starter that will make children's minds stretch and bodies stretch, that will deepen their social awareness, and widen their emotional responses. Stimulation is the reason why children, no matter what their age, come to school. They must sink their teeth into something meaty or they might just as well stay at home.

In all education, this flood tide of stimuli is followed by a second stage: ample and generous time for response. Three-year-old students, thirteen-year-old students need the chance to react to the stimulus, to organize their own impressions and sensations, to incorporate in themselves all that has flowed in. First stimulus, then response—this is the standard pattern of education.

Colleges provide stimulation through top-flight lectures. Colleges and all the upper levels of education open up new vistas through books: "Read the next ten pages." . . . "Read the next chapter." . . . "Check the books in the bibliography." Movies—documentaries, teaching films—can also provide the initial ferment for older children.

Teachers of young children start with reality.

For boys and girls who have not attended school before, the sheer fact of school is itself stimulating. School is a stimulus simply because it exists—it is "there." This is a great challenge for the three-year-olds, for new four- and five-year-olds, for Head Start children. The new setting, the companionship of children, the wide array of indoor and outdoor equipment are a rich feast.

This initial impact is like that of a campus on the college freshman. The buildings, the grounds, the statues, the traditions, the dorms, the student union, the library, the new freedom and new responsibilities, the songs, the football games, roommates, professors, the style of dress—there is so much to take in. Every sight and sound, every personality, every location starts wheels

turning. In the same way, the well-equipped classroom for the very young, filled with the right materials and with children, provides the initial flood tide of sensation, impression, challenge, invitation—as much as beginners can take.

The Many Faces of a Teacher

The teacher does a major part of her teaching before the children ever come to school by setting the scene so that it is stimulating. No one sees the teacher do this. Small wonder again there is that rumor that anyone can teach young children! Yet making this initial stimulation right for the children is skilled work.

A Teacher Must be an Astute Purchaser

It is costly to equip a laboratory for young children, just as it is costly to equip a science laboratory or a business education or home economics education laboratory. A skilled teacher exercises selective judgment in what she buys and what she passes by.

She especially needs highly developed sales resistance. Workbooks are promoted that have zero-stimulation value and inappropriate response value for children at this age. Sales campaigns promote overly expensive learning kits, especially ones allegedly designed for Head Start children, which are made up of more attractive packaging than content. It is easy to spend a disproportionate part of a budget on high-priced equipment that offers only minimal return in child stimulation and response. Big sums can be wasted on expensive swings, fancy merry-go-rounds, on elaborate overhead and motion picture projectors. Money can be also wasted on materials not sturdy enough to withstand hard use by a group of active children.

A teacher who is a wise spender looks primarily for materials that are "unstructured." She wants open-ended materials that can be used in many different ways for the countless purposes that children themselves think up. In the indoor classroom, the sets of unit blocks; the easels, paints, and clay; the tubs and water tables; the materials for dramatic play; the small boats, cars, and figures of people and animals; the dolls and doll carriages; the workbench materials—all meet this standard. In the outdoor classroom, large blocks, boards and boxes and ladders, climbing apparatus, tricycles and wheel toys, and the sandbox are similarly unstructured. These are multipurpose materials—they promote intellectual, social, and physical growth. And they are double-edged: These are stimulus materials and materials for children's response.

Some needed equipment is structured. Young children need a generous supply of books. They need puzzles, peg boards, and form boards of varying difficulty. They need high-quality phonograph records.

Our classrooms also need many of the special tools that the various fields of learning use. Typically, under-six education has done exceedingly well in providing good tools in one field, art. A classroom for young children often looks for all the world like an artist's studio. The products that come out are children's products, but the process that goes on is the artist's process. The rich availability of easels, paints, brushes, paper, clay, and collage materials helps young children live like artists.

Our classrooms must be equally as well stocked with the tools of all the liberal arts. Instruments for measurement, for example, are central to mathematics. Instruments for observation are basic to all the sciences. We want our children to act and feel like three-year-old, four-year-old, five-year-old scholars in many fields. We must—with a fullness comparable to what we have done in the arts—make available the tools of many disciplines: rulers, scales, magnets, microscopes, magnifying glasses, telescopes, binoculars, globes, maps, ropes and block and tackle, levers, typewriters. . . .

Children's tools can be used for a variety of interests.

Children's tools must be good tools. Children need small hammers, for example, and small saws, small pliers, wrenches, and screw drivers—*small,* but not toy tools. We have wisely recognized the need for quality instruments in music. Wise teachers insist on pianos of the finest tone (even though young children bang on them at times). They insist on good drums and rhythm instruments, on high-fidelity phonographs that produce music, not noise. Young children need similar *bona fide* quality tools that do well the job they are supposed to do in every area.

A Teacher Must Be a Persnickety Picker-and-Chooser

Everything that goes into her room must meet her precise standards. No picture is posted on the wall simply because it is "cute" or "pretty" or just to fill space. Each picture says something and says it well. No book goes on the bookshelf simply because it is available or cheap. Books are carefully chosen for their relevance to the children, for their artistry, for their style. No phonograph record or music cassette is bought simply because it makes noise. A teacher wants music of the highest quality for her youngsters, music most capable of striking a responsive chord within them. A careful teacher guards the walls in her classroom, the floor, the ceilings, the space. Only the best in her toughest critical judgment gains access to them.

A Teacher Must Be a Scavenger

Much material for both stimulus and response cannot be bought, even when money is available. Teachers have to engage in a never-ending treasure hunt. The extent of children's learning depends greatly on a teacher's boldness in scrounging for clothing for the dress-up corner; for cork, bottle caps, toothpicks, wood shavings, and plastics; acorns, pebbles and shells for collage; thread spools and typewriter spools; a wooden barrel; a discarded adding machine; a log. . . .

A Teacher Must Be a Community Planning Engineer

Many activities go on at once in the young child's classroom. Each activity must have the particular working conditions—room or privacy—that its nature demands. Blocks need ample floor space. Books, puzzles, and table games need protected areas. Dramatic play calls for isolated space so children can lose themselves in their dream world. Painting must be near water. Good space utilization means good use of materials; it means less crowding, fewer conflicts and fewer accidents; it means fewer interruptions and therefore less frequent distractions.

A Teacher Must Be a Safety Engineer

A climbing apparatus must be tested before children use it, to be sure it is steady, firmly rooted and strong. All wooden surfaces—blocks, boards, boxes, and outdoor equipment—must be splinter-free. Nothing should be so weak that it will break under a child's weight: ropes, climbing boards, the surfaces of play houses. A teacher must guard vigilantly against jagged edges, against surfaces that can cause children to fall, against lures that will lead the children into the path of swings or other moving objects.

A Teacher Must Be a Maintenance Specialist

All materials have to be in tip-top shape for maximum use. Blocks cannot be jumbled. They must be stored by size so that their arrangement encourages

children to use them freely yet thoughtfully. Tricycle pedals, handles, and seats must be firmly attached so children are both safe and comfortable. Workbench material must be carefully selected: wood soft enough for children to hammer into successfully, nailheads large enough for children to hit. Sand must be the right consistency: soft and powdery if it is to be poured, damp if it is to be packed. Paint colors must be clear and full-bodied, not wishy-washy-watery. Clay must be moist and workable.

A Teacher Must Be a Cautious, Thoughtful Manager

She has to decide what materials to put out and what to save. She has to think of yesterday, of today, and of tomorrow. Her goal is stimulation, not overexcitement; enough materials must be available for challenge but not so much as to create confusion. She must seek balance in her materials so the children are stimulated socially, emotionally, physically, and intellectually.

A Teacher Must Be a Keen Observer

The initial scene-setting for stimulus leads a teacher into many roles. Each must be played thoughtfully, with self-conscious awareness. At this stage the teacher is teaching largely through materials. Making her materials available in the most telling way is not an offhand job, not one to rush through in the last minute before the children arrive. She must exercise the same precision and calculating decision-making that the most gifted author or lecturer practices in deliberately choosing the best words and expressions.

As the children react to the initial stimulus, the teacher circulates among them. Now she must be a keen observer, assessing whether the scene is well set. Is it retaining its yeasty power? For everyone?

Often no major changes are needed for quite a while. The basic equipment of under-six education does not lose its charge quickly. Even five-year-olds who have been to school for two previous years find new possibilities in sand, blocks, wood, clay, paint, boards, and boxes—and other children to use them with—for long stretches of time.

Small changes may be called for, however. These can mean the difference between stimulation and monotony for individual children. Sometimes the needed new stimulus can be provided simply by adding similar pieces of equipment: new books for children to browse through; new records or tapes for them to play; more difficult puzzles; more clothing in the dress-up corner; new colors of paint at the easels; a new doll; a different kind of clay; bigger pieces of wood at the workbench; different materials for collage at the worktables; a new car or boat or truck brought out of reserve.

Sometimes the needed added stimulation can come by placing the same basic equipment in a new area or in a new relationship. The trucks, autos, boats, and the small figures of people and animals may be moved closer to the block area. Walking boards may be placed between pieces of climbing apparatus or placed at new heights or at new angles. A tricycle and a wagon may be roped together to lead into more complicated play. Paper for the easels may be cut in new and different shapes: ovals, squares, long rectangles,

triangles, many-sided and odd-shaped pieces. Newspaper, instead of un-printed paper, may be hung as easel paper, or the unprinted paper may be col-ored instead of white. The teacher may even start a block construction before the children arrive in the morning. Her small beginning calls attention to the blocks and gives the youngsters a lead on which to build.

New Stimuli Needed

At some point, major new stimuli will be needed. Only the teacher observing the children can tell when. She senses that more youngsters seem at loose ends. Their activity lasts a shorter time. Their products—their paintings, block building, make-believe, woodwork, or clay—seem less innovative.

The time for a change comes sooner with children who have had previous group experience than with those who are meeting group life for the first time. It may come sooner with older children or when children have used some of the school's materials at home. The challenge of the basic room—its equip-ment and the presence of co-workers—is great, but in and of itself it does not last forever.

One point is important to remember: *children may outgrow the initial stimulus of the basic equipment, but they do not outgrow their age*. They are still young children—albeit a month or two or three older than they were at the start of school. They still learn best through experiences. When it is time for a change, the change need not take anything away. The old basic equip-ment, indoors and out, is still needed, but new events, new *happenings* must be fed in. It is time for more "lectures" and for more "books in the bib-liography"—for more stimuli—but in three-year-old, four-year-old, five-year-old style. Children need more real-life action so there can be more and better response.

The *field trip* is clearly the best way of providing added stimulus. Young children cannot read but they can see. They cannot read but they can touch and hear and smell. They cannot read but they can ask questions. A field ex-perience is the prize learning stimulus for any age: for adults, for graduate students, for college students. We can be thankful for the young child's il-literacy. It forces us to do the best thing, to take the youngster to firsthand sources.

Young children's field experiences are short trips, not exhausting journeys. There are good possibilities that should not be overlooked within the school itself, on the school grounds, and within the immediate neighborhood of the school. Their trips ought not to be to sites teeming with mobs and crowds and masses; these are simple trips, not overexciting and fatiguing.

Most of all, a good trip allows children to become active par-ticipants—not mere onlookers or a captive audience for a lecture by a guide. This criterion is of prime importance.

A trip to an airport where youngsters can only look at planes in the distance from a viewing balcony is not as good as a trip which allows the children to get into a plane, sit in the cockpit, talk to the pilot, listen to the intercom, and perhaps even taxi along the landing strip. A trip to a farm where the children can only see a cow from behind a fence is not as good as a trip which allows them to pat the cow, smell the cow, and try to milk her. A trip to a supermarket where the children can only walk up and down the aisles is unsatisfactory. The youngsters need to get into the refrigerator room to feel its cold, to climb into the delivery truck to know its hugeness. They need to stamp prices on canned goods, to use the scales, to ring up their purchases on the cash register with the cashier's permission and guidance. A good trip will be short but packed with direct, personal impact.

The longest part of the trip will be the hours the teacher spends getting ready for it. A good trip is never an offhand excursion and seldom a last-minute inspiration. It requires much detailed planning. Careful arrangements must be made ahead of time to guard against "experts" at the site lecturing the children—adults love to talk! Arrangements must be made so that children have the maximum opportunity to touch, to handle, and to use. Real dangers must be spotted, but imaginary dangers must not be allowed to hold the children back. The teacher needs to make a dry run of the trip to test out its length; children should be stimulated, not exhausted. And the teacher herself must learn ahead of time some of the teaching opportunities that can arise.

Visitors coming into the classroom from the world outside—if the children cannot go out to them—serve the same purpose of stimulation with almost, not quite, the same intensity. And the same criterion applies to visitors as to trips. The visitor should not be simply a talker or a distant performer on a stage putting on a demonstration. The children should not be a sitting audience—they must be in on the act.

The visiting firefighter comes complete with truck. The children climb on it; they turn on the siren; they clang the bell; perhaps they help hold the nozzle while water streams through the hose. The firefighter is in uniform. The children try on the fire hat and wear the badge. The visiting police officer comes in the squad car. The children turn on the searchlight and hear the two-way radio. They touch and use the police officer's handcuffs, billy club, whistle, pad and pen, cap and badge. The reason for bringing in a fire fighter (or whoever the visitor may be) is not for the children to see one; it is so they can *be* one.

Many *activities* are possible within the classroom or in the play yard which also serve well to carry children's thinking into new areas. These "at-home" happenings, like everything else, are usually at their best in smaller subgroups. Then everyone can take part. Cooking is one good example. Four, five, or six youngsters and the teacher may make a gelatin dessert, pudding, cookies, pancakes, a stew, or applesauce. But there is no end of possibilities: Four or five may dig a garden spot and plant seeds outdoors; four or five may bring in some garden soil for an indoor bulb or seed planting; a few youngsters

may work with the teacher in setting up a terrarium, in building a pet cage, painting a playhouse, or setting eggs in the incubator to hatch.

Exhibits are another way of bringing stimulation into the classroom. A good classroom ought to be a lively museum—you never know what you will see! Today's exhibit may be a snake, a mouse, baby ducks, a kitten, a bird, pollywogs or minnows—it may even be a human baby. The exhibit may be a bird's nest, antlers, a musical instrument, a ship's bell. Teachers, with the help of parents and others, can reach out into a community that children cannot get to and bring that community right to the children's home base. A classroom "museum" can be like the very best of our public museums, not a "hands-off" place where you simply stare, but one which invites you to handle and touch.

Provisions for Follow-up

The injection of new stimuli means that the teacher must now also make additions to the room equipment. The dramatic play corner, for example, need not remain a housekeeping corner for all eternity. Children who have been to the supermarket ought to find, when they return to their room, the props that will reinforce their trip experience and open up relevant opportunities for response. A grocery cart, a telephone, a cash register, a scale, paper bags, a stamp for marking prices, pads of paper and pencils, white aprons—these are all needed now, just as stoves and refrigerators were timely when children were acting out their home living.

The outdoor playground of youngsters who have been to a firehouse should be stocked with garden hose and ladders, a siren and bells for tricycles and wagons, and the dress-up clothes—boots, raincoats, helmets, badges—that will help the children recreate their visit more vividly in their minds. The teacher must make available whatever closely relates to the children's most recent experience: steering wheels or stethoscopes, tickets or toy money, nurses' caps or pilots' caps, flashlights or tire pumps . . . .

This is the time, too, for good *pictures*—large blownup photographs and poster-size art work—that will refresh and deepen children's impressions of people and places they have seen, of jobs they have done. Illiterate children can read pictures. We ought to exploit this fact as a valuable tool for stirring their memories, and for bringing them new, more detailed, and exciting information. The trouble is that pictures that say something—ones not merely bland or "cute," not dull, not dead—are hard to find. Teachers who seek mind-stretching experiences for their youngsters need to pester the public relations offices of industries and businesses, the trade associations, travel agencies, and newspaper offices. It takes persistence and hard work to build up a lively picture file so that the right pictures to cap a stirring firsthand experience are on tap.

The *books* a teacher makes available for browsing as well as those she reads to children can also strengthen the real-life experiences youngsters have

had. Not all stories or pictures need tie back to trips and visitors. Many a story or picture stands on its own, a new adventure and a new challenge in and of itself. But good teachers are alert to the possibility of using words and illustrations — the symbols — to carry children back to their happenings, to carry them more deeply into those happenings.

Theoretically, *movies* could prove effective reinforcement of the stimulus youngsters have gotten from their real-life adventures. Now and again, a commercially produced film comes close enough to the actual experience children have had to serve this purpose. Usually, the best films for classes of young children, however, are amateur films — parent-made or teacher-made — taken of the children on their trips or as visitors have come to them. Slides and displays of still photographs of this same home-produced kind also make it possible for youngsters to relive and to talk about a happening they have shared.

Educational TV someday also may reach a point where it can be a true stimulant and a sound reinforcer. If mobile camera crews could capture the details of local community life, this would be a great service to young school children. Educational TV, studio-bound, is more of a sedative than a stimulant. Too often, it is tied to doing on the screen what the teacher should not do in the classroom: Talk at the children and give them artificial lessons.

None of these back-up experiences — pictures, stories, movies, slides, photos — need be all-group experiences. The "organized" quality of the usual all-group Show-and-Tell session has set a bad standard that ought to be dropped. It is beautifully designed to let one person talk, to let one person feel involved, while all the others wiggle, doze, or let their minds wander. Young children need the fullest sense of being "in" on what is going on. The larger the group, the smaller the likelihood that children will care. They will be present but unmoved. Stimulus is strongest when it touches each person. We ought always to strive for the small setting — the subgroup of a teacher with three or four children, the private group of the teacher with one child alone.

None of these back-up experiences, especially not story time, should be used to keep children quiet. The aim is to stir them. A story is not a tranquilizer to be taken before lunch, before going out-of-doors, or before going home. It ought to be a springboard for interruptions, for questions, for comments, and the stimulus for a train of thought.

The Sequence of Learning: Where to Begin?

Which new added stimulus should be chosen first? Where should a teacher begin? One answer seems to make the greatest sense: *Begin wherever the liveliest action is.*

No trip is so precious that young children everywhere must take it first. No one visitor must always be the first to every classroom. No activity is so fundamental that all others depend on it. Nor is it crucial that certain facts, skills, or concepts be mastered first.

Only one thing really matters: A teacher must stay close to the cutting edge of children's enthusiasms. She must choose significant happenings, rich in potential learnings — this is not amusement or busywork. But a teacher must have the freedom to seize upon the most gripping event available to her group.

This policy of maximum leeway for a teacher to plan specifically for her own particular group is contrary to common practice with older children. The prevailing approach—one many kindergartens follow, too—is to have a course of study for a year or a sequence of units for a semester: Our Community Helpers, the Home, the Farm. It is contrary to the recommendations of some scholars, newly interested in the problems of child education, who believe that their particular field must be mastered in a step-by-step orderly progression.

The adult logic behind a planned sequence of units looks fine on paper. In practice, however, it often conflicts with the young child's psycho-*logic* makeup. The child under six has an unpredictable attention span. The fixed units become binding in the classroom. They often force teachers to try to hold youngsters to activities long after interest has flagged. They make teachers ignore events that unpredictably capture children's concern. They force teachers to ignore unusual teaching opportunities that come along unexpectedly: the steam shovel digging at the corner, a house being moved down the street, a bird building a nest outside the window.

These are egocentric children. The happening has to touch *them*. This personal involvement is the key to their motivation, the key to holding their attention, the key to their caring. Units planned in advance, units planned for children in general, can leave young children cold. Happenings at their doorstep can arouse them.

These are beginners. They are making their initial investigations and discoveries in many areas. At a later age, they can put what they have learned in some logical order in their minds. Now there are significant learnings wherever they turn, and their high interest is more important than the logical order. A trip to the bakery, a ride in a truck, the visit of a mother and her baby to class, the experience of cooking stew or establishing a terrarium — all can open up new, provocative trains of thought to these children. These boys and girls are new to this world, not old hands who have been everywhere and done everything.

The temptation of school systems to write out a kindergarten or Head Start course of study is great, but we ought to resist it. A much better use of teachers' time is the development of a comprehensive list of the many significant happenings available to a particular school, an all-inclusive detailing of the resources available of trips and visitors and activities. A teacher can then wisely choose from such an extensive list the stimulus most needed by her group at the time.

Energy would also be well spent elaborating the possible developments stemming from one of these happenings, spelling out the varied teaching opportunities that might emerge. Such a prototype could serve as a guide and useful eye-opener as to how other happenings might be exploited. The prototype would be a sample, a taste. Like the list of Happenings, it should not tie a

teacher's hands. The right place to begin and the right steps to take next cannot come from paper. They must come from the teacher's assessment of her children. For any one teacher, the right place to start is with whatever significant happenings will stir up her children the most.

Response

Once the teacher has set the stimulation in motion—whether through the initial equipment of the classroom, through alterations of it, through trips, visitors, or through classroom activities—the next step is the children's response. The youngsters go to work. The teacher stands back a bit.

The day may begin indoors or out. Time and weather are key factors. The day care center, because of its early hours, will probably start indoors. But wherever the day begins, the greatest gift the teacher can bring to the children at this point in the instructional process is freedom. The children are free to choose what they will do. They are free to use materials in whatever way seems important to them. They are free to stay with the materials as long as they choose, and free to work with whomever they choose. Through setting the scene for stimulation, the teacher has done her initial teaching. Soon she will have more teaching to do in other ways. But right now, starting the very minute they arrive, the children need the chance to go work on their own, to get involved in their own learning.

Play Time and Work Time

Words to describe this important part of the young child's day are hard to find. At the college level, you would probably call it "discussion time," time for "committee work," or "buzz sessions," or even "bull sessions." At upper grade and high school levels, this would be the time for themes and reports; the students organize all that has been coming in to them and try to make some of it their own. At the under-six level, this period is most commonly called "play time," sometimes "free play."

This name *play* applies to the largest part of the young child's school day. The teacher-instigated stimulus periods—trips, visitors, real-life classroom activities—are not play times. Juice, toileting, story time, and music are not play times. But play does fill most of the important blocks of time on most days. The children play for thirty or forty minutes, indoors or out, at the start. As their energy runs down, the teacher changes the pace briefly with toileting, snack, story, or music. Then play or free play begins again, outdoors if the group started inside, indoors if the day began in the outdoor classroom.

In the day care center, the same basic sequence continues. Lunch and sleep form the next transition—these are not play times. Nor are the waking, toileting, dressing, and snack times. After that, the children customarily go outdoors to play and then come indoors to play, or vice versa. The one exception

occurs as the day nears its end. If the children are tired from their long spell of group living, or if they become anxious as the arrival of their mothers draws near, the teacher may have to inject herself into a more central position—perhaps as a story-teller—to become a stabilizing force.

Schools with no outdoor classroom of their own basically follow this same sequence, too, but they cannot change location. The children play, there is a break, and then children play again with different materials available, all indoors. The absence of an outdoor classroom puts pressure on a teacher to fill the time with more teacher-dominated and all-group activities than young children need: organized games, assemblies of the class, workbooks. But a wise teacher resists the pressure. If her original stimulus has played itself out, she seeks additional happenings, rather than busy work, so that her children can have a springboard into better play.

Play sounds wicked as a central activity of a school. Free play sounds worse. But young children's play is not light-hearted activity. Least of all is it wild, running-screaming activity. Play is a time for concentration. Children become completely absorbed in blocks, make-believe, paints, or at the workbench. Play is a time of earnestness and intensity. The instant a teacher senses a lackadaisical quality, a random or scattered quality, she knows something is wrong. Either energy is at a low ebb, or the stimulus has run down, or the setting is wrong, or something—it is time for a change. Children at play are like men and women at work they love; like students at study that enthralls them; like artists in the act of creation.

Play for young children is not recreation activity, not recess activity. It is not leisure-time activity nor escape activity. Free play is thinking time for young children. It is language time. Problem-solving time. It is memory time, planning time, investigating time. It is organization-of-ideas time, when young children use mind, body, and social skills in response to the stimuli that have come in to them.

"Independent work" could be the label for this activity. Many schools call this "work time," not "play time." It is that. The instant a teacher senses a letdown or pointless repetition—anything less than hard work—she knows something is wrong. It is time for a change.

Free play is "free" because children choose what they do, how they do it, how long they do it, with whom they do it. Free play is "play" because the activity strikes so deep a chord of pleasure within them. But free play is learning. When the learning stops, something is wrong. It is time for a change.

The Talking Teacher

In free play, children are learning through their use of materials. They are learning from each other. They are learning from their busy, continuous, internal process of puzzling, wondering, and organizing their thoughts and impressions. These are sometimes spoken of as "incidental learnings." The term is not one that minimizes these learnings. The children's drive to play makes some of these

learnings, the most acceptable, most retained learnings of all. "Incidental" suggests only the unpredictable content of the learnings. Active playing-working children can literally cover the waterfront in their verbal and physical explorations.

But while the children freely play, they learn from the teacher, too. The teacher is not passive—play time is a busy time for her. Play time is a time for "incidental learnings." *It is also the time for pinpointed instruction.*

The teacher circulates from group to group, from individual to individual. She stays close to the children. Children's play time is the time for the teacher to use her knowledge of subject matter. To do this well, she has to hear what is on children's lips, read what is on their faces, sense what is in their minds. She is constantly seeking for every teaching opportunity that can arise out of the youngster's activity.

The teacher of young children needs a lot of information at her fingertips. Each of the fields of learning has its own body of facts; each has its broad concepts which emerge from those facts; each has its own terminology, the precise words and the technical words that scholars use in their fields of study. When a teacher has planned a happening in advance—a trip to the filling station, a train ride, cutting out the pumpkin and baking the pie—she can anticipate some of the children's questions that may come up, and some of the opportunities she may have to teach specific points. She has to spend a lot of time organizing her thoughts. What are the key facts involved in this activity? What are the big ideas and important generalizations that can emerge? A teacher has to be a source of information, not misinformation. She has to be able to pass on accurate facts, not myths or old wives' tales.

A teacher needs more information than she can store in her mind. She must have access to resources to supplement her knowledge. A good encyclopedia and a good dictionary should be available in the classroom. They should be as commonplace a resource for the teacher as easels, books, dolls, and blocks are for the children. Other source books are needed, too, such as adult reference books in areas in which the children are commonly involved—bird life, engines, mammals. It should be standard operating procedure for the teacher to say many times a day: "I don't know. Let's look it up." Or: "I think I am right. Let's double-check to be sure."

The resources need not always be books. The teacher should also have access to specialists whom she can consult in person and by telephone. It is important for children to be brought into this process of uncovering new information and of checking information with firsthand and secondary sources.

To build sound information, good language, and valid generalizations, the teacher is ever alert for the chance to say the right words to the right person at the right time. It is all too easy to talk too much *at* children. Talking creates the illusion of teaching, but the wise teacher knows that little learning goes on unless someone is listening and unless someone cares.

Some teachers cannot resist the temptation to be center-stage. They cannot resist the temptation to over-use flannel boards—a chance to talk and play the role of actress-magician! Such teachers love planning times when all the

children come together at the start of the day to tell what they expect to do and to receive the teacher's blessing. Such teachers have badly-named "Work Times" when they do all the work, asking questions, prompting answers . . . and maintaining order.

To be sure, other teachers of young children talk too little. They participate too little. Once they have set the stage for stimulus — they often do this too little also — they become mere bystanders. They want the children to be active, they want them to be free. But they have not found the way of playing a constructive role themselves while the youngsters are constructively engaged.

A wise teacher knows she can always safely and constructively speak "welcome words," words a child will be glad to hear. She also recognizes when she must speak less welcome words, and she is skilled in saying them so they have the best chance of sinking in. And she can keep quiet, too, if talking would make her seem an intruder.

Welcome Words

Praise for what a child has done is always welcome. The teacher gives support, every chance she gets, to the qualities she wants to build into children: curiosity, creativity, independence, generosity, thoughtfulness. . . .

Communication that firms up what a child has said is always welcome. "You're right. That is a pyramid." . . . "That cloud is a thunderhead. How did you know that?" . . . "You *do* have nine blocks. Let's count them together: one, two, three. . . ."

Answers to questions a child voices are welcome communication. The youngster listens to the response because he or she thought up the question. "Water freezes when the temperature drops to thirty-two degrees. Let's get the thermometer and I'll show you where thirty-two degrees is."

A teacher close to children can volunteer the answer to the unspoken question on the tip of a tongue or in the back of a mind. She does not always have to wait for the words to come out. Or she can ask a leading question, a slight step ahead of where the children are in their thinking: "What could you do with that?" . . . "Does that remind you of anything?"

The teacher plays this same welcome role when she makes the signs that go on children's block-building: *Airport . . . Ticket Office.* She is in tune with what is on a child's mind when she embellishes tricycle play with an appropriate sign: *Stop . . . Slow . . . Gas . . . No Parking.* Or when, indoors or out, she helps to elaborate dramatic play: *Quiet. Hospital . . . Tires For Sale . . . Men at Work.*

The active, circulating, listening teacher speaks welcome words when she gives children the help they need when they need it. She may speak words of general encouragement — "You're getting it. Keep trying!" — if those words are enough to spur a child on. She may speak words of specific advice, if a child needs this kind of help: "Try lifting one end first." . . . "That pole is too short, isn't it? I know where we have a longer pole that you can use."

Less Welcome Words

All teachers, of course, speak many less welcome words in the course of a day. Often the words are unnecessary and wasted. A child gives some clue — a ques-

tion, a puzzled look — and we start with welcome words but don't know when to stop. We are so eager to teach that we fail to teach. We tell more than the child wants to know. A wise teacher never overstays her welcome. She stands ready to exit gracefully when a child's interest flags.

Some of our less welcome words need to be said, however. They are words of prohibition, words of correction. The child has not asked for them, but the words are necessary to keep children from hurting themselves or others, from damaging property, or from persisting in some error. Words of prohibition and of correction are hard words for any of us to take, but a teacher does not back away from saying them when she has to. If she is wise, however, she searches for the way of saying them to make them as palatable as possible to the child. She wants these less welcome words to sink in. She has no desire to have them shrugged off because the child finds them too unpleasant.

The less welcome words should not be wishy-washy. They should not sound like a suggestion when they are meant to be a command. They should not sound like a question when they are meant to be a statement. They should not sound like a choice when there is no choice, when the child is expected to do what the teacher is saying. Wishy-washy words only add to a child's confusion and almost always lead to more trouble.

The less welcome words should be firm but they should not be angry. A youngster may have behaved badly or may have made some irritating error. But when we jump all over children they react by defending themselves. If the words sound like an attack, the lesson gets lost. Children become so busy defending themselves against the attack, so busy with conflicting emotions, they cannot think straight. And straight thinking after all, ought to be the goal of all of our words, the welcome and the less welcome ones.

The less welcome words should not be broadcast. When they must be said, they are best said in eyeball-to-eyeball, private conversation. Young children have to save face; we all do. The public reprimand, the public correction, puts even a young child on the hot spot. The child's thoughts go more into how to escape, than into how to do better the next time.

The less welcome words should not be nagging words. If a teacher has to say the same thing, day after day, a hundred times, she gets no medal for doing her duty assiduously. The chances are that she is wasting her time, merely going through the motions of teaching. The child obviously has tuned her out — the words are not getting through. Whenever she finds herself nagging, the wise teacher reassesses what is going on. More talking — even louder, tougher talking — probably is not the way to reach the youngster at this time.

A better approach may lie in backing up the words with action. The teacher may have to stand by a child so that her presence helps the youngster act better. She may have to take a hand or an arm — as a friend, not an arresting policeman — to give extra support to what she says.

Or a better approach may lie in making some change in the classroom environment: rearranging the equipment, removing some troublesome material, changing the time schedule. Settings can say No for us — or Yes — in an impersonal way that often can be more effective than any spoken word.

There are times, too when the best answer is to bite our tongue and bide our time. The smart approach for the moment may be to do nothing.

A teacher usually can afford to play this waiting game when only language is at stake, when the trouble is what a child *says* rather than what the child does. One example is the problem of changing Head Start children's street language to the language of the school, both their linguistic peculiarities and the more colorful expressions. The children's words may offend us but the world won't end because of them. In language—in many other areas too—young children have to make "mistakes" first, a whole batch of them, before they are ready to change. Teacher-words that are unwelcome today become welcome words in some tomorrow when the youngsters themselves begin to see a reason for changing.

Silent Teaching

Some of the best teaching any of us ever does occurs when we don't say a word. We are not telling anyone anything. We are not showing anyone anything. We don't even know we are teaching, but the children have their eyes riveted on us. They don't know they are learning, but they are lapping up our behavior.

This process of silent teaching is called *identification*. Children feel with us; they like us; they want to *be* like us. Identification is one of the most potent educative forces, and it operates at all age levels and everywhere. In homes, the well-loved parents of young children are style-setters—they teach more through their love than they ever could through words alone. At school, elementary youngsters, adolescents, even college students, have adult "heroes" and "heroines." The process of identification goes on, too, among young children. Older brothers and sisters at home as well as older boys and girls in school serve as models. This is one reason why Head Start strongly urges using junior and senior high school volunteers in its program. Every growing person has eyes that look up.

The youngest children, most of all, hitch their wagons to a star.

Their dependence—their smallness, their newness on this earth, their ignorance and impotence—makes them exceptionally open to the lessons that can come through identification. Identification has an unusually valuable place in the good teaching of young children. What a teacher is, what a teacher does, how a teacher acts form a large part of what a teacher teaches.

There is one qualification, however, under-six or over-six: Children identify only with the people they like! The rest of us are mere passersby, parts of the scenery, wallflowers. We may set spectacular examples, but if children have no deep feeling for us, they won't tune us in—we have to reach them some other way. Identification only operates when relationships are close, warm, and friendly. Silent teaching is nil when relationships are cold or casual.

The good teacher of young children goes out of her way to build intimate bonds. The prize way for her to do her wooing is to spend time alone with each child. She searches for the intimate touch: visiting the child at home; saying something personal when the child arrives in the morning; giving concentrated help when a youngster is in trouble; working a puzzle or reading a story or taking

a short walk with one child alone; holding a youngster's hand, sitting by the child's side, or tousling hair.

Every youngster has to feel: This is *my* teacher, as if that one child alone was the apple of the teacher's eye. It is no simple job for a teacher to convey this sense of caring to each one. Some lucky youngsters are magnetic—they immediately attract a teacher's warm feelings. But often a teacher must go to extra lengths—arranging private chats, making personal telephone calls—to reach other youngsters who are less quickly lovable. Yet it is often the quieter children or those who get in our hair who most need someone special they can pattern themselves after.

Once children are crazy about a teacher, they listen better to what she says and—more important—they keep their eyes on what she does. The teacher is on the job when she is talking and knows she is teaching—she is also on the job *all* the time, teaching through everything she does.

The massive learnings that come through identification are often unappreciated. The learnings are so quiet. The learnings only show up later. They are less apt to be specific, the kind that can be measured on a test. But broad attitudes, values, the points of view, the style and approach of a teacher do become part of children, if the children think their teacher is really a prize.

A teacher's way of talking becomes a part of them. If children feel close to us, the language we use is the language we teach.

A teacher's sense of beauty sinks in. The gaiety, color, and good taste of her clothing, the attention she gives to the charm of the room, her selective response to objects of beauty—to a flower, a bird, a cloud, a color—all teach the child.

A teacher's openness to experience is absorbed. Children who love her are aware of her freedom from fear of snakes, mice, bugs; of her enjoyment of snow and cold, of thunder, of the wind; of her relish for new tastes; of the way she reaches out to the different and the unusual.

Everything about a well-loved teacher gets under a child's skin: her patience, her humor, her reasonableness, her kindness . . . her helpfulness. Walt Whitman spoke of "a child (who) went forth every day and the first object he looked upon, that object he became and that object became part of him for the day, or a certain part of the day, or for many years, or stretching cycles of years." When that object is a well-loved teacher, the child's learning can be manifold.

_____ **The Scope of the Curriculum**

Covering all the fields of learning is a formidable task, not an easy one for any level of education. The traditional elementary school approach to this question of the scope of the curriculum, as well as to the question of sequence in the curriculum, has been the development of curriculum guides. This approach, however, is not well suited to programs for young children.

We do better to follow the approach of the colleges. The college solution to the problem of a balanced diet in the curriculum is to have "distribution requirements." Colleges try to provide experiences in each of the four broad areas of knowledge: the humanities, mathematics and the sciences, the social sciences, health and physical education. Early education can do the same thing. Periodically, perhaps once a month or so, a teacher can look back over a group's total happenings and each child's involvement in them. Has there been an unnecessary lumping in any one or two broad areas of study? Has there been a reasonable balance among all four? This periodic checkup can alert us to whether we need to strive to open up experiences in new directions.

The goal cannot be, nor need it be, an even-steven approach—equal time for every field of study. For one thing *the age of children* means that some fields must be treated lightly now, to receive more emphasis later. In general, the younger the children the less apt they are to become excited about or truly to understand the faraway in either time or distance. The younger the children, the less apt they are to become concerned about the inert and the immobile. Three-, four-, and five-year-olds are more likely to respond to what they can see, touch, and use. They are more apt to become involved in whatever crosses their path in some noisy, active, functional fashion. A fossil may intrigue a few young children—the chances are slight that it will excite many. The Washington Monument—tall, statuesque, dead—is more apt to become a center for running up and down steps than for any meaningful lessons in history, art, or community planning.

Secondly, a *school's location* also makes complete, balanced, A through Z coverage difficult and undesirable. An urban school might have an occasional chance to teach geology when an excavation is being dug. All schools for young children have few chances to teach astronomy. Inland schools, seacoast schools, suburban schools, warm-weather schools, all schools have special opportunities—and limitations. No school has all the resources close at hand to promote the utmost of what children could learn if a specific location and setting confronted the children with a challenge.

A *teacher's own background* is a third factor affecting any effort to achieve complete coverage and a curriculum of perfect balance. Colleges face up to this fact: "We have a very strong physics department." . . . "Our work in psychology is rather weak." But colleges are fortunate. They can subdivide human knowledge and parcel out the specialties. In contrast, the teacher of young children is the entire faculty, all by herself. She is the physicist, psychologist, philosopher, artist, musician, mathematician . . . the A-ist through Z-ist. And no one can be good at everything.

A teacher's enthusiasm is the secret ingredient in all good teaching—it must not be lost. A teacher has to be excited about what she and her youngsters are doing. Teaching cannot be her duty—it has to be her love. You can count any child lucky whose teacher is a little "unbalanced," head-over-heels in love with activities that involve mathematics or science or art or literature. The curriculum may be somewhat uneven, but the children are apt to be in a good class.

A need does exist to guard against avoidable imbalance, that which occurs through inadvertence, bad planning, or from blindly following tradition. One way of doing this is to check a classroom diary periodically against the framework of the liberal arts. Then, if need be, we can always set out aggressively to correct any imbalances and to fill in any important gaps.

The Common Strands in Subject Matter

Another safeguard for insuring adequate coverage and a balanced curriculum is for the teacher to be aware of some of the themes that permeate the fields of study and to take every opportunity to drive them home to the children.

The subject-matter labels make the disciplines sound separate and specialized. Yet there are broad strands which ignore the labels. These concerns are a part of each and every field. A teacher who keeps these across-the-board themes in mind can teach simultaneously in more than one field. Whenever she hits at one of these themes, she teaches many subject matters, no matter how the label might read on the activity in which the children are engaged.

All scholars hold one overall view which can be stated like this: *Man lives in a universe of mystery in which there is order, continuity, and interrelationship.* Broadly speaking, this is the stance of ichthyologists at their particular site of operation, the stance of the geologists at theirs; this is the set of psychologists as they study individuals, and it is the attitude of sociologists as they examine groups. The archeologist studies the past; the political scientist is more involved in today, but both hold this outlook. Each and every one—and biologists, nutritionists, geographers, philosophers, *A* through *Z*—is trying to unravel the mystery by finding some part of the inherent order, continuity, and interrelationship in order to give man more control over the universe.

This one broad, shared viewpoint leads to other common attitudes and approaches. Some of these attitudes are felt more keenly by specialists in mathematics and in the social and natural sciences; some more keenly by workers in the humanities. But there is overlap and interplay. When the classroom rings with common themes, it makes little difference whether the children are cooking applesauce or digging a trench, visiting a fireboat or planting a garden. They are working in no one subject matter—they are working in all of them.

A Sense of Wonder

Regardless of the label or area of specialization—astronomer or artist, botanist or author—adult scholars look at life around them with a *sense of wonder*. They take nothing for granted within their own field. Because this is their training, they bring this same sense of wonder to all of life. Nothing passes them by. Nothing is too small, too insignificant for their curious notice. Nothing is or-

dinary. Scholars—psychologist, statistician, musician, biologist—are open. Their eyes are open; their ears are open; their nostrils are open; their pores are open.

Scholars are aware of and captivated by the phenomena around them. The anthropologist is aware of the way babies are held when they are bathed. The criminologist selectively hears the sternness in a mother's voice. The agronomist stoops to feel the crumbly quality of the soil. The nutritionist tastes with the tongue the thickness of a pea hull. Each specialist has a particular focus, but all have an identical response: The world is full of fascinating phenomena.

The young child's world can seem everydayish to adults. In that world, there are few seemingly spectacular incidents. The child's life is made up of the plop of hot cereal, the whistling of the teakettle, the dew on the grass, the frost on the window, red and green paints running together, wood floating in the water table and a metal ring sinking, blocks toppling, the whirr of wind, chocolate melting in the hand. The scholar's sense of wonder transforms a similar, "ordinary" world into the "extra" ordinary.

A good classroom helps its children to look on their small world as a part of a universe of never-ending mystery. We do this when, no matter what happening the children are involved in, we teach them to stop, look, and listen . . . and feel and taste and smell. We foster a sense of wonder when we give fullest support to the questioning mind: What is it? Where does it come from? What is it made of? What is it for? We do it when we spur close-up examination, through our own example and through the encouragement we give to children. When we work in these ways to build a sense of wonder, we move toward a balanced curriculum because this openness, this excited awareness, is a common quality of every discipline.

A Commitment to Evidence

Regardless of the label or area of specialization, adults scholars approach all phenomena with a *commitment to evidence*. They want the facts. They are not content with surface appearances, quick impressions, say-so, or hearsay. Scholars are driven by insistent questions: How do you know? How can you tell? How can you be sure? They experiment, so that they can be clearer about what they are seeing. They compare, so that they can be certain. They dig into the background to get the facts. They record all the evidence so that there is no forgetting and no misunderstanding. Scholars are skeptics until all the facts are in. They then become believers, but only as far as the facts will carry them. Scholars are the detectives in this universe of mystery.

A good classroom prods its young children to get evidence. We push them into the detective role whenever we encourage puzzling and wondering: Why does the Jell-o gel? Why did the blocks fall? What made the aquarium water turn green? Why did the wood split? Why do you think Bobby hit you? We foster the detective role whenever we support experimentation and comparison: "Can you think of another way of doing that?" . . . "Let's try it again to see what

happens." . . . "We will look carefully tomorrow to see if it stays the same." We build a commitment to evidence when we take every opportunity to write down facts for children so that they can see a record kept: of their height, of the temperature, the rainfall, the weight of a frog, the number of days the eggs have been in the incubator. Whenever we emphasize the need for evidence, we cut across every subject-matter line.

Searching for Relationships

Regardless of the label or area of specialization, adult scholars also are concerned with *classification and grouping*. They try to relate one observation to another. They search constantly for the broader meaning. They push from the specific to concept, from concept to broader generalization. They search everlastingly for unity, through time and across-the-board. They are persuaded that there is order, if they can discover it; that there is continuity, if they can discover it; that there are interrelationships.

We help children think along these lines when we lead them into seeing connections: "What does the marshmallow taste like?" . . . And what does it feel like, look like, what does it make you think of? We teach in many fields at once when we introduce children to the search for similarities and differences: "Have you ever tasted anything like this before?" . . . "It's round and soft, almost like a what?" . . . "Do you think it bounces like a ball? Try it and see." We push the subject-matter walls down when we lead children into thinking back to causes, when we prod them into puzzling about future probabilities, and when we help them connect what they are doing to something else they know.

Man as the Potential Master

Adult scholars hold one more passion in common: Regardless of the label or field of specialization they all see *man as the potential master of the mystery*. They believe man can control his environment. In particular, the artist and the musician, the playwright, architect, author, poet, and sculptor hold this vision. They see man as a creator. But so, too, do the mathematicians and scientists. This is the image when they build planes, develop space programs, seed clouds, control population, and multiply our food and water resources. It is the image of the social scientists as they wrestle with the problems of war and peace, internationally and interpersonally. Man, a creator, is the underlying concept of health workers as they battle disease. All scholars believe that the whole point of getting the facts, and comprehending the law, order, and interrelationships among phenomena is so that man can make the universe a better place in which to live.

We build this same spirit—we teach what every discipline wants its students to feel—when we support children's own fresh, innovative ways of responding to their world. We do it when we liven their language: "How else could you say 'quick as a flash'? Quick as a . . . what?" This is not language teaching

alone—it also teaches the creative spirit that floods the sciences, mathematics, and the social sciences. We do it whenever we give special support to a child's originality: "I like the way you painted your picture. It is different from everyone else's." This is not a comment on art alone—it also boosts a spirit essential to the sciences, mathematics, and the social sciences. We build the sense of man as master when we foster independence, when we spur problem-solving. The particular field does not matter, the spirit cuts across all of them.

Evaluation

Evaluation is so important that we all ought to be good at it. The pressing practical question of retention or promotion, a matter of vital importance to parents and to children, is involved. In addition, as teachers, we need to know whether we are achieving what we set out to do. And if we are ever to end the shortage of programs for young children, our country has to know: Do nursery schools, kindergartens, child care centers, and Head Start pay off?

Unfortunately, under-six education has grave problems with evaluation.

The Measurable and the Meaningful

A persisting reason for the difficulties with evaluation in under-six education is the heavy reliance on *objective* evaluative instruments. Americans like to come out with a score, a grade, a number, a percentile. This seeming precision is one of the reasons why reading readiness tests sound better to many people that the "test" of a child's actual reading behavior, even though the artificial tests utterly fail to measure desire as a part of readiness. The love for the sound of precision is a reason why research that evaluates the efficiency of Head Start, or the impact of kindergartens, turns to tests that measure vocabulary, IQ, and items of factual knowledge instead of in-depth studies of individuals and their families.

There is nothing wrong with objective tests *except* that there are too few tests available, and the ones available often measure the wrong things. Yet we stay wedded to objective instruments. The easy availability of the wrong tests gives us empty answers, but we persist in using them.

The tests we use and go on using tell us whether children have learned to distinguish a rectangle from a triangle, and whether they know the right word for each figure. The tests are no help in telling us whether the youngsters have been made more dependent in the process; whether they have been made more competitive; whether their hostility to adults has increased; whether they have been made more conforming or insincere; whether they see themselves more as stupid, brilliant, or unimportant youngsters. We know whether they can give the right answer, but we have no objective evaluative techniques for revealing whether the right answer has made them better people more able to live with them-

selves and better for the rest of us to live with. The devotion to objective evaluative techniques makes us confuse the measurable with the meaningful.

We are like the man, down on his hands and knees, searching under the street light for his lost wristwatch. A helpful policeman joins the search, but when they are unsuccessful, the policeman finally asks: "Are you sure you lost it here?" "Oh, no," the man replies, "I lost it up the street, but the light is better here."

Evaluation of early education has to center on the goals of under-six education. These are twofold. *For the individual,* as stated on page 4, early education aims "to help each child learn as much as he or she can in all areas of human experience and to do this in such a way that the youngster lives the years of three, four, and five in the richest, most satisfying, most constructive way possible. The one big job (of nursery school, kindergarten, day care, Head Start), once a child is enrolled, is *to teach* and to do so in such a way so that each youngster is more glad to be alive during these early years." This ultimate concern is the quality of the child's living at the time, the youngster's sense of self-fulfillment.

For our society, early education aims to develop boys and girls with the qualities our country needs most. It seeks to produce people who are rugged individualists, for example, and free people, people who will use their heads, and have a heart. The second ultimate concern is the development of human attributes, the qualities that make up the person.

A year's growth in any subject, the mastery of any skill, the addition of any knowledge are all important, but these are not the end goals. Subject matter is the means through which we work. The goals—evaluation has to center on them—are a different thing. We must not let the availability of objective instruments in some few areas sidetrack us. We must not let their availability make us concentrate on measuring our means while we ignore the end results we really seek.

Subjectivity

The easy availability of objective tests and the lure of the shiny scores they yield need not force us into measuring the wrong outcomes. We can continue to use intelligence tests and vocabulary tests for the help they provide in understanding individuals. At the same time, however, we can use, much more fully than ever before, *subjective* measures as our major evaluative tools.

Subjectivity has its pitfalls, just as do the objective approaches. But subjective measures have one overriding virtue: They free us to evaluate what under-six education is all about. They free us to examine the quality of children's living; they free us to look at their qualities as human beings. They do not force us into focusing on side issues or tangents.

We have been needlessly scornful of subjectivity and afraid of it. We have been halfhearted and hesitant about using it. We have underplayed the value of observation by humans and overprized the importance of a machine's score,

number, or grade. We need to appreciate more the value of concerned-parent and trained-teacher insight. We especially need to create better machinery so these insights can operate.

Teachers live with children in school. Parents live with them at home. The shared observations of these two sets of people add up to a sensitive evaluation for gauging children's state of mind. Do they seem alive and alert? Do they seem vigorous? Do they seem enthusiastic and responsive? Are they eager to come to school, or do they appear bored, untouched, and apathetic? When they return home are they fussy? Feisty? Tense? It is not difficult for people who live close to children to assess how they feel about life. There is no reason to downgrade this assessment. This is the important job to be done, and parents and teachers can do it.

We do need better machinery through which to do it, however. One great aid would be major blocks of time set aside for parent-teacher conferences, throughout the year. In addition, we need the continuous flow of communication through brief, informal telephone and face-to-face conversations. Evaluation is not a job for June. If we wait until then, too often we will only be able to look back in anger and dismay. Our communication system must be so open that parents and teachers can move into action the minute a signal comes, from home or school, that a youngster is not full of zest.

We also need a framework, a common focus, as we observe children and as we talk together. Both parents and teachers must understand what matters most to children during these early years. Building a deep awareness of the basic growth tasks young children face should have top priority on the agenda of nursery-kindergarten-day care-Head Start room meetings.[1]

Basic Growth Tasks

The basic growth tasks are children's private learnings. They make up the meaning *they* take from all that happens to them. They are what children learn about people, about the world into which they have been born, about themselves—over and beyond whatever else we teach them. These learnings are the ones most apt to be remembered. They are the learnings that will most affect how children feel and what they will do in every future situation.

In the under-six years, all young children work to discover how much trust they can put in adults and how much safety there is in their world. This search for a sense of trust is a basic growth task, one uppermost in children's minds. It is the first meaning they take from how they are handled and treated in every little event at home. As they move on into a group, this remains the lesson of prime importance: What are big people like? The poorest child searches for answers;

---

[1] Sharing this top billing should be discussions on the kind of human our society needs presented in Chapter 3. These two items—the basic growth needs of children, the qualities our society prizes—give parents and teachers a solid framework for their evaluative conferences.

the most privileged child searches. Without good adults, the world looks frightening to the young.

In the under-six years, all young children also work to discover ways of living with their own age-mates. The search is a complicated one that can cause pain, discomfort and hurt, just as it can bring sweet rewards. It is a fumbling process of trial, error, and experimentation. It is a slow process and a delicate one. Children must feel more fully themselves as they build their wider social bonds, not less true to themselves because they are socialized. Finding out how to live with their own generation and with older and younger people is a matter of consuming importance, a growth task children are aware of all of the time at home and at school.

In the under-six years all young children want to grow in their own powers, too. Children are born dependent, but no child wants to stay that way. They are curious about the world in which they find themselves. They want to build mastery over their own bodies, the very first "house" in which they live. They want to develop skill in spoken language so they can further control their environment. They also face the difficult task of developing emotionally. Without an expanding range of emotions, the child's life stays thin, empty, meager. Without expanding control over the expression of emotion, the child's life is turbulent, troublesome to the rest of us, and frightening to the child.

Young children need strong, helpful, big people to care for them for many years. But during all these years, they seek to feel strong and powerful so that they can care for themselves. Children seek to discover that *they* are good. They can hold their heads up. They *are* somebody. They can manage in this world.

Young children's search for trust in adults, their search for joy in their age-mates, their search for confidence in themselves is called the development of self-concept. Children are "little nothings" at birth. They must move from that nothingness. The whole point of their living, its very significance, lies in the movement toward self-concept.

Healthy self-concept means dignity. It means the child becomes a person, alive with a full feeling of self-awareness, self-direction.

This is what children come to school to learn: *selfhood.* Proud selfhood, and the development of the special qualities our society needs, are what evaluation has to focus on. Parents and teachers, pooling their thinking, must both come to see these as the crucially important points—not reading readiness, not getting ready for first grade, not countable language or intelligence test scores.

Anecdotal Records

Teachers, more than parents, can collect written evidence which bears on these central goals. Anecdotal records—brief descriptions of behavior—can provide specifics for discussion as parents and teachers confer. In the busyness of a day, a teacher may need some kind of prop to make herself keep records—the job can so easily be overlooked. One technique is to set a concrete goal of writing up every day a fixed number of behavioral incidents. The exact

number makes no difference, but a set number can help to fix the pattern of writing down specific happenings so that they are not forgotten. Another aid is to carry a pad and pencil tucked in one's pocket for instant recording. Still another is to preserve some minutes for writing up records immediately after the children leave, when the incidents are still fresh in your mind.

Such anecdotal records, incidentally, become an excellent means of spotting children who are being overlooked. At the end of a month you may discover you have no records on some children at all! Anecdotal records are also a means of discovering whether some areas of development are being passed over. You may have records galore on social behavior but hardly any that reveal intellectual, physical, or emotional response.

Anecdotal records can be supplemented by planned and scheduled observations of each child. There should be spot-checks from time to time, with a full recording of what a youngster does for fifteen or twenty minutes, as if a motion picture camera were making a documentary of how the child spends those minutes of life. November's documentary compared with February's documentary can throw light on whether a child's behavior is expanding or whether the youngster seems to be standing still.

Conferences, conversations, meetings, anecdotal records, planned observation mean added work for the teacher. There is no getting away from it. Much of it can only be done when the group includes a teacher and an aide. Much can only be done when class size is right for the age. But unless we actively and aggressively seek evidence on the measures that count, we will everlastingly find ourselves at the mercy of easy evidence on measures that count for less.

Accountability

The problems of evaluation are intensified today by the demand for accountability. All levels of education are being told to prove that what they do pays off. Under-six education, making its bid for wider public acceptance, especially feels the brunt of this demand.

The insistence on accountability strikes a note of reasonableness. We all need to know whether our educational efforts are succeeding. But underlying accountability is one unfair assumption that *schools alone* account for all outcomes. *Schools* are to be held accountable, every other force is absolved.

Parents and homes are not to be held accountable. Newspapers, book publishers, television stations are not to be held accountable. *Accountability,* as the term is used now, assumes that schools and teachers alone control all outcomes and therefore ought to be held responsible for all learning.

A medical analogy can make this injustice clearer. Imagine an automobile accident in which the driver is badly injured. Is it fair to hold the doctor alone accountable for whether the driver's life is saved? Does it make any difference how badly injured the victim is? Does the victim's previous health make any difference—whether the driver is recovering from recent surgery, has a history of malnutrition, or heart disease? Does it make any difference whether the driver

wants to live? Or whether the doctor can treat the patient in a well-equipped hospital or do the best that can be done at the accident scene?

Obviously, it is not fair to hold the doctor alone accountable for whether the patient lives or dies. Too many other considerations enter in.

Doctors can be held accountable—doctors *should* be held accountable—for doing their professional best. Accountable not for *outcome*—that is almost in the lap of the gods, so many variables are involved—but *accountable for input!* Doctors must do all that is possible for them to do. They must work as skillfully as any professional could expect them to. For this, their input, they can be held accountable, fairly and with justice.

Input

Schools—under-six schools in particular—must insist more and more on being judged in this same way. Outcomes can be assessed fairly only if everyone—a total society—is willing to become involved in the study. *Input* is the fairer measure.

If accountability can be redirected to focus on *input*, under-six education can amass compelling evidence of its worth. The input of the good school for children under six is impressive indeed.

Any good school for young children can say to its parents, to the community: "We promise you. You can hold us strictly accountable. If your children are with us for forty weeks of a school year, we will read to them 120 of the world's very best books for children their age, 120 pieces of the world's very best literature."

This is input. This a school can promise; this parents can measure; this a school can be held to. And this promise everyone of goodwill, every parent, would recognize as being very worthwhile.

Will this input turn children into readers? That is *outcome,* and outcome depends on many factors a school cannot control: the example of the child's parents; the availability of a public library; the cost of children's books and the availability of bookstores; the child's eyesight. The variables are endless. But the school's *input* is clear.

"Send your children to us for forty weeks. We promise, and you can hold us to it, to let your children travel. We will take children to at least twenty of the most exciting, mindstretching, provocative sites in their part of the world close to the school." Most thoughtful people would have to say, "That is impressive and that is good."

Send children to school for forty weeks.

They will hear 120 pieces of excellent music, the very best for their age.

They will sing forty different songs.

They will handle twenty different animals.

They will meet at least ten new adults.

They will see forty eye-filling, wonder-inducing pictures on display.

They will taste twenty new foods.

They will handle twenty new tools.

They will hear 10,000 words not yet in their spoken vocabulary.

They will be praised, honestly, a minimum of 200 times.

They will have 1,000 chances to carry out an idea of their own.

They will follow directions 1,000 times.

They will make at least 2,000 decisions.

They will weigh, measure, or compare at least 1,000 times.

And 1,000 times—at least—they will hear justice explained and decency defined.

All this, and more, a good school can promise to do and be willing to be held accountable for.

Quantitative evidence on *outcome* is hard to come by. It often is inconclusive when it is available. It frequently is very limited in its coverage. The countable, measurable, quantitative evidence on *input* can be very persuasive. It ought to lead any reasonable human to say, "I would be glad if every young child could experience all of it."

TEACHING THE BASICS: READING

Many parents express one specific anxiety about the education of their young children: They want their youngsters to learn to read. This wish runs so deep that it merits special attention.

Parents state this concern in a particular set of words: They want schools to "teach the basics." The wording is right. Teaching reading *is* basic. It deserves top priority both from parents and from early childhood educators. Children who grow up not able to read, or not reading well, or not liking to read are severely crippled in our complex society.

Teachers of young children must find ways to assure parents that we share with them a high priority for teaching reading. We must leave no doubt in their minds that we, too, want children to learn to read as quickly as is right for them. We must make it crystal clear that we do not want to hold any child back in reading skill, any more than we would want to hold a child back in the development of any capacity. Some of parents' intense obsession with reading comes because they think teachers are fighting them—they want one thing and we want another.

We feed the flames of this unnecessary conflict when we say, "No, we do not teach reading in kindergarten (or in nursery school, child care, or in Head Start)." We feed the flames when we say, as many more teachers do, "No, we do not teach reading, but we *do* teach reading readiness." The pedagoguery leaves too many parents feeling unsure and unsettled.

There have been sound reasons for these traditional teacher-responses. Teachers have wanted to protect children. They know that few youngsters at these early ages are ready for technical lessons in reading or to stay with such lessons for long. Teachers have not wanted to increase the pressure on children, but our negative words and our weasel words have unfortunately promoted that very result.

We can help parents feel less anxious about the problem if we tell them that we *do* teach reading; we work very hard to teach it; *but* we teach reading in ways that fit under-six children.

We need to work hard to communicate this point of view to administrators, too. In particular, we must reach principals, but we must also reach the "higher-ups": supervisors, directors of curriculum, superintendents of schools. These are able educators—they would not have risen to their positions of leadership without good ability and training. However, very few of these leadership people have ever worked with young children, studied about young children, or thought specifically about the materials and methods of programs for young children. Able in their own fields, they are understandably ill-informed about early childhood education. Their tendency is to think in terms of tests, books, paper-and-pencil, the seated children, the assigned tasks of the upper school.

The result of bad communication with parents and with administrators has been great pressure on kindergartens, in particular, to teach reading in ways that do not fit young children. This pressure forced one professional association which had fought for public kindergartens to conclude: "If the curriculum for entering (kindergarten) children is to be focused on group instruction in the academic skills . . . the Association feels it would be wiser to postpone school entry to age seven."[1] The pressure led seven national organizations to issue a *Joint Statement of Concern About Present Practices in Pre-First Grade Reading Instruction.* Their worry: "Highly structured pre-reading and reading programs." Specifically: "In attempting to respond to pressures for high scores, teachers of young children feel impelled to use materials, methods and activities designed for older children."[2]

Although the heat has been on kindergartens, in particular, other and younger early childhood groups are also feeling pressure. Teachers of four-year-olds and of Head Start groups both report an increasing rigidity creeping into their programs. This is not good for children. It is not good for reading. We must become skilled in communicating both with parents and administrators so they will not push for inappropriate teaching techniques, but be glad instead to see teachers of young children teach reading in ways that are right for the age.

Some Basic Understandings

We will make progress with parents and administrators if we zero in on certain basic understandings. These understandings ought to be the focus of conversation after conversation, parent meeting after parent meeting. They ought to be the subject of bulletin after bulletin sent home by teachers to parents. They

[1] The Virginia Association for Early Childhood Education, 1977.
[2] The Association of Elementary, Kindergarten, Nursery Educators; Association for Childhood Education International; Association for Supervision and Curriculum Development; National Association for the Education of Young Children; National Association of Elementary School Principals; National Council of Teachers of English; International Reading Association. 1977.

ought to form the content of memos, notes, and continuous conversations with administrators. We must try, every way we can, to build agreement on four central points.

An Early Start on Reading: Boon or Boondoggle?

The first basic understanding has to do specifically with early formal teaching of reading. We must help everyone to see that an early start, in and of itself, is not necessarily good. The one right time to begin the formal teaching of reading is each child's own time.

In our country we have long been persuaded that "the early bird catches the worm." Coming in first always gets high acclaim. In sports some say, "Winning isn't the main thing. It is the *only* thing." In area after area we have believed in the slogan, "The sooner the better." *But* this does not necessarily hold true in the formal teaching of reading.

Some children—very very few—read as early as age three. A handful read as early as age four. A few more children—still a handful—learn to read at age five. Given our energetic, pushy, dynamic climate you can hardly blame parents for wondering about these early readers: Are they all set for life? Have they piled up a lead they will never lose? You can hardly blame parents for wanting to do something at home to give their child a head start. And it is understandable when both parents and administrators want schools to start sooner on formal reading instruction so that a lot of children can have the advantage of an early beginning.

It sounds so logical, but we have to help everyone see that learning to read at an early age may or may not be a good idea for a child. *It all depends.* It depends on why a child learned to read before most other children. The simple, straight fact of coming in ahead of others is not the crucial point. Only one thing matters—what caused the speed-up? Why is that child reading early? What triggered the early reading?

Some children who read early do so because they inherited the right set of genes. They were probably early developers in every facet of their growth, and their parents, or one of them, probably were, too. These children crawled earlier than others, they walked earlier than others, they talked earlier than others.

Some children who read early do so because they have "the right kind" of intelligence. Words and letters come easy for them. All of us are "smart" in many ways, but these particular children have minds that soak up figures, symbols, signs, and verbalisms.

Some children who read early come from homes where mother and father are bookworms. They come from homes where the walls are lined with bookshelves, where books are the prized presents at holiday times. Ever since they were born these children have been learning that reading is a favored way to spend time.

Some children who read early have older brothers or sisters who are good readers. Often these older ones become honest-to-goodness teachers at home, passing on their knowledge to the younger ones through endless games of make-

believe school. The thrill of reading rubs off on the younger ones; a lot of the techniques do, too.

Some children who read early are "loners" for one reason or another. They turn to books the way others their same age turn to people, to busy activity, and to play.

No matter what the reason—often there is a combination of reasons—some children who read early learned because reading was "a natural" for them—it simply flowed out of their nature or from the kind of family the children lived in. You could almost say that the early reading . . . just happened. It was no big deal.[3]

When early reading comes about in this simple, easy way youngsters do benefit. They are apt to be good readers. They are apt to love reading. The chances are that they will do well in their early school work. Some other children who learn to read on "standard time" may catch up. One usually can't tell, for example, at age three which child happened to crawl, stand, or walk a little earlier. But often, when early reading comes about in this unplanned, natural way, children hold their gains and are always more book-minded than other children.

These particular children had the right genes, and/or they came from the "right" homes, and/or they had the "right" siblings. Reading was a snap for them.

Other youngsters are pushed and prodded into reading at an early age.

They are urged and goaded.

Sometimes the pressure on these children is obvious; sometimes it is subtle. The younsters simply sense, rightly, that it matters very very much to their parents that they learn to read.

These children are not so lucky.

A few of them—no one can predict who they will be—learn to read early, and everything works out satisfactorily for them.

Others may or may not learn to read earlier, but there is a price tag on their effort. The price may be that later they will reject reading the way some youngsters pushed into piano lessons too early reject the piano when they grow older. Or the price may be that these children will reject authority or "the establishment." They read all right, but they are more touchy, more stubborn, more resistant than they normally should be. Usually you cannot push young children around without getting a backlash—the children get even in strange ways as they get older.

For the largest number of children pushed into early reading, the efforts are primarily a waste of time. Despite all the drill, fuss, strain, and countless little unpleasantries, the children learn to read at about the time they normally would have. At its best, the time and trouble of too-early teaching went down the drain; at its worst, the time and trouble of too-early teaching led to unhappy side ef-

---

[3] I have written a series of twelve *Notes for Parents,* intended to be distributed free to parents by schools. One of them is entitled, "Learning to Read At an Early Age." They are published by the Southern California Association for the Education of Young Children, 6851 Lennox Ave., Van Nuys, CA 91405.

fects. Many parents have seen similar results from too early and too strenuous efforts at toilet training.

What, then, is the right time to begin formal, technical reading instruction? Early—at age three, four, or five? On what is "standard time" for more children—at six or seven? *The one right time is each child's own time.* This is one basic understanding we must hold, and one we must help parents and administrators to see clearly. No child must be shoved ahead. No child must be held back. Each child must be taught at the time and in such a way that learning to read flows naturally, with all the great benefits that derive when that does happen.

Levels of Lessons

A second basic understanding is that, in reading as in all learnings, there are different levels of instruction. There are the foundational lessons—these are the beginner's learnings. And there are the more specific, more advanced, more technical and detailed lessons for later on.

Most parents and administrators assume that in reading the only lessons that count are the more technical ones. They believe that to teach reading, children must sit at a desk or a table; that you have to put a book in front of them or a paper and pencil; that you have to focus directly on the letters of the alphabet or the sound of the letters or on words. Unless parents and administrators see this particular scene in the classroom they are likely to say: No reading instruction is going on.

We have to build the understanding that we teach reading when we teach the foundational lessons, *and* we teach reading when we teach the more technical lessons. The one important commitment is that we give all the help each child needs at the time when the youngster can make the best use of it.

Parents and other adults are aware of these different levels of instruction when a child is learning to swim. A mother carries her five-month-old in her arms as she stands in the waves at the seashore, the water up to the mother's knees. This mother is teaching her child to swim. She is giving a beginning lesson, a very important one—a foundational lesson in enjoying the water, a lesson in not being afraid.

Three years later the mother watches while her child builds sand castles at the water's edge. Now the waves lap up and touch the child's knees. The mother is still teaching her child to swim. This is another beginning, foundational lesson.

Three more years and the child is in a swimming pool, a member of a swimming class. But the child's learning to swim did not begin with the technical lessons now going on in ducking the head under water, holding the breath, practicing the kick. These lessons are simply another stage in a continuous instructional process. In this process both the foundational lessons and the technical lessons have their place—one cannot succeed without the other.

In teaching reading, the foundational lessons almost never take place in a didactic, sit-down-and-I-will-teach-you kind of way. Such blunt instruction does

not fit the nature of the foundational lessons (and offends the nature of the beginner). Foundational lessons are "absorbed." Children breathe them in by being surrounded by them. Children observe. They listen. Children soak up what is going on. What they see and hear gets under their skins and into their minds.

Almost all under-six children need beginner's lessons taught in this unobtrusive, pervasive way. These foundational learnings center on the development of a positive attitude toward reading and toward books. They center on motivation, on children developing a positive attitude toward themselves as people who can, of course, learn to read. These foundational lessons center on key ingredients in the reading process: the development of the child's spoken language; the sharpening of observational powers; the deepening of attention span. They center on the essential idea in the whole reading process—that reading is language written down. The foundational lessons also involve various elementary skills, such as how to hold and care for a book, how a book proceeds from a beginning to an end, how our words and sentences read from left to right.

Foundational lessons in reading are never single-barrel affairs in which a teacher aims at one point and one point alone. Foundational lessons come along with bundles of other learnings, all mixed together. A great deal of learning goes on at once—in social, emotional, and physical areas, and in intellectual areas other than reading.

Although these foundational lessons are the most common at the under-six ages, there are times when under-six children are also able to benefit from more direct, more specific, more one-shot-at-a-time, more technical instruction. There is an almost sure-fire test of a child's readiness for such instruction. It is not a paper test, but the test of the child's actual behavior. A child's free choice —what captures interest and holds the youngster persistently, what a child rejects and ignores—is the best evidence of a child's readiness. It reassures parents when they know that a teacher is collecting this evidence day after day, not simply on one "test day" alone. And it is comforting to them to realize that a teacher is as eager as they are to move on into technical instruction whenever the signals come that a child is ready for this kind of help.

One clear evidence of a child's readiness for more technical instruction is when a youngster specifically asks: "Show me how to write my name" or "Tell me what that sign says" or "How do you make a 'W'?" But the request need not even be framed in words. An observant teacher can sense from a child's whole body that a question is there, and then the teacher takes the lead: "Would you like me to show you how to . . . ?"

Some children show through their total behavior that reading holds a high priority with them. A teacher, ever-watching, gets the signals and is ready to respond in the most useful way. These children are aware of the signs, labels, and writing in the classroom. On field trips they are alert to the street signs and house numbers, the signs in stores and on products, price markers, the wording on buses and trucks. These are the children who ask the teacher to write out words to embellish their dramatic play. They are apt to be the ones who want to dictate stories. They are the ones who, when they have completely free choice, turn to books. They are apt to choose games that call for matching. Other

youngsters, exposed to the same opportunities to read, pass them by. The chance to read never catches their eye, as it does with these more-ready youngsters.

Often these more-ready children need no special help—it would be intrusive to offer any. But the teacher is alert to give any kind of instruction, whenever any seems called for. At times it may seem wise for her to provide a word: "That says 'cottage cheese'." Or it may be wiser to prod the child's thinking: "Does it look like any word you know?" or "What do you think the word is? Can you tell from what it says just before it?" or "Can you sound the word out?"

With under-six children who exhibit an especially keen interest in words, teachers have experimented with a variation of an approach first described by Sylvia Ashton-Warner in her 1963 book about Maori children, *Teacher* (New York: Simon and Schuster). These teachers set aside a specific time in their program for direct reading instruction, but they do this only with child volunteers—no pressure is put on any youngster to take part. This is a personalized approach, done on a one-to-one basis. The teacher asks, "What word would you like to learn today?" The child chooses a word that for some reason is a favorite. The teacher then proceeds in various ways to help the youngster master the chosen word.[4]

All the more technical lessons—even so gentle an approach as that of a "favorite word"—are bound to look to parents and administrators like the only "real" teaching of reading. But, if we work at it, the conviction can grow that *all* children are being taught to read. *All* are getting the maximum help they are ready to use. *All* are getting lessons, foundational lessons or technical lessons, whichever is most appropriate for them. No one is being held back, no one is being pushed.

Reading Is Everywhere

There is a third basic understanding we must strengthen—that *reading is everywhere in today's world*. We can lessen some of the early reading pressure from parents and administrators, and some of the pressure to concentrate only on the more obvious, technical forms of instruction, if we hit hard on this point.

In some favored children's homes reading is superabundantly prevalent. Mail comes to the house. Reminders are posted on the refrigerator. Magazines cover the living room table. Books line the wall. There are calendars, bulletin boards, advertisements, shopping lists: words, words, words wherever a child looks.

Other homes are not so deluged with the flood of symbols. Even in the most nonliterate settings, however, words upon words bombard children. Words that tell what trucks carry: *Oil . . . Gas . . . Carpets. . . .* Words that tell what stores sell: *Wines and Liquors . . . Hardware . . . Groceries. . . .* Words that tell the

---

[4] Elizabeth Goetz gives a good description of this approach in "Early Reading: A Developmental Approach," *Young Children,* July 1979.

names of products: *Coca-Cola . . . Wonder Bread . . . Hostess Cupcakes. . . .*
There are signs everywhere, rich neighborhood and poor: *Stop . . . No
Parking. . . . Street signs: Market . . . Main . . . Mission. . . .* Bus signs: *City
Center . . . Parkside. . . .* There is writing on the TV screen, writing on the candy
wrapper, writing in the newspaper that blows against the steps. Automobiles
display their name plates; cereals flaunt their names on the package; the grocery
store posts signs for its "specials" in the window. Today's child—rich,
poor—grows up submerged in symbols.

Such total submersion makes it easier to teach all children to read than
would be true in a far-off corner of the world that had not yet been invaded by
print. Yet we let anxieties about reading mount as if it were some strange,
abstruse, unused, seldom-seen part of life.

Children Want To Read

Closely related is the fourth understanding—*that youngsters love to learn to read
when the time is ripe for them.* The skill ties in to one of the most solid human
satisfactions. Reading makes a child feel big. Reading makes a child feel powerful. Reading makes a child more independent. Reading is not some bad
medicine adults have to force on children. Learnings are difficult when they go
against children's grain, but this is not true of reading. It has built-in rewards that
make the teaching of reading, when the time is right and the methods are right, a
very easy job.

Only on rare occasions in human development does a child's self-concept
shoot up sky-high. One of those times is when a baby first stands and sees a new
world from an exciting new height. When a child first walks, moving out to that
world, is another such time. When an adolescent first gets access to an
automobile. . . . When a young adult first lands a good job. . . . Included in this
precious, limited listing of life's prize times is *when a youngster first reads.*

This joy in reading is evident early when youngsters first recognize their
name, even before they know any other words. "That says my name," is the
proud over-and-over refrain. The joy is evident later when the new reader
reads . . . and reads . . . and reads and reads. The new reader reads street signs,
house numbers, road signs, everything the eye happens to rest on.

Later, still, the special pleasure of children who have created their own
books is further proof of the elevating, stimulating impact of knowing how to
read. These children experience one of the simple wonders of the world—that
reading is nothing more than language written down. But the book they create
is *their* language, *their* words, *their* story. They said the words and now they can
read the words, and anyone else can read their words, too. This is power, this is
pleasure.

Lessons that make children feel small are hard for them to learn. Lessons
that belittle them are hard for them to learn. Lessons that involve developing
control over impulses are hard for children to learn. So, too, are lessons that involve behaviors we seldom practice. Reading is not tangled up with any of these
hazards. With the chance to read so omnipresent, with the pleasure of reading

so persuasive, helping children to read ought to be a snap. We simply must take care not to mess up the process.

We can make reading seem dismally difficult by trying to teach the technical lessons too early.

We can complicate the process by ignoring certain crucial preconditions: A child must see well to read well; a child must hear well to read well; a child must be in a reasonably healthy emotional state.

We can use stupid teaching materials not tied in to anything young children have seen or done or heard or felt—boring materials, idiotic exercises in abracadabra.

We can give up on children who learn slowly. We can call them "failures," "stupid," or "immature," needlessly and harmfully. It ought to be obvious that youngsters whose home backgrounds give less support than others to reading will need more time before they come to the technical lessons than do those children who are favored in this regard.

We can forget how great the odds are stacked in favor of reading. We can let over-anxiety lead us into tightening up and pressing, and then skimping on the teaching ways that are appropriate to our youngsters. We can mess up the process. But we don't have to.

"No" To Workbooks

On one point teachers of young children ought to take a firm stand. We ought to say "no" to workbooks—there should be no place for them in kindergarten. We ought to say "absolutely NO" to workbooks for still younger children. We ought to make it perfectly clear to parents and to administrators that workbooks, exercise books, paper-and-pencil riddle and drill books, simply do not fit the under-six age.

These are not sitting-down children. These are not quiet children. They are not meant to be taught all at once in a group, not twenty or twenty-five at once, not even six or eight together. At this age, such mass instruction only breeds inattention and creates discipline problems.

This is the wrong age for the heavy emphasis on right and wrong, win and lose, on following the rules of the other fellow's game. Five-year-olds—certainly younger children even more so—almost never seek out this kind of experience for themselves on their own, it has to be imposed on them.

This is the wrong age to expose to command after command: "Draw a line" or "Make a circle" or "Put a mark." Such adult control and domination is appropriate when the learner is consciously seeking help. It is inappropriate—it is indecent!—with young children, beginners.

This is the wrong age for stereotyped line drawings of life. Young children need a richer, fuller diet—they need to deal with life itself.

The workbooks, exercise books, the paper-and-pencil riddle and drill books violate individual differences; they spoil teacher-child relationships; they negate significant developmental characteristics of the children; they distort the flow

of a program. Their content is dull; their methods are inappropriate. Their goals can be achieved in better ways at less expense in money and with fuller returns in learning.

Perhaps a classroom might include *one* workbook or exercise book, or paper-and-pencil riddle and game book, but never one for every child. The one book could be put on the open shelves, along with all the other materials from which children choose. On rare occasions an individual youngster may seek out the book and be eager to work on it, either alone or with a teacher's help. Under these special conditions the vices of the book are minimized, and whatever strengths it has are maximized.

Holding the line against workbooks is not easy. People who are eager for play to stop, those who think learning is listening, those overly aware that First Grade (!) is coming are always eager to begin "formal teaching."

Adults who are aware of how much knowledge today's young children seem to possess sometimes lean in this direction, too. Somehow these grown-ups leap to the conclusion that formal sitting-down lessons are the only way of teaching what they regard as "today's smart young children." They forget how these informed youngsters got that way. Not through workbooks. Not through specific exercises and drills. Those among today's children who really are informed had the chance at home for firsthand experiences. Their parents took them places; their parents did things with them; their parents talked with them. These children were not caught up in vacuous readiness exercises, and such experiences won't make them smarter now.

Inexperienced teachers, unsure of themselves, not at home with children's activities, are also often eager to begin on workbooks. These colleagues welcome all-group, sitting-down lessons. Life becomes more peaceful for them, but not more productive for children. We cannot let their insecurities change the nature of a good program for children.

Perhaps most of all, we have to be aware of the commercial pressures to use workbooks. Until 1965—the beginning of Head Start and of the national focus on young children—the field of early childhood education was so small that it was hardly worth a publisher's notice. Since 1965 young children have become the bright new market. Authors and publishers have assiduously sought ways to use their resources to tap the burgeoning kindergarten field. They anticipate with relish the time when child care centers will be more available and when we will have public four-year-old groups. Today early childhood education holds the promise of big money.

There is, of course, one way in which publishers can serve young children: They can publish *bona fide* books. They can publish honest-to-goodness books written by creative authors and illustrated by creative artists. They can publish "real" books that have something informative and provocative to say to the reader or listener. In publishing parlance these are called "trade books." Unfortunately, very few trade books are hugely profitable. The big money lies in workbooks, packaged kits of formal teacher-dominated lessons, and expendable paper-and-pencil materials.

It is doubtful that any words of interpretation about young children by teachers could turn publishers away from this new gold mine. The more aware

we become, however, of the conflict between big profits and little children, the keener our sales resistance can become, and the more possible it may be for us to build up the sales resistance of administrators. Considerable sums of money could be saved taxpayers, or spent in more rewarding ways, if we could all learn to say "No, thank you" to inappropriate materials.

Appropriate Methods with Young Children

Holding the line against workbooks is easier to do when it becomes apparent you are not being simply negative. Say "no" to workbooks, but be sure everyone knows that you say a very enthusiastic "yes" to other, more appropriate, more effective ways of teaching reading to young children. The point emerges clearly: You are not opposed to teaching reading, you simply insist on using methods that fit the under-six age.

Stories Galore

One of the best methods of teaching reading—a foundational method, one welcomed by all young children regardless of their degree of readiness—is reading stories to youngsters.

You should take great pride in your skill in choosing books that have a fundamental appeal to your children.

You should take great pride in your ability to load your classroom with book after book—bought, borrowed; from the school collection, from your own collection; from libraries; from parents, from friends. Your room should be a treasure trove of good books.

You should take great pride in the wide scope of the books: fact and fancy; prose and poetry; screamingly humorous, and sad and moving; adventure books and books involving human emotions; books of photographs and books done in stunning artistic style; books about the whole array of human experience—anger, death, illness, fear, loneliness, great joy and glee; books about animals, trucks, boats, birds, machines, about everything under the sun; books just of pictures, books with few words, and books with enough text to challenge an advanced reader.

You should take great pride in the fact that you and your children "publish" books of your own. In addition to tens of store-bought books, you should have tens of homemade books, too. Your children experience exciting adventures. Funny things happen to them. Sad events take place in their lives. They encounter mysterious happenings, with a note of suspense. Individually or in small groups the children can dictate these stories to you. You should take great pride in your ability to capture children's words, to simplify some words and sentences, and to bring the story together between covers, bound, a book. One

child, or a small group, or the whole class and you are the authors. This homemade book obviously has special powers to lure and entice local listeners. In many cases, since the words are their own, some children also easily become "local readers."

You should take pride in the prominence given to books and story times in your daily schedule. You surely will always have one "official" story time when most of the children come together to hear you read. Even those few youngsters who read well themselves enjoy story time. Being read to is a pleasure that doesn't wear out. Listening to a story is pleasing early in life; it continues to be pleasing for many years after.

Because stories are so welcomed by young children, you do not need to insist that everyone come to story time. On most days everyone will, gladly. Occasionally a child or two may prefer to continue with another activity that for the moment is more engrossing. Some may prefer to half-listen while they sit apart from the group. Your pride ought to be in the relaxed atmosphere of the story group, and in the children's enjoyment of it, rather than in 100% attendance.

In fact, the smaller the listening group the better. The smaller the group, children have more chance to choose the stories they most want to hear. The smaller the group the more chance for them to raise questions and to react in other ways, making their listening an active rather than a quiet process. To achieve this important give-and-take quality you may want to schedule two or three "official" story times during the day, as well as other opportunities for smaller groups of children and for individuals to hear stories. An aide, for example—a parent volunteer perhaps—can be the "designated story-teller," always on tap available anytime to anyone who wants to hear a tale. Or if not an adult aide, a youngster from the upper grades who enjoys reading to one or two children could carry this assignment.

You should take great pride in your own ability as a story-teller or perhaps the word "story-teller" carries the wrong emphasis. You should read stories well. You project. You add enough dramatic touches to hold children's interest without being so dramatic that you become the star, putting on a show. But for all your story-*telling* ability, your greatest skill lies in getting children to respond. Story-time should not be "shut up" time. It should be a time when children's eyes, ears, and minds are superactive. You stir them into action by soliciting responses to some noteworthy feature in a picture. Or by pointing out something special about the sound of a word or the shape of a word or the newness of the word. Or by encouraging children to relate what they have just heard to some event in their own lives.

Story time must be thinking time. Story time must be remembering time. Story time must be observing time. It cannot be all these good things if you are the story-*teller,* the one doing all the talking. Nor can it be all these things if your story group is always large. The smaller the number of children—1, 2, 3, 4, 5, 6—the easier it will be for you to read, not only the words on the page, but "read" the eyes and faces of the youngsters, too, and adapt your process accordingly.

Of course, you should also take great pride in the presence of books everywhere in your classroom. Your adult books on your desk, or wherever you

keep your possessions, set an example so children will know: Grown-ups read! You also need quiet, private corners where individual children can sit comfortably, looking through a favorite book. You also need a library corner where several children can sit, each child reading at whatever is the youngster's level of skill: reading words, reading pictures.

Books should be a part of every child's day.

This strong emphasis on books is one of your foundational lessons in reading, geared neatly to the age of your children. Some parents and others will, of course, wonder: Does it really add up to teaching reading? With a little help from you anyone should be able to see that the answer is a clear *yes*.

Exposed to good books and stories galore, children cannot help but learn to enjoy books, to appreciate them, to anticipate them as one of the pleasures of life. This is a fundamental reading lesson, and you make a good start on it.

Hearing those good books, in some cases reading those good books, children cannot but help expand their vocabularies.

With your gentle guidance they can hardly avoid sharpening their interest in words: the sounds of words, the shapes of words, the lengths of words, similarities in words, strange words, funny words, unusual words.

With books so much a part of their days, children are bound to pick up various specific learnings: that sentences move from left to right, for example, and words do too; that books have a beginning and an end, and a topside and bottomside; that books must be handled with reasonable care. There will be occasions for you to make these points unobtrusively, but even more important: The children will see over and over the care with which you handle books and they cannot but help pick up your leads.

Reading-and-Writing Supplies Galore

In addition to having books galore, you must equip your classroom with the widest possible variety of the tools, materials, and equipment that stimulate reading and writing activity.

You will want crayons without doubt, but don't stop with them. You also need pencils, pens, magic markers, and chalk—anything and everything that make it easy for a child to put an idea down on paper—in the form of a letter, in the form of a word, in the form of a hieroglyphic.

Your easels, paints, and brushes serve this same purpose. We think of easel painting as art, but it is at the same time a form of writing. A youngster has something to say and sets it out for others to see. Occasionally four- and five-year-olds use the brush specifically to form a letter, or to spell out their names. But all painting is practice in writing, whether the product looks simply like a design, or whether we think we can recognize a house and a sun, or whether we know that it is a "K."

You also want to have on hand ink pads and many rubber stamps—stamps that say *PAID* or *F.O.B.* or *FIRST CLASS, AIR MAIL* or *SPECIAL DELIVERY,* the specific wording doesn't matter. Sometimes youngsters will use a rubber stamp in their dramatic play exactly as the stamp is used in adult life, to mark a paper with the right date or to mark something *PAID* or *RECEIVED.* The youngster uses the stamp to feel big and to do what an adult does. But whether the stamp is used "correctly" or for a purely "pretend" purpose, the child is picking up a basic learning: Writing conveys an idea, and people can read it (or pretend that they do).

A printing set with individual letters and an ink pad gives children an excellent chance to write out what they want to say. Most youngsters will ask you for a model they can copy: "Write out my name for me" or "Write out *Cash*" or "Write out *Menu.*" A primary typewriter is another valuable piece of equipment—essential in the five-year-old classroom but useful even with four-year-olds. Some rules are needed, of course: Don't pound, don't jam the keys. But a typewriter is a wonderful tool which brings youngsters a great sense of power—you push down here and *P* shows up there!—while luring them happily into the business of writing and reading.

Rubber stamps, printing sets, and the primary typewriter are not always used in the way some adults consider the "one and only right way"—to make the correct sign, the correct letter, or the correct word. All these tools, like crayons and paint and chalk, at times serve a purpose that is clear to the child, even though it may not be clear to us. A youngster repeats a string of *R*s, makes a face with *O*s, or creates a design along the edge of the paper. This personal experimentation can look like waste or "fooling around," but don't be misled by appearances. You must allow leeway for experimentation. Out of this testing and exploring the limits of materials, this seeing-what-will-happen-if, a child's later confident ease in expression comes. When we push too soon for the one right way, we cut off what is for the child valuable "basic research" and laboratory work.

In the same vein, children around age five frequently come through with reversals when they try to write their names on paintings and elsewhere. Individual letters are turned around; sometimes the word itself is written from right to left. Don't be in a rush to correct these beginning efforts. There are two steps you can take without running any risk. First, you can be careful that *you* write correctly the child's name (or whatever word may be involved). And, second, anytime the child indicates dissatisfaction and asks for help—"Did I do that right?" or "Is that how you spell it?"—then you have a golden opportunity to show gently whatever is the correct way.

Puzzles also make a contribution to learning to read. They demand careful observation and attention to detail—the same abilities that let a child distinguish *cat* from *cot*. Some puzzles, when completed, tell a story in sequence, another useful foundational reading experience. All of them, when completed, add up to a picture that conveys meaning, just as the straight lines and circles of the printed word do.

Board and table games also teach reading. Not all under-six youngsters are ready for the competition and the winning-and-losing aspect of games. Not all are ready to read the printed words that some games involve. But for those who choose to play, the fun of the games makes learning whatever reading skills are involved an almost unconscious process—a good way for the foundational lessons in reading to proceed. Picture dominoes and regular dominoes call for careful observing, for matching, and for following rules. The many variations of Lotto call for the same skills. Other games—some you can buy, some you must make yourself—require written instructions that tell each player what move to make.

Games illustrate the basic ideas underlying all the reading-and-writing supplies. Have a lot of them on hand. Aim for the widest variety, from the easiest to the more difficult. Then you leave it up to each child to take the next step: to use the materials or to ignore them, to choose which ones to use, to choose how long to stay with them, while you stand ever ready to give any help a youngster may need.

Writing Everywhere

Another appropriate way of teaching reading to young children is to surround them with writing. Everywhere their eyes turn there should be symbols that carry meaning to youngsters. You are after meaning, not clutter; you are after sense, not a superfluity of symbols. But you try not to miss any reasonable, appropriate opportunity to write down ideas of significance. You want your children to see you using paper and pencil, using paper and pen, paper and crayon, paper and typewriter, paper and print, *and* you want them increasingly to become active partners in the enterprise.

One familiar example is the practice in two- and three-year-old groups of identifying each child's locker with a small picture. Usually the picture is of an animal, but it may be any familiar object: a truck, a telephone, a bottle of milk. The picture says to the child: This locker is mine; my "name" is on it.

Another good example is the practice of teachers of three-, four- and five-year-olds of writing clearly the artist's name on each child's painting. The letters say to the child: This picture is mine; it has my name on it.

The symbol, whether picture or word, conveys meaning, and the child cares. Those are two essential ingredients. The alert teacher keeps looking for every setting where these two qualities come together.

You put labels on everything where a label makes sense. You don't mark the door *door*—the label doesn't add any meaning—but if there are two doors you mark one *in* and the other *out,* or one *boys* and the other *girls.* A chair isn't labeled *chair* but if the chair, for some reason, is reserved for a particular person's use, it is marked *Jerry's chair.* You label drawers if the label makes clear what is inside. You label shelves so one can tell where objects are supposed to be stored.

You write announcements and plans on the chalkboard or on the easel: *The nurse is coming today . . . You may take books home today.*

You also write reminders on the chalkboard or easel: *We need 15 cartons of milk . . . We need more red paint.*

You write job assignments: *Fred feeds the fish . . . Sally waters the plants . . . Peter sets the table . . . John sweeps the floor.*

You write directions that must be followed: the recipe when the children are cooking, the amounts of food for each animal, the formula for making salt and flour dough. . . .

You write important notices: *The four-year-olds have gone to the Zoo.* You write permission letters, first on the chalkboard or at the easel where the children can see them—"May the five-year-olds visit the fire boat?"—and thank-you letters: "Thank you for letting the five-year-olds visit the fire boat."

You write important records that should be kept for later reference: *On April 3 our hamster weighed three pounds and six ounces . . . On May 5 our tomato plant was two feet tall. It had six blossoms . . . On March 15 we fertilized all the plants.*

You write words, signs, labels or markers that add depth to children's dramatic play. For example, if children play gas station: *Premium . . . Regular . . . No Lead . . . Out of gas . . . Air . . . Tires for Sale . . . Anti-freeze . . . Credit cards. . . .* The chances for helpful writing are endless whether the play centers on gas station, hospital, store, train, or airport.

Sometimes you take the lead: "I have a sign that says *Tickets* for your ticket office." Sometimes the youngsters take the lead: "Make us a sign that says *Danger. Explosives.*" It doesn't matter where the idea for the writing originates. Only one general rule is important: The teacher should do as much writing as is appropriate *but no child should have to read it.* That step is up to each youngster.

A few will read every word of writing around. Some occasionally will show interest and occasionally ask for your help in figuring out words. Many won't even be aware of the writing any more than they notice a smudge on the window. The writing doesn't interfere with their lives any more than the smudge on the window does. That is the essence of so much that you do as you teach

reading: The experiences are all available. They are as attractive as you can make them, but they are not mandatory, and you are not coercive. The chances to read are available just as your easels are, for example, but no child needs to read the writing any more than the child has to paint simply because the easels are there.

Pictures Galore

There is one special form of writing uniquely suited to the reading abilities of the whole under-six age range. Your room should be a showcase for it. You should display the most exciting, alluring, informative pictures on your walls—pictures that "grab" young children as they pass by.

The pictures can be of many kinds: reproductions of adult art work (and originals, too); photographs; posters; pictures cut from magazines; materials from travel agencies, from government bureaus, from industries. The content should not be so far removed from the experiences of your children that the picture is unimportant and meaningless to them. The greater danger, however, is that our pictures are too often dull and ordinary and commonplace, adding nothing to what children already know. Worse, too many pictures are "cute." You would do well to think of "cute" as a one-word criticism, saying that something is childish but not childlike.

Action becomes one of the standards to keep in mind as you build up your picture collection. You don't want "portraits" of chickens, rabbits, horses, cows. These animals should be shown doing something that children would not normally know about. So, too, with pictures of ships, planes, boats, cars, and trucks. Good pictures show these involved in activity that makes a child stop and say, "Look at that!" or better still: "What is that?" The only kind of still life—the object is simply sitting there looking at the camera or the artist—that is apt to catch a child's mind is a picture of the highly unusual, an animate or inanimate object that does not cross a child's path every day.

Detail is another important element in good pictures for young children. A picture fails if a youngster can take it in at a glance—one quick look and that is it. The way a baby's eyes and hands go to a speck on the crib, the young child's eyes are eager to go to the minutiae of a picture: the little but significant points that make the picture an engrossing story-telling agent.

Customary practice has been to use the precious wall space in our classrooms for displays of children's art work, and it is not easy to argue against this use. The displays are a means of showing that art is a treasured experience. They are also a useful means of heightening children's self-concept—there is glory in having your product displayed.

As useful as this historic practice has been, it is probably wiser for teachers to urge parents to display their children's products at home, freeing the classroom walls for pictures from your collection. You turn your walls into "writing space." The writing is not in the standard form of letters and words, but in hieroglyphics—pictures that tell a story. Younsters surrounded by such pic-

tures, drawn to them because they titillate the mind, find it easier to make the transition to that form of a picture we call a "word."

Two old evils associated with displays of children's work can creep into your displays of pictures, unless you guard against them. First, don't end up with a cluttered room. Don't display so much at once that the dominant impression is one of confusion. Take pride in your ability to display a picture dramatically in an eye-catching (mind-catching) fashion. Second, don't leave your pictures up forever—once up, never down. You must allow time for children to absorb what you have displayed, but don't end up with a monotonous room. Change the exhibit. Your goal is to excite your viewers so they call out to friends: "Look at this!" That is the way you want your children to feel about all reading—about this basic form of picture-reading, and about the more advanced form of word-reading.

Language Is the Heart of Reading

One more important way in which you teach young children to read is to help their vocabularies grow. A child can learn to sound out the word *hurdy-gurdy;* a child can remember what to say when confronted with *hurly burly;* but a child isn't *reading* unless he or she knows what the words mean. Calling out nonsensical sounds or mouthing unintelligible mumbo jumbo may look like reading but is, in fact, some totally different activity. Children who begin their "reading" this way all too often never take up books as one of life's pleasures as they grow up. Real reading is different. Reading is language one knows, understands, needs and uses, written down so one can come back to it, and written down so others can have access to it. Language is the heart of reading.

All the natural, logical, mutually pleasing experiences that deepen and extend language are foundational lessons in reading.

When a teacher uses a rich vocabulary as she talks with children, this is teaching reading.

When a teacher seriously listens to a child or a small group of children as they talk about a matter of concern to them, this is teaching reading.

When a teacher makes it easy for children to play together, talk together, and share the words that come from their different home backgrounds and differing experiences, this is teaching reading.

When a teacher stimulates many and varied activities within the classroom—cooking, gardening, building, selling—that involve new words and clarify the meanings of words children partially know, this is teaching reading.

When a teacher makes trips a basic part of the curriculum, this is teaching reading. Firsthand experiences with reality add depth to children's language. *Barge* becomes real; *silo* becomes real; *chef* becomes real.

One quality of these reading lessons is important to note—these are lessons in reading *and* simultaneously they are lessons in other significant areas of life: lessons in the social studies, in science, in mathematics. . . . The reading lessons come bundled up with other lessons. They are not separate, not isolated, but a natural part of a total program of good living for young children.

Reasonable Expectations

Even when we are at our best—the best of foundational lessons and the best of technical lessons in reading—all any child can learn is one year's worth. When we say, "We teach reading," we must not mislead parents or administrators or anyone into unreasonable expectations.

No level of education—not education over six or under six—ever teaches all there is to know about anything in any one year. It simply teaches one year's worth.

A freshman in college takes a course in literature. If it has been a good course he has learned a freshman year's worth. He had studied literature before. He studied it in nursery school, in kindergarten, in elementary and in secondary school. Now, in college, he studies it again and he will study it again and again. There is American literature, English literature, and world literature. There is the literature of special periods: writers of the Eighteenth Century, writers of the romantic novels . . . the literature of special styles of writing: prose, poetry, drama . . . there are intensive courses in the writings of one author: Shakespeare, Emerson, Molière. . . . The freshman has only scratched the surface. He has learned one year's worth, but what more could one ask . . . of a college year, a nursery school year, a kindergarten year? The study of literature, if it was done well, enriched his living in that year.

Learning starts early and it goes on. It is absurd to think of children learning to read in nursery school or in kindergarten or in first grade. A child learns a nursery school year's worth in nursery school, a first grade's worth in first grade. Then, if the lessons have been done well, the learning continues in all the years to come. In reading, for example: learning to read with more ease; with greater ability to cope with new words; to read with greater speed; with better understanding and with more critical comprehension; to read foreign languages; to read shorthand; to read technical literature. . . . Good instruction teaches as much as the student can master at the time. In reading, good instruction uses methods that are right for the student at the time.

Administrators know this from their experience with older children. If we keep talking with them—especially if we lure them into our classrooms so they can see the emphasis on reading—they will increasingly be able to carry over their understandings to younger children.

Parents can also see the logic of this, if we meet with them and if they have a full and open chance to talk out their doubts and to voice questions. Their support will come more quickly if they also have the chance to see at first hand the emphasis on "the basics" that goes on in an active, stimulating classroom. When we leave parents out in the cold, their anxieties mount. Then the pressures mount for teacher-dominated, formal, inappropriate approaches to the teaching of reading. If we extend a friendly open hand, parents can become strong supporters for more fitting ways of helping their young children to learn.

6

TEACHING THE BASICS: GOOD BEHAVIOR

Many parents feel a second specific anxiety about the education of their young children: They want their youngsters to learn good discipline. This strongly held concern also merits special attention.

Parents seldom speak of "teaching the basics" when they talk about discipline. But they should. Nothing is more basic than teaching children to behave so that they are a joy now for others to have around, and so they grow up to become good citizens. Children who threaten people and who threaten property are menaces to themselves and to all of us.

Parents who value good behavior need to know: We agree with them, we are on the same side they are. Call it character education. Call it moral education. Call it discipline. Teaching the ways of decency is a basic job of early education.

Clearing Up Misunderstandings

Once this clear agreement with parents is understood, it can be easier to talk through some of the misunderstandings about discipline that frequently arise. Some adults, for example—parents, some teachers, too—equate good behavior in an early childhood group with ... no childlike behavior! They want the children to be quiet—*that* is good discipline. They want them to walk in line—*that* is good discipline. They don't want free choice, or moving about, or experimenting with materials, or the easygoing give-and-take of social relationships. They don't see any of this as good behavior. These adults think that three-, four-, and five-year-olds are "good" only when they behave like *thirty*-three, *thirty*-four, and *thirty*-fives.

Through continuous conversations, through shared readings, through group meetings we must strengthen understandings about the essential nature of young children: their activity, their noisiness, their strong social drives, their need to feel big. . . . Good discipline for three-, four-, and five-year-olds lets these children healthfully act their age. Standards and expectations, both at home and at school, must be keenly attuned to the capacities of honest-to-goodness boys and girls, not to the capacities of angels or adults.

We must also firm up agreements on the goal to strive for. Some people, because they prize discipline so highly, are willing to settle for a veneer of good behavior that lasts through a school day, forgetting about building values and commitments that will last through a lifetime. This leads them to equate discipline only with obvious, showy, and sometimes noisy methods that lean heavily on fear and shame.

Teachers and parents must confer frequently so that ultimately we agree that youngsters shall be so treated and so taught that they come to *want* an ethical society for themselves and for others. They, the children, must come to believe in and choose a life of thoughtfulness, generosity, kindness, consideration, and helpfulness. They must come to believe in the careful nurturing of resources and in the sensitive treatment of people. Most important: They must be so sold on these values that they will carry them around with them wherever they go.

Dictatorial societies have their secret police and spying neighbors. Our "police force" must be larger than that. We must have one "police officer" for every child! One, in every child's head. One, in every child's heart. One, that goes with children wherever they go. Children live in a mobile, changing society. Only this kind of inner discipline can stay with them no matter where they are (and in their brave new world of tomorrow they may end up on a space ship). Only this kind of inner discipline can give children standards that will guide them in new situations (and in their changing world they will face countless new situations not covered by any past specific rules).

Our discussions with parents can clear up one more common misunderstanding: Inner discipline need not rule out instant obedience. In fact, the reverse is true. Children who have been so taught and so treated that they themselves believe in decency are prepared to obey a command—one! two! three!—should such a need arise. In life there are occasional times when someone in authority says "stop" or "no" or this way or that, or fast or slow, or left or right. The need for instant obedience is not an everyday occurrence, but when it happens, good citizens of conscience are prepared to believe that there must be a good reason. Not having had to fear authority, it is easy for well-treated children to respect authority and to trust authority in life's rare emergencies. Youngsters with inner discipline do not need to choose whether to respond.

Methods—Not Some One Single Approach Alone

Because they prize discipline so highly, some adults think exclusively in terms of punishment as the way to achieve it. They always want to use a heavy hand.

Other adults, because of their over-eagerness, constantly search for some miracle method, a simple, surefire bundle of tricks guaranteed to work wonders.

And perhaps all of us, without our knowing it, tend to rely more than we should on some one favorite approach, be it talking things over with children, smothering them with love, or using "behavior mod."

We all have to come to see that helping children to develop an allegiance to good behavior is not a simple job. It takes time to build inner discipline. It takes time to develop that sense of trust that lets a child (or adult) instantly obey when quick response is called for. It takes patience and perseverance. It takes hard work. It takes thinking and puzzling. *And* there is no one quick answer, there is no one guaranteed method.

A good way to protect yourself against over-simplification is to pursue three distinct approaches to teaching good behavior.

Each of these three is different from the others.

Each is equally important.

Each is finely tuned to the ways and style of young children.

Each must be pursued continuously and all three must be pursued simultaneously—you want all three of them going for you at once.

All three approaches are as applicable at home as they are at school. The more you can persuade parents to do what you do, to follow at least these three approaches at home, the better the chances that a child will learn, believe in, and act on the values that make good human society possible.

What are these three approaches to teaching good behavior? Work on your classroom setting; work to build understandings; work to develop healthy feelings within children.

Work on the Setting

This approach to teaching good behavior is quiet. You carry on this activity "off stage." A casual observer might not even realize that you are working on discipline.

In this approach you direct your energies on the classroom environment. You work on your program. You work on your schedule. You work on your daily plans for the group. You work on the atmosphere in your class. You do everything you can to create a setting where it is easy for a child to act well. You weed out every temptation, you weed out every sore spot, you weed out every pollutant that pulls behavior down.

Even though some observers might not realize that you are working on discipline, this quiet, behind-the-scenes way of working is an honored approach in widespread use. It is, for example, a standby of police and highway departments. The behavior problem they confront is how to make people safe drivers. One of the basic techniques is to work on the setting: Straighten the roads, take out the dangerous curves . . . Put dividers in the middle of highways . . . Build bumps into the road to remind drivers that they are approaching an intersection . . . Paint white lines to indicate the edge of the road . . . Build underpasses

and overpasses to eliminate intersections . . . Create slight curves and other little challenges so the monotony of the freeway doesn't lull a driver to sleep. . . .

This is also a technique parents have long relied on. It is useful to remind them of how helpful the approach has been, and to urge them to continue to find new uses for it. Parents removed the breakables, for example, so their baby could crawl and touch without being "bad." They removed the poisons so their child could explore without being "bad." Parents know that hungry children become irritable, and fight and cry more easily. When the family goes on a shopping trip or on a long car ride, parents carry a bag of raisins or cookies with them. A little food makes it easier for children to be at their best.

Parents know that bored youngsters easily become trouble-makers. A story, a game, a toy to fill in blank time helps children to be good performers; unemployment makes them act worse. People other than parents have picked up this lead. Airlines provide books and puzzles for young passengers. Doctors and dentists stock their waiting rooms with books and games. Restaurants provide paper-and-pencil puzzles for their young customers. The underlying wisdom is as old as the Bible — the devil makes work for idle hands.

When teachers use the approach of working on the setting as one means of producing good behavior, they take on the role of environmental expert. Each day — almost every minute of the day — they send themselves an "Environmental Impact Report." In the classroom, on the playground, in the hallway, in the lunchroom, what makes children act worse than they have to? A teacher committed to good behavior has roving eyes: What are the sore spots? What rubs children the wrong way? What are the worst times of the day? What changes — in room arrangement, scheduling, equipment, content — would lift children up, letting them behave better than one would have thought possible?

The longer you teach, the more you come to know some of the common classroom settings that pull behavior down.

Whenever you line up children, you invite misbehavior.

Whenever there are empty time slots — the children are just waiting — trouble is apt to begin.

Whenever the days become monotonous — too few surprises, too little excitement — behavior tends to disintegrate.

Whenever school becomes just talky-talk, bookish, and paper-and-pencilish . . .

Whenever work is too hard . . .

Whenever work is too easy . . .

Whenever you limit freedom of choice . . .

Whenever you bring your whole group together, as if your classroom were a congregation, behavior tends to disintegrate.

The behavior pollutants range from the tangible — the room is too hot, the chair is the wrong size, the walls are too cluttered — to the intangible: too little praise, too little laughter, too little love and joy in the air.

Working on the setting — fixing up this, modifying that, removing this, adding that — is no easy job. You must work hard and you must work constantly — this is not a job you do once and then it is done. It is an everlasting task, *but* it is a provocative, challenging, creative one.

Working on the setting is also a highly rewarding expenditure of time, energy, and thought. Whenever you make a change that hits the nail on the head, you stand some chance of getting immediate, pleasing feedback. Shift the midmorning snack time a few minutes earlier; if hunger was the villain, you immediately see better-behaving youngsters. Put more challenging equipment on the outdoor playground; if the fatigue of running-chasing was the villain, you immediately see improvement. No other approach to discipline pays off so quickly.

Working on the setting also has quite special usefulness with young, not-yet-verbal children. It is, of course, the approach wise parents of infants and toddlers rely on most of all. But even two-, three-, four-, and five-year-olds often find words too hard to grasp and too hard to remember. And these ages are constantly led into dangers and hazards too abstruse for them to grasp or to anticipate. Fixing the setting becomes even for them a way *par excellence* for stimulating good, safe, constructive behavior.

If you want to cut down conflicts when block constructions are "accidently" knocked down, protect the block-builders with a barrier of some kind.

If you want to guard against accidents that occur when impulsive young children run in front of swings, create a fence of some kind around the swing area.

If paint-spills on the floor lead to one crisis after another, protect the floor with some kind of covering.

Don't think, however, that this approach is only for the very young. If you ever want the whole audience at a lecture or the congregation at church to sit in the front rows, close off the rear rows with a ribbon. You will transform the adults into very well-behaved humans, neatly sitting up front. The approach of working on the setting is applicable to all ages. It happens to have special usefulness with under-six children whose world is not yet completely a world of words.

One Special Benefit

When you work to build good behavior by improving the setting, you talk little. In fact, most of the time not a single word is spoken. The setting does the talking for you. You do not have to be the one who says, "Don't go out that door." The way you have fixed the space carries the message clearly.

In the course of teaching there will be many occasions when you will have to speak out. Putting into words a clear-cut "no" or "yes" or "you may" or "you may not" is an important part of a teacher's job. Never shrink from such direct, verbal insistences when they are the right approach. But the more you let the setting speak for you, the more you save your verbal ammunition for those times when it can do the most good.

This is sheer gain for good discipline.

When you create a setting where it is easy for children to act well, you nag them less. You remind them less and prod them less. *You* prohibit them less, because the setting you have created does a part of this job for you. You are free

to build more relationships with children of a totally different kind: friend, helper, companion, appreciator, supporter. . . . *These roles play a crucial part in building good behavior.*

Children feel close to you. Without their knowing it, without your knowing it, your values sink in to them. Your standards reach more than their ears. You—your ways, what you do, how you respond—get under children's skins. This is the process called *identification.* Children like you —they want to be like you. Unless youngsters do identify with grown-ups whom they like, admire, and enjoy, they face an almost impossible task in taking on the pleasing ways of our society.

Boys and girls who feel that adults are always on their backs have the odds stacked against them. The air surrounding them may be filled with the sounds of discipline—*no, yes, don't, must*—but too much talking, especially unnecessary doses of it, turns children off. When grown-ups are always after them, children stop hearing or, if they hear, they tune us out and reject what we say. Worse: They reject us, what we *do* as well as what we say.

What seems like such a soft approach—the happy times children and adults have together, the laughing times, the productive times—is a basic prerequisite for sound discipline. The process of identification is a slow process—the results will not show up for years. But you can count on it: You get in good licks for good discipline through all the close personal pleasing relationships you have with children.

Work on Understandings

Working on the setting as a means of building discipline has one serious deficiency. In a good environment children act well *but they do not know why they do.* Children build no bases for generalizations. Nothing is raised into their consciousness to guide them in other settings which may not be so skillfully arranged. By all means, work continuously on improving your classroom setting, but do not fall in love with this one idea. Don't stay stuck with it alone.

Simultaneously youngsters need to *build understandings* about good behavior. They need to know the reasons that underlie good behavior. They need to accept those reasons. They need to be persuaded that good behavior is the path to choose. In this second approach to discipline you work on reaching the child's mind. You try to be sure that children understand the reasons in back of whatever rules and regulations exist. You would be glad if your youngsters could say (assuming they had the language), when someone asked them about the laws governing their group; "We'll tell you what they are and we'll tell you why we need them."

Ours is a country governed by law. There are no hidden, secret prohibitions, nor can any charge be made simply on some leader's whim. Our rules and regulations are out in the open. It is an important part of children's civic educa-

tion for them to learn from the beginning: There are such things as laws; the laws protect us; the laws are our friend.

One television commercial, occasioned by the energy shortage, tells the American way very beautifully. A highway patrolman is talking about the 55 m.p.h. speed limit. "Fifty-five miles per hour saves lives. Fifty-five miles per hour saves energy. . . ." Then, very impressively: "*And* it is the law!" In America we have laws and we must respect them.

Some classrooms, of course, set up sixteen million rules and regulations. Too many!

In some classrooms there are only the most general rules: "Be kind to other people" or "Take good care of property." Too vague.

The way to build *understanding* is to have two, three, four, or five *specific* regulations, along with any other *general* standards that make sense. Youngsters must live in classrooms where, like our country as a whole, definite laws govern what goes on.

Step One, then, to build understandings: Establish some classroom rules and regulations.

Step Two: Don't set up so many that children gag on them.

Step Three calls for great sensitivity. Your classroom rules and regulations must fit your boys and girls. You want reasonable requirements. If you ask more than youngsters can live up to, only evil results. The laws are broken, the children become hostile. You work exceedingly hard to make the laws stick, but youngsters scoff at them or skirt them or ignore them, as adults did during Prohibition days.

To set up reasonable rules you will have to draw on all your knowledge of the age-level characteristics of your youngsters. Remember that at every age children—naturally and healthfully—do some annoying and troubling things. You don't want to legislate against these behaviors that flow from the stage of growth your youngsters are in. Your laws must not go against the grain, prohibiting four-year-olds from being four-year-olds and five-year-olds from being five-year-olds.

Almost surely you will have to rely somewhat on trial-and-error. If your youngsters have great trouble abiding by a rule (it is a law they simply cannot seem to remember and to obey), your struggle to enforce it can be the tipoff: That rule must be at fault, not geared to the age. A law is no good that is so easy for children to obey that they hardly know it exists. But when the standard is much too high, when you have to work excessively to enforce it, you do well to drop the rule and to cope with the behavior in some other way. You may decide simply to live with the behavior; the annoying things children do because they are the age they are do not last forever. Or you may decide to control the behavior by working on the setting. You always have that approach to fall back on.

Choosing reasonable rules calls for great sensitivity, but *Step Four* is the heart of this particular approach to discipline. Your children must know good reasons for whatever laws you have. Your case cannot be: "Because *I* say so." And it should not be a simple appeal to group conformity: "*We* don't throw

sand." You must be able to set forth sound, important justifications for each requirement. You must be able to show how good behavior supports, defends, and protects the well-being of the child, or the well-being of others, or the good care of the surroundings. You must search for the best words to help youngsters see why the law is important.

You talk. You persuade. You give examples. You do your best to make the case for decency. You are not long-winded, of course. And you do not necessarily do all the talking. Often your best role is as listener while youngsters say their side of the case. Sometimes your role is as discussion leader, asking in effect: "How do *you* see it?" To make the case for law and order does not mean that you alone preach a sermon. It does mean that building understanding is a *verbal* approach. Words are the essence. You reach for the best way to penetrate a child's mind so the case for decency goes along wherever the child goes. You use words and you stay at the job until finally a youngster says, in effect; "I see it. I've got it. I believe it. The idea is mine as well as yours."

Most of your best persuading will be done face-to-face, one-to-one. Talking with your children individually or, when need be, in small groups of two, three, or four is wisest. Always with young children, and especially with something as important as good behavior, you do well to minimize talking to the class as a whole. Young children's egos are too strong and their attention spans too weak to make the public-address, whole-group approach fruitful. Person-to-person you stand a much better chance of capturing a youngster's thought processes, and you are better able to adjust what you say to the child's response.

Step Five calls for consistency and persistency. Be sure you enforce whatever laws you have. Upholding the law each time is not easy when you are responsible for a whole group of busy children. But your goal should be: Never let any child "get away" with breaking a law, not even once. No one is a greater threat to the society of the classroom or of the wider world than the scofflaw. You don't want any boy or girl in your group ever to feel bigger than the law, or that the law does not apply to him or her.

If a rule is broken, right then and there talk with the offender if you possibly can. When that is impossible—often you cannot break away from whatever else you are doing—seek out the child at the earliest possible moment. Then step by step go over what happened. Go over the rule and why there is such a rule. Without exception all youngsters must feel that what each one does is important. They need to know that you care and that you want to help them understand. If necessary, track them down by telephone in their homes!

You enforce the law *but* with young children that does not mean that you punish them. When children break the law, you talk with them. *That* is enforcement. When children break the law again, you talk with them some more. *That* is enforcement. When children break the law again, you talk and talk and persuade and discuss and listen and seek new words to make the reason for the rule and its importance even clearer. You are *teaching* good behavior. You are trying to persuade children, to touch their minds. You want the standards and values ultimately to become their standards and values, ones they will live by because they accept them as their own.

Punishment

The question of punishment, is, of course, a thorny one. It makes an excellent topic for discussion for a whole series of meetings with parents—meetings at which you tell your thinking and parents tell what they do.

The question is thorny because the idea of punishment leaps into most people's minds whenever a child disobeys, and especially when the misdeed happens more than once. Some adults even feel let down if the possibility of punishment seems ruled out. "What can you do?" they almost moan. In despair: "All you can do is talk at them." Talking is made to sound like the feeblest of all possible responses.

You should be clear in your mind on that one point: Talking is not and must not be feeble. Talking need not be harsh and it need not be angry. It need not be loud and it need not be threatening, *but:* Talking must not be feeble. When you are teaching a child about good behavior your whole tone and manner must convey great seriousness, great earnestness. Down at the child's level you look the youngster straight in the eye. Everything about you has to make it plain that a matter of first-rate importance is under discussion. There is not, and should not be, anything wishy-washy about using words to get an idea across.

On the issue of punishment, there are several excellent reasons why it makes sense to minimize punishment when you work with young children. One is that punishment is too effective . . . *for the moment!* Once you lean on punishments you will be able to control much bad behavior . . . *for the moment.* Punishment can "work" magic. Just be sure to hurt the child—that is the one thing you have to do. Sometimes the pain is a physical hurt; parents are more apt to do that. Schools are more apt to inflict the pain of deprivation. When you have lived with children for even a little while you quickly get to know what they enjoy the most—and there you have your punishment, handed to you on a silver platter. The child has to sit while the others play . . . The child must stay indoors while the others are outside . . . The child must sit apart from the group. . . . You hardly have to think any more, and that is one of the vices of punishment. The impact is not on the child but on *you,* the teacher.

A reliance on punishment—knowing you can always use it, knowing that "it works" for the moment—stops your thinking. It keeps you from asking: Should I have handled this behavior be changing the setting? Is the rule truly reasonable? Have I found the best words for building the child's understanding? Should I concentrate, not on the setting and not on trying to reach the child's mind, but on moving to still another approach? The greatest break a child can get is to have a *thinking* teacher, a *puzzling* teacher, a teacher who constantly keeps searching for the best answer. Once you start punishing you lessen that quality in yourself.

The impact of punishment on the child is bad, too. The punishment "works" but sometimes this means it simply hides the symptoms. The youngster moves on into the next class or the next year or the next community with problems unresolved, less ready than ever to become the self-directing citizen the world needs. Or the punishment "works," but only as long as you and your

punishment are around. And you can't go on with the child forever, into that next class or next year or next community.

Another weakness of a punishment approach is that it is susceptible to "inflation." You choose a penalty and it works for a while. Then at some point the child says, in effect: "Aw, that doesn't hurt me." Then you have to jack up the ante with some new punishment that hurts even more. In a sense, the child is in control. The child decides how hard you have to apply the screws. It is not healthy for young children to sense that they are the bosses. They very much need to know that wise, strong, sensitive adults are in charge.

Punishment also opens up a bargaining process. The child has a choice: Shall I be good, or shall I take my punishment? Youngsters should never have that option. Our society cannot tolerate a situation where children "buy" the right to be bad by agreeing to take some pain. Somehow we must strive to get the idea across: We all *must* be good—there can be no two ways about it. The notion that one can choose to pay the price and take the punishment is insupportable.

We are talking, of course, only about young children at the sheer beginning of their lifetime learning. We are not talking about adult offenders or how society should treat its grown-ups who cause trouble. At life's beginning, when there is still time, when values have not yet been set, the weight of our effort ought to be on establishing decent behavior as *the* way, the only way, a nonnegotiable item.

Punishment holds still one more hazard, especially with little children. Young boys and girls are uniquely dependent on the goodwill and support of nurturing adults. The hurt and the fear that punishment entail put this basic relationship in jeopardy. This is a high price to pay for the momentary good behavior that punishment might bring. The adult's angry face, the glare, the sharpness in tone of voice can strike more terror in young hearts than a grown-up might realize. Our displeasure is so frightening because young children need us so much. We should be wary of playing fast and loose with goodwill and trust in our relationships. Those add up to the strongest forces going for us in our effort to persuade youngsters to join the human race.

It goes without saying that goodwill in relationships does not mean that children can walk over adults. It does not mean that children "get away with it." It does not mean that adults should never say "no" for fear of damaging a child's psyche. The goodwill that counts is the love and caring of a strong adult who has standards and who upholds them.

You must stop the child each time a law is broken. You must enforce the law each time by making the reason for it more clear and more impressive. Sometimes you add strength to your words by using your body while you talk. You hold the child's arms or shoulders to convey the seriousness of the occasion. Perhaps you lead the child away from the scene of the trouble to make the point more clear that the particular behavior must not go on. But your body, like your words, is not a device for hurting—it is a means for building the understanding you want.

Panaceas

At one time isolating children who misbehaved was thought to be a wonder-worker. Every early nursery school had its isolation room, where children could be sent when they were bad. Kindergartens were more apt to stand children out in the hall. Upper grades—some lower grades too—used the classroom clothes closet as a place to shut up misbehaving youngsters.

Shame has also long been regarded as another wonder-worker. We no longer make children wear dunce caps in school. It is not uncommon, however, to make children stand or sit in a corner in full view of everyone. Nor is it unusual for classrooms to set aside a chair which takes on whatever name fits "the crime" of the child: the "crying chair," when children are in tears and a teacher thinks they shouldn't be; the "baby chair," when youngsters are not acting sufficiently grown-up; the "mean chair," the "spiteful chair," the "selfish chair"—name the offense, and the chair is available as a tool for embarrassment and isolation.

Behavior modification fits into this long line of panaceas. No matter who does what, or why, use "behavior mod"—it works wonders.

You need to be careful that reasoning with children—trying to teach them, reaching out with words to touch their minds—does not fall in with this almost endless list of cure-alls. You must be prepared to do a great deal of talking, reasoning, and explaining. Good behavior is not easy for children to learn. Much that we want them to do goes counter to their impulses. Learning to remember; learning to hold back or hold in; learning to use words instead of force, are all hard tasks for children to master. When you set out to building understandings you begin on a long, slow journey. Parents sometimes say very impatiently, "I've told you a thousand times!" Good behavior sometimes takes a thousand-and-one tellings. *But* don't stay wedded to this one approach alone. Work continuously to improve your classroom setting. Work continuously to build understandings. At the same time you must work on still a third approach.

_____ **Work on Children's Feelings**

To act right, a child has to feel right.

Feelings are so important that they can overwhelm what any one of us knows. They can drive any of us into actions that all good sense tells us we shouldn't do.

In turn, when our fundamental emotional needs are being met, we—children and adults—are free to use our brains, free to think, free to act the very best way we know how.

One important approach, then, to developing good behavior is to help children develop good feelings about themselves, about their peers and the other humans around them, about the world of reality in which they live. The

goal is to be sure that each and every child develops these positive attitudes, not simply the lucky handful who are blessed by healthy experiences at home and who have pleasing experiences showered on them at school.

The Warm Flow of Supporting Feelings

There are many ways of listing the positive feelings that matter so much to humans. One way is to group these basic needs under two large umbrella headings. The first heading covers all the warm feelings that flow in to us from the world outside: the supporting, comforting feelings that come from being known and cared for, loved and appreciated.

The need for a steady flow of these warm feelings is paramount in infancy, and holds A-1 priority through all the early childhood years. The newborn and the child in the first year or so of life is completely at the mercy of all of us. This tender child has to be certain, without doubt, that the world will be peopled by strong and loving adults, willing to do all that the child cannot do. When the child needs food, food will come. When the child needs holding, loving hands will be there. When the child needs company, pleased people will be around. When the child needs stimulation, adults will provide it. Human life begins as a time of tremendous dependency, when everything hangs on the generosity, the caring, the giving of the stronger and more able.

The best term ever coined to convey the feeling that matters above all at this helpless time in development is *unconditional love*. Youngsters are loved with no strings attached. They are loved without having to earn the love. They are loved and run no risk of losing the love. They are loved because they are here. Love is theirs, unconditionally.

The word "love" itself is, of course, an overall term. For the infant it means food, gentle hands, the happy sounds of pleased grown-ups; it means having one's physical needs met. As children become two, three, four, and five "love" is expressed in some of the same ways, and in variations. These slightly older boys and girls don't need to be carried, of course. But they do still find great assurance from many forms of physical relationships: games of ride-a-cock-horse and piggyback; holding the hand of someone big; a little rough-housing; some hair-tousling; a pat on the back; a squeeze of the arm.

As children get older, smiles say "love." Friendly words say it. A listening ear. An attentive look. Praise and notice and recognition. Comfort and care when there is a physical hurt. Sympathy. Even limits say "love" to a child; when the limits are reasonable and not harshly applied, they are proof that someone cares. Out of all of these experiences the child, stamped by dependency, builds the feeling that the world is safe. People are glad the child is here; people will do what has to be done.

Lucky children get continuous proof of unconditional love from nurturing parents at home. Then these youngsters—and all youngsters—come to school. The fact that they are two, three, four, or five does not mean that they have outgrown their need for love. Actually, in a new setting, the basic need rises to

special heights. Going to school creates the question for the child: Can I count on these unknown people in this new place?

Teachers who value good behavior have classrooms that reflect all the warmth and support any child could need. Teachers' personal relationships are, of course, the most important element: their ready smile, friendliness, cheerfulness, their interest in each and every youngster, their personal touch. But the style and mood of the classroom itself also express good feelings: color, gaiety, laughter, a lack of tension, the absence of competition and rush, no fear of punishments. Specific classroom arrangements convey the same messages: sofas and easy chairs for a teacher and a child or two to sit on; good food; flowers; animals in the classroom who need care and who, in return, give affection. Simply put: If you value good behavior make sure your classroom is a happy place for children to spend hours of their lives.

The classroom must also be a generous place. Each individual is assured of getting all the love he or she needs, and it is recognized that needs vary. There are times when a youngster's need for love goes sky high. The newcomer to a class has this heightened need for love, for example. So, too, does the child whose home is having some temporary upset, and the child who momentarily is having a rough time with classmates.

Other children daily and continuously show a sky-high need for love. They are emptier than their classmates because of the peculiar happenings of their personal pasts. Somehow—the ways can be manifold—these boys and girls did not get a full, comforting sense of support when they were infants and toddlers, and before they came to school. The chances are that they are not getting this full sense of support at home now. The result is that their need is more intense than that of their classmates.

The need for love in its various forms does not simply fade away if the need is not met. Children become hungrier and hungrier for the warm flow of supporting feelings. Unmet, the need presses more and more on all their thoughts until it dominates everything they do. But when a child's need is satisfied—initially at home, then in the warm and generous classroom—the need for love falls back into a more appropriate place. Just as someone who has been ravenously hungry finally pushes away from the table, ready now to move on to the next activity.

From the standpoint of learning—learning good behavior or anything else—the youngster whose feelings are in good shape can now think. And remember. The child is not at the mercy of powerful surges for proof that someone cares. The child *knows* that people care. The youngster is free to use his or her strengths.

Discipline often has a hard-nosed hawkish sound, but not in this instance. If you treasure good behavior, one way to build it is to warm up your classroom. Be sure that each and every child finds your classroom—that means largely *you*—overflowing with warmth, good cheer, praise and affection, friendliness. All this warmth may not look like a direct attempt to build discipline, but don't let anyone talk you out of it. Good feelings are absolutely essential ingredients of good behavior.

The Clear Thrill of Growing

Children need a flow-in of satisfaction *and* they need a flow-out. They need to get, they also need to give. The second umbrella heading covers all the good feelings that flow from growing, from bigness and independence, from contributing.

The first sign of this kind of pleasing feeling comes in the early months of life. The infant loves to be cuddled, held, appreciated, enjoyed. Then, delightful as all the flow-in of warmth has been, the infant soon wants to move out—to crawl, to stand, to walk. A drive for power and independence which will last the child's whole life begins to show itself.

Infants delight in crawling.

Just as there are times when the need for affection rises to the top, so too this need for bigness reaches peaks. The high points sometimes come because of developmental reasons, and sometimes because of events in the child's life.

Developmentally, toddlerhood—the time when the new skills of walking, talking and hand control are coming into flower—is one peak time for the satisfactions of being big and independent. The two-ish years are another such period. Tantrums that so frequently erupt at this age are a reflection of the youngster's striving, reaching, trying. The tears and fierce bursts of emotion often result from the child's pushing against limits which adults impose; equally often they result from the child's straining against the limits the youngster's own body sets. But strain and push the child will—the need to grow is deeply embedded.

Under-six children in school groups are greatly involved in the search for independence and bigness. The sheer fact of coming to school feeds this need.

Then, once in the group, children seek all opportunities to test their own wings. Youngsters who are in school at this stage are fortunate. There ought to be no better place for a child to taste the thrill of growing. Power, skills, knowledge, mastery, independence are right down our alley. Helping children to feel pride is our business. We ought to be very good at it.

Every under-six group ought to take glory in the wealth and variety of experiences it provides, the abundance of its equipment both indoors and out, and the freedom of choice it opens up. Under-six groups should not settle into a rut; they should not narrow the paths; they should set no rigid limits on the kinds of abilities that they prize. An under-six group — with its opportunities for physical activities, for many forms of artistic expression, for all kinds of dramatic play, for intellectual adventures — can be an excellent place for every child to satisfy this second broad emotional need.

The group itself offers countless chances for children to feel they are a valued part of something larger than themselves. These opportunities include carefully planned chances to contribute: Who will set the table? Who will water the plants? Who will feed the fish? They include daily built-in opportunities for children to share in cleaning the room, putting outdoor equipment away, moving furniture. Most of all, the comfortable free-and-easy social give-and-take of the small self-selected groups opens up the chance for children to present ideas, to take leadership, to contribute to planning, to speak out, to be listened to.

The individual attention that characterizes the good under-six group is another source of this important satisfaction. Teachers have countless opportunities to "tutor" children, to give one-to-one help so that youngsters perfect skills they are developing — in tumbling, for example, or with tools at the workbench, or at the easel. Teachers, sensitive to individual children's interests, can extend children's knowledge — pointing out details on trips, answering questions at story time, talking with boys and girls at the science table. The challenge is to be sure that each and every child knows the clear thrill of growing.

There is a further challenge. Some youngsters come to your group with more than just the normal developmental need to be big and to be important. These children have special hungers just as inevitably as some children come desperately hungry for more love and warmth. It usually isn't the least bit difficult to spot these power-hungry children. Their behavior will soon show you how much it matters to them to feel important. The real difficulty comes in bringing ourselves to meet their need. These children make it all too easy for us simply to be angry with them.

No matter how they act — and they can act badly — these boys and girls do not need more anger. They need doors opened. They need unusual and individual chances to develop skills; they need unusual and individual chances to contribute to the group's well-being; they need chances for leadership jobs; they need chances to succeed. Your other youngsters must not feel that you are skimping on them, but somehow you must contrive so that these few special children get the fullest possible glow of growing. If you prize good discipline you will make sure that they — and all your youngsters — leave your classroom less ravenous for power and for bigness than when they came.

Your actions may not look on the surface like major efforts to build good behavior, but what you do is fundamental. When the need for bigness and importance is unmet—at home or at school—the need stays uppermost in the child's mind. Pressing on the child, it takes away thinking powers and weakens controls. It can drive young children—later, big children and adults—into destructive and attacking deeds, dangerous to themselves and to others. But with the need well met—at school and at home—it settles into its appropriate place. Children are free to think, free to learn, free to act well.

When Children Still Misbehave

Despite your work on the classroom setting, despite all you do to build understandings, despite your efforts to develop healthy feelings, there are bound to be times when you will feel you are making no progress with particular children.

It is at this point that some teachers say: "O.K. Punish them now." They have saved punishment, often a little reluctantly, as the last resort and now this is it. Or if not punishment, at least the threat of punishment. Or the harsher, sharper voice of command which carries an unspoken threat.

There is a wiser alternative to these stern ways.

An old adage (slightly modified) says exactly what to do: "Don't just *do* something. Stand there!" Stand there . . . and mull. Stand there . . . and puzzle. Stand there and search for a handle on what has gone wrong.

This thinking process, of course, has to go on quickly so that you are not immobilized. Children won't stand still while you mull; you can't actually "just stand there" either. You have to think, but some answers can come to you almost in a split second.

Because of this pressure on you to act, one helpful technique is to have what you could call a checklist firmly fixed in your mind. Have some definite questions you ask yourself, exactly as pilot and co-pilot do when they are readying a plane for flight: a fixed, invariable set of inquiries, always gone over in exactly the same order, leaving nothing to chance. In a jiffy run down the list each time you feel puzzled by a child's behavior.

Such a checklist could take many forms. No one could make a winning case for any one particular order to the questions. But a strong case can be made that there be an order. You will be glad if you have a fixed listing of questions in your mind, one you stay with every time—no skipping around, no leaping to favorite explanations.

Following is one such checklist. You may develop another that suits you better. But the checklist that follows illustrates the process. To get the hang of it, no matter who does what, whenever you are puzzled, in each instance ask yourself the following questions in the same, fixed unvarying order.

The Stage of Growth

First, could the behavior that is puzzling you stem from the stage of growth the child is in?

You need to know, first of all, whether you really do have a problem on your hands. The behavior may be annoying; it may look hurtful; you may not want it to continue. *But* there is the possibility that the behavior may be a normal, healthy expression of the child's stage of development. Although troublesome, it may nevertheless be a contributing factor to the individual's growth.

To make a judgment on whether or not the stage of growth could be the cause, ask yourself whether you have seen or heard or read that a great many other children around this age do this kind of thing. Go back in your mind's eye to the behavior of other children around this age whom you have taught. Dredge up what you have read about this age, and what the books and the experts say. Call to mind pictures of children this age and how they act out of school, on the street, and in stores.

Your quick flashback can give you a tentative answer to whether the puzzling behavior is universal among children at this point in their maturing, or whether it is peculiar to the child about whom you are concerned.

If your best judgment is that the behavior is universal—the cause is probably the stage of growth the child is in—you immediately get one note of comfort. You can rest assured that the behavior won't go on forever. Age-appropriate behavior—the good and the bad, the pleasing and the hard-to-take—stops of its own accord as children get older, just as spring stops when summer comes along.

In addition, two constructive courses of action immediately open up to you. Both stem from the fact that age-appropriate behavior, while at times annoying or irritating, is a building block in a child's total growth.

One course of action is to learn to live with the behavior, to accept it and not worry about it. You tolerate the behavior. You may even be able to bring yourself to be glad to see the behavior and to appreciate it. And if there are rules and regulations prohibiting the behavior, repeal them.

"Permissiveness" is the word often used to describe this response. It is a good description and, *in this instance,* a good response. The behavior is "permitted" to continue—not because a teacher is weak; not because a teacher has given up in despair; but because a thoughtful teacher has decided, on the basis of the best evidence available, that the behavior is intended to occur. To put the matter bluntly, God seemingly made humans this way. Age-appropriate actions, troublesome though some of them may be, are built in to the way humans are made. It would be harmful to rail against them.

The second possible course of action is identical in its basic attitude, but different in its approach: The behavior is channeled. You open up a detour. You fix matters so that while the behavior cannot go on *here,* it can go on *there.* The

behavior cannot go on *now* but it can go on *then*. The behavior cannot go on with *this* but it can go on with *that*. Permissiveness, not prohibition, still sets the tone—this is healthy behavior, after all. But when you channel, you find ways for the behavior to continue that make it easier for the adult or for the group to live with it.

It is more difficult to channel age-appropriate behavior than simply to live with it. To channel you need to think creatively and quickly. Channeling is not prohibition. Neither is channeling a substitution or a diversion. It is *not* channeling to say: If you want to take a walk, read a book instead . . . If you want to read a book, go swimming instead. In good channeling children feel that they have done what is natural to them, but simply in a different time or place or with different materials—a change so slight as to be inconsequential. They have, in fact, no great awareness of having been channeled. This contented state of mind is the best proof that you have channeled skillfully. But such channeling isn't easy to do; sometimes it seems almost impossible.

The easiest way, the safest way, *if* you feel the troubling behavior stems from the stage of growth the child is in, is to learn to live with the behavior. It is true that none of us can force ourselves into accepting behavior that makes us uncomfortable—permissiveness means a glad tolerance, not a grudging and defeated air. But none of us has to stay set forever in our ways. Slowly we can learn to live with more and more of those behaviors that occur because a child is a healthy child. And our acceptance of such truly childlike behavior will give us healthier schools and healthier communities.

Unmet Emotional Needs

Your best thinking, however, may lead you to reject the hypothesis that the behavior stems from the child's stage of growth. As you quickly recall what you have seen and read, the behavior does not strike you as being almost universal around this age. Go on then to the next query on your checklist.

Second, no matter who does what, in every instance, ask yourself: Could the behavior stem from the child's search for ways to satisfy unmet emotional needs?

You have already made one useful observation: The child is not acting his or her age. If the youngster had been, you would have stopped with the first explanation—the stage of growth. But you rejected that.

Sometimes you get further confirmation that the child is not acting up to age from what other adults say about the child's behavior. You frequently hear a parent or another teacher say to the youngster: "You're acting like a little baby" or "You're acting like a two-year-old." Such words are not useful to the child, but they can be useful to you. Seemingly something is dragging down a child's behavior and keeping it down. Unmet emotional needs have that power. When needs are not met, a child gets mired in infancy or toddlerhood or in some

younger age span when the needs usually are fulfilled. A boy or girl acting *continuously* like a younger child—"Why don't you act your age!"—may be tipping you off that unmet emotional needs are involved.

Something people tell you about a child can also be of value. Some children, even under the age of six, despite the short time they have lived, have acquired reputations and labels. If those who know the child immediately say, "That's him all over," you have another lead. Or if they say, "That's her to a 'T'" or if they call the child a "bully," a "whiner," a "baby." The name-calling is hurtful to the child, but it can be useful to you. It suggests that this youngster has acted this same way over and over, for a long time and in many places. Unmet needs have this capacity to dominate behavior.

Your own observation may confirm this fact. You may realize that the misbehavior does not occur only in one place or at one time or only with one person. The misbehavior goes wherever the child is: indoors and out, on the street and in the group, in the hall and on the bus, at juice time and music time and story time. This sense of "always and everywhere" strengthens the likelihood that unmet needs may be involved. The cause is within the child, wherever the child goes. And it is not something the youngster can turn on and off.

If you are also taken by any special note of force behind the child's behavior, this, too, can indicate unmet needs as the probable cause. Sometimes parents or other teachers imply this note of force when they tell you about the child: "We've tried everything." Whether they really have "tried everything," their words make it clear that the cause of the misbehavior is no light-and-easy matter. Something drives the child into the behavior "despite everything"— despite shame, pain, angry words. Unmet needs, with their great churning within, have that strength.

By putting several of these clues together, your best judgment may lead you to think that unmet needs are at the root of the behavior. If so, two "negatives" come through immediately to help you. The stage of growth is *not* the explanation—you have ruled that out—therefore you will not simply be tolerant of the behavior. And you *don't* face the task of *teaching* understandings. This child is not yet in shape to act on understandings; needs come first.

You know one other fact, too. Helping this child to act well can be a long process. Unmet needs usually do not develop overnight; they cannot be satisfied overnight. The job that lies ahead of helping this youngster to develop good behavior may, therefore, take a long time.

You know still one more fact of the greatest importance: You know how to help this child! The way to start good behavior rolling is clear: *Meet the child's needs.* The job is as simple as that. This child was somehow short-changed in the past. The thing to do now is to lavish life's emotional goodies on the youngster. This child somehow got skimpy portions in the past. The way to help is to give this boy or girl massive doses of as many of life's positive feelings as possible.

The temptation, of course, is to do the opposite—to hold out on such a youngster. The child is misbehaving, after all. The temptation is to say, in effect: You be good *first,* and then we'll be good to you. This sounds fair. With mentally healthy youngsters whose needs are well met this may be the path to follow. Not with this child, however, With the hungry, empty one you must reverse the process. You must be good first—very good to make up for life's past stinginess—*and then* the child will be able to behave.

Of course, this approach is not truly a reversal. You are following, on a delayed time schedule, the normal sequence that other, now-better-behaved, healthy children experienced. Their needs were met in the course of their growing up. People were good to them first—and early—and for long periods of time. The result is that now they can think and act on their understandings. With the empty youngster you need to do a major catch-up job. Then, over time, that child, too, stands a chance of reaching a point where needs will drop down into their appropriate place. Then that child, too, will be able to act on what he or she knows.

It is easy, of course, to say: *Meet the child's needs.* This seems to leave unanswered the question: What needs? Often this sounds like an overwhelming poser, almost impossible to answer. But the fact is teachers often know what children are seeking. The children's behavior has told us. Their behavior has almost shouted an answer—with force—time and time again —always and everywhere.

The real problem is not that of knowing what needs the child is seeking to satisfy. The difficult job is to persuade one's self that needs are important. We say about so many children: "Oh, he *just* wants attention" or "She *just* wants to be first" or "He *just* wants to show off." "She *just* . . . " and "He *just* . . . " We *know* what the child is after. We know the areas where massive doses are needed. We know what we must pile on, all of us, in every conceivable way and for a long time. We *know* but we will not take our insight seriously. We belittle our knowledge with that minimizing put-down word, "just": "He *just* wants you to notice him."

One area we may not know. We may not know how the unmet needs arose. We were not on hand in the child's infancy and toddlerhood. Rolling back time, helping those who were on hand in the child's early days to recall what actually happened, is a long, skilled job, one most of us are not equipped to undertake. Sometimes we do learn snatches of background. It almost always sensitizes us and puts us more on the child's side. It builds our determination to stick with our catch-up efforts to meet needs, no matter how long they take. But knowing the child's history, as valuable as that is, ought not to be crucial. We can so easily see the child's present behavior, the persistent and forceful, almost pathetic searching. That ought to be enough to tell us: The child has unmet needs, and it ought to be enough to tell us something of what those needs are.

There will be times, of course, when you cannot grasp what the child is seeking. This often happens when a youngster's search has gone on so long that the behavior has become distorted. It happens when the child's search has met

with such frustration that the behavior has become disguised. This is a complication but not an insurmountable obstacle. The remedy? If you cannot tell
for sure what a youngster is seeking, give the child massive doses of all the
things you know are good for children. Pile on, in every way you can, massive
doses of warm, nurturing love *and* open up massive opportunities for achievement. This is essentially what fortunate, healthy children experienced in the
course of their growing up.

Some notes of caution are in order. When children who have long been
empty suddenly find themselves with adults who appreciate what they need,
the children sometimes behave worse! They are like famished people at a ban-
quet table, gorging themselves and grabbing. They are like parched people, at a
well, slurping and pushing. To be so close at last to what one has feverishly
sought can trigger out-of-bounds responses. Don't let this behavior put you off,
and don't let it make you land on the child. These over-responses may be the
final clue that you really have found the cause of the child's trouble, and that
you are moving the child toward good behavior.

The other note of caution: Someone has to act as each hungry youngster's
policeman while the child's needs are being met. Such a child needs a watcher,
a person continuously on guard, ready to step in when unmet needs burst
through the surface and propel the child. Until needs are met, words of warning, prohibition, or instruction are not strong enough to do the job. A friendly
body intervening, a friendly hand on the arm, an idea for diversion can work.
You and/or your aide must be ever-ready to play the role of friendly guardian.

Teaching is not easy when children with unmet emotional needs are in
your group. Unfortunately there is no way to avoid it. Bringing up children so
that most of their needs have been reasonably well met has always been a difficult task for all homes. It is a much harder job today. The increase in single-
parent families; the increase in divorce and separation; the increase in the
number of mothers working at a time when help with good child care is so
scarce; the mobility of our families; the poverty so many families experience—many factors increase the likelihood of your having a goodly
number of emotionally hungry, troubled children in your room.

The many changes in our social fabric are a strong argument in favor of
aides in every classroom, either paid aides or volunteers. Their presence makes
it more likely that someone will be available to play the role of protec-
tor—protecting other children, protecting property, *and* protecting the driven
child until the seething of unmet needs subsides.

A Specific Bad Local Situation

Your best thinking may lead you to reject the hypothesis that unmet emotional
needs are the root of the problem. To be sure, the child is not acting up to age.
However, if you see none of the compulsion and persistence that go with unmet
needs, you have to continue down your checklist to the next possible explanation.

Third, are there factors in the immediate present setting that may be making the child act in a worrisome way?

Unmet needs arose in the past—you have crossed that off as a possibility. But there can be pressures in the here-and-now that keep a youngster from responding well. These pressures may be in the classroom; they may stem from happenings on a child's way to school or at the breakfast table or as far back as supper last night. You want to explore, in your mind's eye, the specific, immediate, local setting in which the child is functioning.

Once you think about this possible cause you may become aware of out-of-school events that could be causing the misbehavior. Sometimes, with great good luck, you are able to do something which alleviates the out-of-school problem. Even when you cannot reach out that far, however, at least you know that something in the setting is the villain—not the child. This knowledge will temper your treatment of the child, and keep you from adding more complications to the youngster's life.

More often the source of the trouble is a specific situation in the school program, occurrences while the child is with you. The complication here is that you are a part of this "specific bad local situation." You developed the program. You developed the time schedule, the room arrangement. You set the spirit and tone of the classroom. It is very hard to look at one's self and decide: Ah, yes! I have found the source of the trouble. *I am!*

Sometimes one clue makes it easier for you to arrive at this painful decision. When something in the immediate classroom setting pulls down behavior, usually more than one child is affected. If the room is too hot, it will be too hot for many. If the wait is too long, it will be too long for many. If the challenges are too dull and routine, many youngsters are apt to be bored. If the assembly program is wrong for the age, several children are apt to get restless. One child's behavior catches your eye, but a second look makes you realize that many are not acting as well as they could, not just one child alone. What to do is clear. Don't do anything to the child. Concentrate on fixing the sore spot in your classroom or program.

Unfortunately, (for understandable reasons), often only one child responds to what is, in fact, a bad situation for many. Young children are dependent on their teachers; they are predisposed to like them. Young children are new children who haven't seen a lot of the world yet. They are predisposed to accept much that comes along as simply in the nature of things—they try to take in stride whatever comes.

These factors shield teachers of young children from reactions other teachers get from older, less dependent boys and girls. The junior high school age, for example, makes no bones about showing dissatisfaction. Their acting-out behavior can be hard on a teacher, but it can be a tip to anyone who wants classroom living to go right. Young children are more apt to keep to themselves the uneasiness they feel. This puts a burden on teachers of the young: We often have no one except ourselves to make us be at our best!

A saving grace is that in every group there are likely to be a few children you could call "the agitators." They may be the youngsters with more sensitive feelers—life hits them a little harder. They may be the more volatile children.

These children "speak out" through their behavior, protesting what probably also bothers some others. These are the few out on the picket line. You won't be glad to have them in your group every minute of the time. In the long run, however, you are lucky they are there. These youngsters can tip you off to specific parts of your classroom program that are bad for them *and* probably not right for many other children as well. Follow the leads they open up—changing the setting, improving the setting—and you will improve their behavior and the behavior of the whole group.

The Need for More and Better Teaching

As you think about your classroom you may well come to the conclusion that nothing seems especially wrong. Your children seem to have enough choices, enough freedom, space, an at-ease sense, not too much all-group activity, not too much talky-talk, ample experiences with reality, ample intellectual challenges . . . But some youngster still is not acting up to age. Something is still wrong. You need to go on to another area of exploration.

Fourth, ask yourself whether the child does not yet understand the rule and the reasons for it.

Perhaps you have not yet succeeded in your job of teaching. Maybe you have to search for a better choice of words. Maybe somehow you are not conveying the seriousness and earnestness you feel. Maybe, by tone of voice or by your posture, you can better convey the gravity of the need for good behavior. Or maybe you have been too serious and too earnest. Maybe you haven't given this youngster enough lift, haven't praised enough or showed your delight when behavior has been good.

Maybe you haven't given enough chance for reactions to come out so the law has remained "your" law and not become the child's. Or maybe you have counted too much too early on words alone to carry your message. It might help if you used your presence or the position of your body, or perhaps your hand and your arm, to make sure the misbehavior stops, at least for the moment. There are many possibilities to explore, but if you have come this far on your checklist—reasonable rule, no unmet need, nothing terrible about the setting—the solution may well be to "hang in there." Continue with your teaching. Continue trying to build understandings.

You may feel that you have been trying to make your point "for ages," but cheer up. You really have been at it for only a short time—young children simply haven't been around very long. They are new to the world, they are new to school. Living with a group of youngsters, living with a teacher who is not their parent, using unfamiliar materials, living in new space, having countless new experiences: all the strangeness is bound to complicate each child's task of learning how to behave. And some children need more time than others.

A young child may be getting a regulation reasonably straight, but does the rule hold in this particular situation? with this new person? and this new material? Our answer—"Of course!"—seems pat and clear to us, but then we have been around a long time. Newcomers need patience, persistence, more

time for ideas to sink in. We would all like to see good behavior come quickly, but building values and building controls take a long time. There is no way you can rush the process.

Perspective

If you work effectively on your setting, if you work skillfully to build under-standings, if you work sensitively to develop good feelings, you will succeed in every instance in teaching good behavior. Right? Wrong! Unfortunately, life does not work out that way. Despite your best efforts you will fail at times.

You do well to recognize the odds against you in some instances. And you do well to help parents, administrators, and citizens recognize the odds so that you don't blame yourself too harshly, and so that schools are not unfairly criticized.

Some of the children you will teach live their lives surrounded by poverty. They are immersed in all the evils of bad housing, bad nutrition, neighborhoods of crime and vice, the absence of hope and motivation. . . . You cannot expect a perfect batting average against such an array.

Some of the children you will teach have neurological and organic prob-lems which force them into misbehavior. In these instances, your classroom ef-forts are of value, but they cannot get to the causes of the difficulty. Unless what you do is backed up by skilled medical resources, your efforts alone will not suffice.

Some of the children you will teach arrive in your classroom severely damaged emotionally by the lives they have led. The causes of the damage still persist in their present-day living. In these instances your efforts to enlist parents' help may fail, usually because the parents themselves need help. They, too, have been badly damaged by the lives they have led—they are in no posi-tion to function at their best. You cannot always expect to succeed with such children.

Medical doctors learn to face situations where the odds are stacked heavily against them. Despite their best efforts, doctors at times see their pa-tients die. The forces stacked against health and survival were simply too strong.

The lesson from medicine is clear: The one legitimate demand *cannot* be for 100% success. The one legitimate demand is that you do your best.

Unlike medicine, teachers have an important positive element going for us. Sometimes what we do seems to result in no payoff at the moment. Our words of praise for a child, our moments of closeness, the chances for success that we open up, the friendly conversations, seem wasted. We feel we have accom-plished nothing. But sometimes a spark lies hidden that does not burst into flame until years later.

Humans are social beings. Humans want to live with other people and want to be liked by other people. Humans want to learn to behave so they can live with other people. You are not fighting human nature when you teach good behavior—strong drives within the human are on your side. These, plus your ef-forts, sometimes keep that spark glowing. So: Plug away. And get all the help you can from any parents who have help to give you.

THE TOOLS AND THE FREEDOM TO TEACH

Many teachers know how to build a good program for children. They understand child development; they hold good democratic goals; they have a rich cultural background, and they know good teaching methods. *But* their hands are tied. They are blocked from using all they know. External pressures determine their curriculum, not good theory.

Teachers are frustrated by these external pressures. Too many good teachers leave the profession in despair. Too many who stay are worn down by the circumstances under thich they work.

To establish a good program for young children, the first step is often to tackle these external pressures. Until they are overcome, theory never gets a chance to operate.

Class Size

The strongest of the malignant pressures is large class size. There is no more pernicious obstacle to a thoughtfully planned program.

Large class size is a roadblock to meeting individual differences.

Large class size is a roadblock to working with parents.

Large class size is a roadblock to an activity program of firsthand experiencing, of learning by doing. It limits the kinds of experiences that can be offered. It rules out activities that make a mess, that call for much teacher supervision, that create any noise.

Large class size limits children's choices. It cuts down on their movement, their conversation, their social give-and-take.

Large class size makes teachers talk more *at* children. It forces them to give more commands. It leads to lining up, to waiting. It breeds more all-group activities; it cuts down on the number of small-group and individual experiences.

Large class size makes us pretend that young children are older than they are. It spawns teaching methods that are inappropriate and goals that are inappropriate.

Large class size spoils everything.

Until we overcome tl.e problem of large class size, we will never have nursery schools, kindergartens, day care centers, or Head Start programs of which we can be proud.

Standards for Class Size

Research cannot prove that any one class size is the optimum for all educational experiences. Class size is relative. It depends on the age of the children, the methods of teaching, the goals of the classroom. Graduate seminars are often limited to three or five students; college lectures commonly serve several hundred students.

There are, however, clear guides to right class size that have accumulated over the years from the practical, personal experience of teachers of young children. The result of this experience has been written into law in those states that regulate private nursery schools and kindergartens. It has set the standard for those excellent private schools that strive, with high tuition and endowment, to achieve top-quality education.

Good class size—not small class size but *right* class size—for three-year-olds is about twelve children in a group with two teachers, a trained head teacher and a teacher's aide.

Good class size for four-year-olds is about sixteen children in a group with two teachers, a trained teacher and a teacher's aide.

Good class size for five-year-olds is about twenty children in a group. Five-year-olds—so like four-year-olds and three-year-olds—also need two teachers, a trained head teacher and a teacher's aide. A paid aide in a public kindergarten of twenty children is a rarity. A volunteer aide should not be.

The Head Start standard—fifteen children to a classroom with a trained teacher, a teacher's aide, and volunteers—seems right for disadvantaged five-year-olds. These children have intensified needs; Head Start is compensatory education. This standard is not good, however, when Head Start serves four-year-olds. The number of children to a classroom should then be about twelve. If Head Start ever moves down the age scale to serve three-year-olds, ten should be the maximum number of children in a classroom.

The class size for day care centers should be the same as for nursery schools and kindergartens, depending on the age of the children. The number of paid adults must be somewhat greater, however, because of the longer hours of operation of the day care center. Usually, one trained head teacher, one full-

time teacher's aide, one part-time teacher's aide, and volunteers can do the job well (plus cooking and custodial staffs, of course).

The standards arrived at subjectively, based on the experience of teachers, received objective backing in 1979 from the National Day Care Study. This was a four-year study, federally financed, of quality and cost in sixty-seven day care centers in Atlanta, Detroit, and Seattle. The study included both observation of the behavior of children and staff, and the administration of standardized tests to the children.

The general conclusion of the study was that "smaller groups are consistently associated with better care." It found that in smaller groups teachers engaged in more social interaction with children. The children, in turn, showed more cooperation, verbal initiative, and reflective/innovative behavior. They also showed less hostility and conflict; they wandered aimlessly less frequently; and they made greater gains on the two standardized tests.

Specifically, the study gave its top recommendation to class size of fourteen with two adults for groups of three-, four-, and five-year-olds. It found this size and staffing to have "the best impact on children": better care, more socially active youngsters, higher gains on tests. Its least enthusiastic recommendation was for a class size of eighteen with two adults, for the same ages of children. This size, which was the maximum recommended, was characterized in the study as "the least effective."[1]

Following the publication of the findings of the National Day Care Study, the federal government in 1980 proposed a revised set of Federal Interagency Day Care requirements. These requirements called for twelve with three adults as the maximum size for a two-year-old group, and sixteen with two adults as the maximum size for groups of three-, four-, and five-year-olds.[2]

The recommendations of the National Day Care Study and the Federal Interagency Day Care requirements are not identical with the historical, subjective standards on group size and staffing. All three, however, hit hard at the same central idea: Decent class size is imperative. And all three are in general agreement on what constitutes decent class size. It is a significant development for the early childhood profession now to have objective research support and national backing to buttress the experience of teachers.

We are so accustomed to crowded classrooms that these standards are bound to seem idealistic. The standard of twenty children in a kindergarten classroom will seem to many people especially starry-eyed. Our good private kindergartens have had to meet this standard, but the standard for public kindergartens has slipped badly through the years. Teacher after teacher feels, "I'm lucky this year. I only have thirty-five." And she means 35 X 2 — morning and afternoon! The battered state of public kindergarten standards may make some compromise a necessary transitional step toward improvement. Good

---

[1] *Children at the Center,* Final Report of the National Day Care Study. Vol. I, Summary Findings and Their Implications. Cambridge, Mass.: Abt Associates, Inc., 1979.

[2] *Federal Register,* March 19, 1980.

education could compromise on twenty-five five-year-olds in a kindergarten—but there should be no compromise on staffing. Kindergartens need two adults. They need one paid professional teacher and one aide, paid or unpaid, parent or nonparent—especially if there are twenty-five youngsters.

These standards do not reflect the prevailing situation in classrooms. But the standards are right—the situation is wrong! *What is* distorts our effort for children. We cannot go on forever accepting as right and necessary what we are now doing. Public education must not become equated with second-rate education. It must be good education—not luxurious, not frilly, but right for the age it serves.

In these present years, we have an unusual opportunity to improve class size. One significant new trend seems firmly established: There are fewer children. The availability of birth control devices and of abortion, the postponement of marriages, changes in how women see their roles—these and other factors account for the steady and continuous decline in the birth rate. It seems unlikely that these factors will be erased or that the trend will be reversed. Newspaper headlines speak of a "baby bust," the opposite of a "baby boom." Schools already have markedly lower enrollments of young children.

This trend opens up important choices. Communities can say: "There is a glut of teachers." They can opt to let teachers go who have no tenure. Or communities can see these years as a time of opportunity to provide well for the youngsters they have.

Wise communities will not talk of "too many" teachers. Our society can certainly use every teacher it can get: to expand our child care centers, to extend public education to our four-year-olds, to establish more Head Start classes. If these advances sound like reaching for the stars, the least we can do is to take advantage of the availability of teachers to bring existing class size down to a decent and reasonable standard.

Responses to Overcrowding

Sometimes we have money for teachers and equipment, but we don't have the room. Overcrowding results from our insistence on squeezing children into the "official" school building. Fortunately, five-year-olds are seldom disadvantaged by being housed in a portable or temporary building on the school grounds, or in an off-campus location such as a rented home, store, or other building which can be converted to kindergarten use. If lack of space within the school is the sole cause of overly large class size there should be no hesitancy about dividing groups into smaller sections and using such auxiliary facilities to achieve right class size.[3]

---

[3] See pp. 178–79 for a discussion of the positive gains in housing a kindergarten in its own small, separate building. One word of caution, however: An aide is imperative, not a luxury in any sense, when a group is housed in a building by itself.

Unfortunately, too often the problem is lack of space, teachers, equipment, and money—a *total* shortage of general support. Teachers must be active citizens working and voting to bring about adequate federal, state, and local support for under-six education. Only one area of general education has succeeded in persuading legislatures and the public of the necessity for right class size. Special education—the education of the mentally retarded, the physically handicapped, the emotionally disturbed—has apparently won the battle. Those of us in early educaiton need to do more than we have done before to help people see that education of the child under six is also "special" education.

While we are working for adequate support, there are in-between steps we can take. These are not solutions—only more money can solve the basic problem. These in-between steps are palliatives and they can bring new problems ot their own. But they can help to tide us over until there is good financial support. Teachers of young children would do well to persuade principals, superintendents, and members of Boards of Education to experiment with the following ideas when class size gets out of hand.

Drop-out Days

One technique for creating right class size is the device of Drop-out Days.

Customarily, children come to school five days a week. Schools run from Monday through Friday. This arrangement is good *if* the enrollment is twelve in a three-year-old group, sixteen in a four-year-old group, twenty in a five-year-old group (or twenty-five, if you are compromising).

When enrollment is higher the Drop-out Day approach says: "We're sorry. We don't have room for everyone five days a week." Each day one-fifth of the children will not attend. The total enrollment in the kindergarten is thirty, but each day, one-fifth of the children will have Drop-out Day, cutting the enrollment on each day to twenty-four, within the range of compromise. Some children will come Monday, Tuesday, Wednesday, Thursday; they drop out Friday. Some come Tuesday, Wednesday, Thursday, Friday; they drop out Monday. And so it goes.

If the enrollment is thirty-five or forty, as it often is, each child has two Drop-out Days. Although the boy or girl comes to kindergarten only three days a week, when the child does come, the class size is right.

The result is a clear definition: A kindergarten is a group for about twenty five-year-olds (or about twenty-five, if the compromise is made). When the number exceeds that, we no longer have a kindergarten, we have a mob scene.

Drop-out Days are neither brand-new nor as revolutionary as they sound. It is true that public education has had a proud tradition. We don't turn children away, our doors are open. This general policy of nonexclusion entitles us to a glorious A for effort, but it often leads to a D in achievement. Although the policy is well established, there have been exceptions when there have been shortages of money, teachers, or space. The two-session kindergarten is one

such exception. Almost all five-year-olds now "drop out" half a day every day! The two-shift and three-shift elementary and secondary schools are also exceptions; these means shorter hours and less attendance than the "normal."

Drop-out Days are not popular with teachers. The continuity of a program is stymied. One-fifth, sometimes two-fifths of the children miss the Tuesday trip to the turkey farm because Tuesday is not their day for school. This discomfort to teachers may not be entirely bad, however. We need the pin-pricks of Drop-out Days to prod us to work more vigorously for adequate financial support. We have learned to put up with the discomforts of large class size. We have learned to close our eyes and minds to how crowds adversely affect children. Drop-out Days cause some distortions of their own, but at least they remind us of the basic problem. That problem is the overly large class size that makes the Drop-out Day necessary.

Drop-out Days also trouble parents. Initially, parents often react angrily: "My child is school age—you must take him!" But parents can learn to understand, if we help them through meetings and conferences, that school personnel do not set the tax rate. Schools are the people's schools. The people determine how good those schools will be, how extensive their offerings will be, how high a quality they will attain. The school, in effect, is simply saying, "We are sorry. You have only given us enough tax money to have a three-day or a four-day kindergarten." School is raising the question: "Is this what you really want?"

We are shielding parents today. We keep them from knowing what actually goes on within our classrooms. Parents send their children in good faith. The children come to school; the parents stay home; and parents never know that their tax money is insufficient. They never know that they are buying a kindergarten in name only. The anger and upset of a community is distressing and difficult to live with. But without the deep concern of parents, schools never become truly great.

Drop-out Months

Varying the number of months in the school year is another expedient for achieving right class size. Usually, children come to school Monday through Friday, September through June. When class size is not right we could say: "We are able to take your child from September to January. Those four months will have to be the 'kindergarten year.'" Or the period might be September through February or whatever adjustment is needed so that at any one time there are only about twenty to twenty-five five-year-olds enrolled.

These are not Drop-out Days but *Drop-out Months*. A child attends continuously, Monday through Friday. The program has continuity during that time. Each child has a shorter school year, but one that permits the youngster to go to a real kindergarten during that shorter year.

Like Drop-out Days, Drop-out Months are not new. Our school year varies now in different parts of the country. In the future, those communities most committed to good education may lengthen their school year to eleven or

twelve months. The school year is purely a man-made arrangement. At the kindergarten level, in particular, the shorter school year is, unfortunately, common. Some school systems which have no regular public kindergarten program do have summer groups for five-year-olds. They cannot or will not provide ten months of kindergarten education—they provide two months.

Summer Head Start—fortunately a disappearing program—is the most obvious example of Drop-out Months. Its children come only eight weeks. They "drop-out" the rest of the time. No one thinks that eight weeks is long enough. It is sheer compromise. Children with disadvantaged backgrounds ought to have twelve-month schooling, and not simply for the year before their entrance into "regular" school. But Summer Head Start, where it still exists, turns to the temporary answer, to the palliative. Eight weeks of something good is better than ten months of overcrowded education, and better than none at all.

There is always the risk that people will forget that short programs—Dropout Days or Drop-out Months—are only expedient strategy. It has been easy, for example, for many communities to live with their abbreviated summer kindergartens. There is the additional danger that summer programs, in particular, will strain to compress into their brief span all that regular-length programs can do. Their summer placement accentuates the idea that kindergarten "gets children ready for first grade." It hides the fact that kindergarten is primarily to make the fifth year of life (or a part of it) more worth living.

There are no perfect solutions, short of solving the basic problem. We cannot simultaneously have inadequacies in support and fully adequate programs. Some price must be paid by somebody, somewhere, somehow. The highest price tag comes with overly large class size—we have to remember that. Any difficulties that flow in the wake of expedients to meet this threat are less serious than the difficulties that come from the main threat itself.

Teacher Aides

There should be an aide in every classroom for young children, even when class size is right. Sound standards call for twelve three-year-olds to *two* adults; sixteen four-year-olds to *two* adults; twenty (or if need be, twenty-five) five-year-olds to *two* adults. But aides are seldom found in public kindergartens, except when class size mounts astronomically. This is a shame.

Some school administrators mistakenly think they have established good working conditions when they provide two adults for forty five-year-olds. They are blind to how grievously they have compromised the standards for right class size. The best that can be said is that they have taken a slight step in the right direction—forty children with two adults is better than the same number with only one! But we have to learn not to wait until class size gets completely out of hand before turning to aides. The teacher with twenty five-year-olds should have an aide. But especially when the number soars to twenty-one—it should not have to zoom to forty!—we should not hesitate a second to find a paid or unpaid helper.

We have been discouragingly slow in bringing aides into the public school kindergarten. The idea is old hat in the nursery school, the day care center, and now in Head Start (although always in these instances with right class size). The cooperative nursery school, in particular, has shown how well parents can serve as aides. Co-ops for years have used parents as their assistant teachers and as assistants in every aspect of their programs: shopping for supplies, office work, nursing services, repairs, and maintenance. In a cooperative nursery school, parer.is pay tuition but they also pay through their services. Each day the trained teacher, tuition-supported, is in charge; one assistant teacher—a parent, whose services are contributed—is her aide.

One support for the cooperative idea is the same old irritant that confronts all under-six education: the ever-present lack of money. Parents wanted nursery education for their children but could not afford to buy what a good classroom must have. They were short on cash but not on time and talent and concern, so they established a co-op. Many side benefits have kept the idea strong and flourishing. Parent-participants understand their children better; they understand the processes of education better; they find personal growth and challenge through the fuller use of their abilities.

It is sheer waste if we continue to limit the idea of unpaid parent participants as teacher aides to cooperative nursery schools. The idea is fully applicable to public school kindergartens.

Head Start has opened up still more possibilities. For reasons inherent in the war on poverty, the aide in a Head Start classroom is paid. Head Start has gone beyond one aide, however. It has tapped many additional volunteers and has shown how nonparent volunteers can help in a program. Preadolescent boys and girls have worked effectively, giving their services to the program. So, too, have nonparents from the immediate neighborhood and from the whole community. The young, the older, the aging, have all pitched in.

Head Start and co-ops have capitalized on a significant truth: There is talent in our population. We have a vast reservoir, especially of able women who are not using all the strengths they have to give. Public education has created this wealth. Public education ought to take advantage of its own creation.

The experience of both programs shows another fact: People want to help. The mechanization and impersonalization of our society push too many of us to the sidelines. Humans have a hunger to be needed, a hunger to contribute to a worthwhile cause. It may sound surprising, but people do not resent being asked to help. The fact is: They are grateful for the opportunity.

Aides in the classroom create problems, of course. Paid or unpaid, they must be oriented to the jobs they are to do and oriented to the children. Conferences must be scheduled after a day or a week's work, looking back at what has happened and planning ahead. Differences of opinion are bound to arise. Lines of authority must be continually clarified. Personality differences crop up. On occasion, individual volunteers, parent participators, or paid aides prove unsatisfactory; someone must handle the always difficult job of discharging a helper. Volunteers must be "disciplined." They need to understand that they

cannot be casual or late or absent simply because they are not being paid. They must understand that they have volunteered for a real job. The teacher must discipline herself, too. It is easy to palm off all the menial jobs on aides, easy to neglect to help them see the significance of their contribution, easy to give them the empty feeling of simply being used.

To avoid the inevitable human problems, the only way is to "go it alone" and have only yourself to think of—allow no other adult in the classroom who has to be taken into account. But a more constructive approach is to recognize the very pleasant side of working with an aide. It is like family life, and family living is usually the most rewarding kind. You need to talk things over. You need to take the teammate's point of view into account. You give a little, but you gain a lot.

We must end the foolish notion that one teacher alone can teach a classroom of young children, even a class of right size. A program becomes outstandingly better whenever there is more than one head, more than one set of eyes and ears, more than one pair of hands and feet. The best advice one can give a teacher of young children who has the right size class but who works alone is: Get yourself a helper! Get a paid aide if possible or an unpaid volunteer. Get parents. Get other adults. Get older children and adolescents. Get one helper. Get two if you can. No one teacher alone can do everything that a sensitive and stimulating program calls for.

This good advice to the teacher with the right class size becomes imperative when class size is overly large and cannot be reduced.

Three Less-Wise Approaches

Waiting lists are another way of achieving decent class size. The obvious difficulty is that of determining who shall be admitted and who shall have to wait. "First come, first served" up to the limit of twelve, sixteen, twenty, or twenty-five can lead to unseemly competition among parents. It is also a questionable approach if it means that the already privileged children of the most conscientious parents are always entered first.

In a sense, Head Start operates on a waiting-list basis, but with a reverse twist. Its economic criterion for admission means that Head Start serves first those who need the experience most. Communities could, with justice, follow this reverse twist. They could use economic level or psychological or developmental status or some other criterion of need. Most such standards, however, would require expensive, skilled, individual testing and would probably yield results difficult for a community to understand and accept.

Increasing the space to fit overly large class size is another common but inadequate solution. Overflowing kindergartens are moved to the gymnasium, to the stage of the auditorium, to a ballroom—but increasing the space misses the heart of the problem. The basic question is: How many other humans can the young child tolerate? With large class size, no matter how large the room, overstimulation and overexcitement and distraction mount. No matter how

large the room, the young child needs the personalization that can come only with right class size. The space standard—preferably forty-five to fifty square feet per child—can mean *reducing* the size of the group to fit the space you have. But even if you have all the space in the world, don't ever increase the size of the group to fill the space!

The third, and least sensible approach of all, is to *raise the school entrance age.* A school can reduce its eligible kindergarten population for one year by changing the entrance age from 4.9 to 5. The improvent in class size is obviously temporary. The solution, however, seems so simple that school after school hopefully asks: "What is the right school entrance age?" The answer by this time ought to be clear: "Most children are ready for school by about the age of three, if the school is ready for them." This answer seldom comforts those who want to raise the school entrance age.

First Grade Reading

Almost on a par with overly large class size as a disruptive force on under-six education is the heavy-handed way in which reading is taught in first grade.

There are as many methods of teaching reading as there are schoolbook publishers. Unfortunately, almost all of these methods have the same characteristics: They ignore individual differences, and they make children give up a part of being age six. The children must be quiet. They must sit to learn. First grade becomes a deadly serious, book-centered study hall. Reading is a separate, isolated subject matter which has nothing to do with the activities of the children. A child learns to read from a commercially produced book that is used nationwide. He learns the approved words or sounds or letters in a step-by-step progression.

The methods pay lip service to individual differences. Everyone claims to recognize that children will be ready for intensive help in reading at different times. But in common practice the real message is clear: *Too bad if you happen to be a late starter or a slow grower . . . We understand but: You fail!* First grades tend to have a fixed grade standard. A child either measures up or lands in trouble.

Obviously, it is difficult for teachers of children under six to influence what is done at the over-six ages. But until changes are made in the teaching of first grade reading, under-six education faces two sorry alternatives: We can fail children in kindergarten to save their failing in first grade; or we can make the same error first grades make—we can ignore individual differences, and exert pressure to get every child ready for intensive reading instruction.

Difficult as the job is, realism dictates that if you want to improve programs in nursery school, kindergarten, day care, or Head Start, you must think about first grade. To protect your own programs, under-six teachers need to know the promising practices in the education that lies immediately ahead and give these practices whatever support is possible in whatever ways are open to us.

Individualized Reading

Any method of teaching reading in first grade that honestly takes individual differences into account will lift some of the weight off under-six education. *Individualized reading* is one such promising practice.

In *individualized reading* youngsters choose their own reading books in terms of their interests and their assessment of their own reading abilities. A classroom offers the widest possible choice, ranging from preprimers and primers to teacher-made books to trade books. There is a reading time each day, but the children seldom come together in groups. Boys and girls choose what to read and read by themselves. The teacher works with youngsters individually, although not with each child every day. She notes a child's weaknesses and problems, and makes suggestions that are a prescription for that child alone. She notes interests and suggests new books that are especially right for that child alone.

In individualized reading, children choose what to read and read by themselves.

Individualized reading is the logical extension of the most prevalent present effort in first grades to take individual differences into account. Once first graders all read from the same page of the same book; the entire class was on the same word and the same line. The breakaway from this mass approach came when we divided children into at least three reading groups. Three groups are better than one. Twenty "groups"—each child reading individually—is a still more sensitive step. One child's reading level may be simply that of looking at

the pictures in books, but he "reads" at his speed at his own desk, unembarrassed, unpressured, unashamed. Another youngster in the same first grade reads a book customarily read by third graders. She, too, is at her own desk, unhindered, going at her own speed, and reading in the area of her interests.

Individualized reading is so logical a "next step," so sensibly rooted in everyone's awareness of how different children are, that it is catching on. *Individualized reading* fits in with some specific teaching methods more easily than others, but it is compatible with a wide range of approaches: with phonics, the Initial Teaching Alphabet, with linguistic approaches, with learning whole words. It is essentially a form of class organization rather than a specific teaching method.

There are problems. Some teachers and parents feel uneasy because the teacher cannot hear every child read every day. The child reads, but the teacher does not hear the youngster. Some teachers feel more important when they have a reading group. They have more management to do; they are more in the spotlight. An economic factor also militates against *individualized reading*. This approach makes use of a large assortment of varied materials. Publishers make less money and book salesmen must spend more time on individual sales of individual books than they do with mass adoptions and bulk orders. *Individualized reading* is catching on, but it has not swept the country.

We shall all benefit as *individualized reading* grows in popularity. Under-six children headed for such a program do not need to be "readied." Their first grade teacher takes them as she finds them, and helps them move on from there. No one has to jump through hoops to prepare them. *Individualized reading* frees the nursery school, kindergarten, day care center, and Head Start teacher to take their children as they find them. This is not pressure; this is challenge. This is not distortion; this is teaching.

Language Experience Approach

Any approach to functional reading in first grade — any method that does not demand that children give up their essential nature in order to learn — will also take some of the heat off under-six education. The method of teaching reading that is most in line with this goal is usually called the *language experience approach*.

The *language experience approach* is an activity-centered way of teaching. The children must first be involved in significant experiences in the sciences, in the social sciences, in the arts, or in the humanities. Then their reading grows out of the things they do. Reading is not isolated. It is not off in the blue. Reading is the inherent, symbolic aspect of real-life activities. The charts, the letters, the stories, the reports, growing out of the activities become the child's primers.

The *language experience approach* allows youngsters to be active, busy, social, independent humans. It allows them to be the distinct individuals they are. Children do as much reading and at whatever level their development makes right for them. The crux is the activity, not a preconceived, mass-

packaged kind of reading. A group of six-year-olds visits a newspaper office. On their return, some will read fiction and non-fiction stories that center around newspaper work. Others will dictate their own stories. The children all read at their own developmental level, but for each of them — as it would be for three-, four-, and five-year-olds — the experience is central.

The *language experience approach* to teaching reading is not new. It is as old as the activity school, at least as old as the 1920s. One cannot say, as one could about individualized reading, that the idea is catching on. But the idea does not die. The teaching of reading is so emotionally charged — and such great financial stakes are involved — that school systems go backwards and forwards, making little gains, suffering little losses.

One thing is clear, however: Under-six education will be more free to do its job whenever six-year-olds are permitted to be active children, involved in projects, free to talk and move about, free to use their hands and bodies, free to respond to the stimuli of real-life situations rather than simply to the printed symbols on a mass-produced page.

The Ungraded Primary

One organizational change affecting reading is making headway and can help nursery schools, kindergartens, day care centers, and Head Start. This is the *ungraded primary*.

The heart of the ungraded primary is the abolition of fixed grade standards until the end of third grade. All children are not expected to reach a definite reading level at the end of first grade as a precondition for their promotion into second grade. There is, therefore, no equivalent expectation that all children will reach a definite level of reading ability at the end of kindergarten as a precondition for their promotion into first grade. No teacher. Children with differing developmental rates or with special problems have four years to reach the standard set for "promotion."

This search for larger blocks of time is the logical extension of a development which began many years ago. Grades became year-long units rather than divided into two: 1A with promotion and retention; 1B with promotion and retention; 2A, 2B, and so forth. The gift of time is a tremendous aid in lifting off the classroom teacher's shoulders the load of tomorrow's expectations.

This gift of time is most fully experienced when the same teacher stays with her group for more than one year. The teacher has no reason to worry about next year's teacher — she herself is that teacher. In some ungraded primary programs, the same teacher stays with the children two or three years, not unlike the "little red school house" where the children had the same teacher for eight years.

Many fringe benefits flow from this continuity. The opportunity to build a continuing relationship with one teacher is significant, even for primary children. Parent-teacher relationships are also usually improved when adults have a longer span in which to come to know each other. Continuity gives teachers a better chance to understand each child and to find the approaches to teaching that will be most effective with each one.

Summer Head Start, where it still exists, brings some of this continuity to education. First grade teachers often are Head Start teachers, if there is a summer program. Not all are gentled by the experience. Some carry with them down into Head Start all of their first grade expectations, plus a frenzied determination to whip the children into shape before "regular school" begins. Many other first grade teachers, however, build a new sympathy for children as children. They develop a fresh awareness of the interrelationships between physical health and intellectual learning, between social and emotional health and learning. They appreciate the strengths of Head Start children and the lacks that the long years of poverty living have built into them. They learn to respect the efforts and strengths of parents who raise their children in poverty's grip. Their awareness of individual differences is deepened. These teachers often bring to their September first grades a fresh determination to make that grade more child-centered, right for all the children who come no matter what the children are like when the term begins.

It would be a real step ahead if full-day kindergarten teachers could remain with their youngsters through first grade. Nursery and kindergarten teachers in private schools would do well to explore the possibility of their staying with the same children over a two- or three-year span.

However, the carry-over of teachers, a wonderful fringe benefit, is not essential to the success of the ungraded primary. A change in attitude and expectation is. Unfortunately, in some schools, the term "ungraded primary" is adopted but the goal stays the same. The beginning years of school are ungraded, but they retain all the old pressures for reading. The new ungraded primary uses new groupings; it speaks of "ladders" for reading, but reading as a separate subject remains the core of the curriculum. When this happens, even under the new name, the kindergarten teacher and the nursery school teacher face the same old demand: "Get children ready."

Transition Groups

Not as promising as ungraded primaries for lifting pressure is the idea of *transition groups*. Children who have had a year of kindergarten but who are "not ready for first grade"—i.e., the first grade is not ready for them—are "promoted" to a transition group. Such groups come with many names. They all stand for a state of limbo. The child hasn't failed kindergarten; the child hasn't been promoted to first grade. The child is in . . . transition.

Transition groups could lessen pressure if they were a temporary placement. Promotion to a transition group ought not necessarily to mean that children have lost a year of their lives. If youngsters gain in their ability to meet "grade standards," whether through maturation or through special help, they should be able to leave the transition group and return to their original age-mates.

The more transition groups are an inflexible placement, the more they stand for failure in everyone's mind: the child, the parent, and the kindergarten

teacher. The old goal remains: Work to get the child up to first grade standard. The result is that kindergarten is but a diluted version of first grade.

Pressure would also lift a little if the transition group were seen as a helping way station rather than a dumping ground. Whenever a child is not ready for first grade, no matter how unreasonable the standards of that grade may be, the child is "different." The difference may be a perfectly normal, healthy kind: slower maturation, or strong, competing, constructive interests. The difference may stem from a troublesome source: a defect in hearing or vision, some emotional upset, or social inadequacy. The difference may be one that should not be tampered with; it may be something remediable; it may be a difference that cannot be corrected—one to which child and parents and school will have to make a permanent accommodation. A transition group at its best is a place for finding out. Fifteen children looked as if they could take the first grade that lies ahead; five seemingly could not. Why? Someone ought to know the answers and then do whatever is called for.

If transition groups are to serve this diagnostic-therapeutic "special study" purpose, their size should be small. Fifteen children would be a full class. Transition teachers should have easy access to supportive psychological, medical, and social welfare services. Given this study approach, given the right class size, given an aide and the needed back-up resources, a transition group would not be a failure-station. The existence of such a group could lessen the pressure on under-six education.

Unfortunately, these two standards—temporary placement, a diagnostic-therapeutic approach—are seldom met. The usual transition group simply staves off the failure that would come in regular first grade. This is settling for little. Children fail, but not quite as obviously as they otherwise would; kindergartens still have to push for first grade standards as doggedly as if no buffer state existed.

The Need for Dialogues

Whether or not there are helpful organizational arrangements, kindergarten and first grade teachers must talk together. A level of trust has to come into being which does not exist at the present time.

Kindergarten and first grade teachers ought to lunch together, where schedules make this possible. They ought to meet after school hours. They ought to ask for time in faculty meetings for joint planning. Somehow, on school time or on their own, kindergarten and first grade teachers need to build a regional pact, an "early education common market" of ideas.

This community of interest must develop if under-six education is to serve as the school's DEW line, as suggested on page 53. But there is an additional need—one of common defense. Both levels of education experience severe pressure to concentrate on formal reading. Both add to these pressures through their own imagination.

There is no conclusive evidence that direct drill on reading readiness in kindergarten makes any difference at all in later reading achievement. About 20 percent of America's five-year-olds do not go to kindergarten; their fifth year of life is bleaker for this, but their later reading does not suffer. There is no conclusive evidence that direct drill on reading readiness in kindergarten makes any great difference, even with disadvantaged children. What these youngsters need is a teacher who will look on them as total people, not simply as prereading creatures. There is reason to believe that even first grades need not center on reading as they do now in order to produce children who will be able to read and who will love to read.

No sharp developmental differences make the six-year-old a fundamentally changed child from the five-year-old. Nothing ought to be taken out of a well-equipped kindergarten room to turn it into a good first grade. New materials need to be added; materials should be more complex, but you add on — you don't take away. First grades need blocks as much as kindergartens do, only more of them. First grades need dramatic play corners as much as kindergartens do. First grades need easels, workbenches, sand, and clay as much as kindergartens do. First grades need their own private outdoor play areas as much as kindergartens do. Given a chance, many first grade teachers will say to their kindergarten friends: "You have exactly what I need: puzzles, toys, boards and boxes, dolls, a workbench, wheel toys." Kindergarten teachers will chime in: "And we need more of them!" Allied, working as a team, kindergarten and first grade teachers can wield greater muscle in getting what both must have.

Working With the School Administration ━━━━━━━━━━━

A third disruptive force hurting programs for young children is the widespread ignorance about early education among school administrators. This is *not* to say that administrators are stupid. They simply do not know. They obviously have shown wisdom and ability in other school jobs, but these have almost always related to older children. Few principals have taught children under six. Few have ever taken courses on the education of children under six. Principals have good heads on their shoulders and their hearts are in the right place. But nothing in their past prepares them for knowing the special needs of the very young.

Uninformed, it is easy for school administrators to throw young children in with the mass. The children are school children now — they are old enough to be treated like the rest. They must walk quietly in the halls; this is what school children do. The kindergarten children must come to school assemblies and fidget through speakers, films, programs that are geared to fourth grade. Worse, the kindergarten class must take its turn in putting on a performance for the PTA. The gross insensitivities are rationalized: "It makes them feel a part of the school." . . . "It helps them to feel big." The actual impact is one of herding young children, of manipulating them. Youngsters learn their own smallness and impotence.

There are errors of omission. Kindergartens cannot get sand — no other group needs it, so why should the five-year-olds? Kindergartens have no outdoor

equipment—other groups use the bare playground, why should kindergarten be special? There are no workbenches. You can't cook in the classroom. Water play is too messy. Trips can be arranged only if the kindergarten has a lawyer to present its case and an expeditor to see the forms through bureaucratic channels.

There are errors of commission. Team teaching, which may have virtues for older age groups, is imposed on the kindergarten. The main result with five-year-olds is to bring too many young children together at once and to segment the program into artificial subject-matter areas. Special teachers in art, music, physical education—valuable resources for older children—are imposed on the kindergarten. The result is that the day is splintered, and the specialists seldom know five-year-olds as well as does the regular classroom teacher.

Sometimes, administrative decisions are issued because there is a vacuum. No one objects. Teachers do not question why and do not offer better alternatives. Some do not even chafe under restrictive regulations. They may feel safer because of them, but their children chafe. Other teachers run scared. They translate "suggestion" into "requirement," "recommendation" into "regulation," "possibility" into "policy." They are unwilling to use the latitude that exists. They themselves lessen their own freedom.

Most teachers of young children are gentle souls. We are quiet. We are self-effacing. But if we stay too quiet, the pressures pile up. A good teacher must stand up and speak out for young children's needs. Without an advocate for young children, school is school is school—but seldom a good school for five-year-olds.

Lobbying for Young Children

Many a teacher has found her own way of standing up for children. She is especially fortunate if her principal regards her as the best kindergarten teacher in the world and wouldn't dream of making her do something she doesn't think is right. Her principal is not the final expert on young children; she is.

The key is the teacher's attitude. A good teacher respects her principal's position as "the boss"—responsible for the school as a whole, responsible to the superintendent and through the superintendent to the Board of Education and to the public.

The principal is "the boss," but the teacher is _the professional_ in her field. She is trained. She is a specialist. She has expertise. Most important today: She is rare. There is no over-supply at any age level of skilled teachers who know their business, and well-trained teachers of young children are especially precious. The teacher has every right to hold her head high, to feel a sense of dignity in the work she is doing. She has the right to assume—without the slightest doubt, unquestioningly—that her point of view, her ideas, her knowledge will, of course, be taken into account.

This does not mean that the teacher always wins the argument . . . at least, not the first time. But it does mean that she has the fullest right to be heard. And the greatest obligation to speak up. It means that no one, arbitrarily or in an authoritarian way, has the right simply to tell the teacher what to do. A professional cannot be pushed around.

Those who have the courage to stand up for what is right for children wisely combine charm with their courage. Making a case for young children's needs does not have to become a nasty business. The first step is to build friendly relationships. The teacher's job is to woo her principal . . . professionally. No one can spell out all the ways of doing this. We each do it in our own way. But the important point is: Do it! It is easy to become so immersed in our work with children that we forget that the success of that work often depends on the goodwill of others.

Clever teachers of young children do not let the principal sit in the office holding his or her head because little children make so much noise. They don't wait until the administrator stalks into their classroom for a state visit. They think up every opportunity to have "the boss" come to their room as often as possible: to say "hello" to the children, to admire some block building, to share midmorning juice. They want the principal to get used to the noise, the movement, the activity, the color, the sound, and smell of a kindergarten. Once the principal ventures in, the children become excellent ambassadors of goodwill. If "the boss" is a man, he can be especially sure of a royal welcome.

Teachers also think of myriad ways of making the program for young children reach out from their room into the principal's office. When the children bake cookies, a plateful always goes to the principal, the gift borne by proud children who are easy to like. Children dictate stories to be given to the principal. Their teacher mounts one of their prize pictures and they present it for hanging on the wall of the principal's office. The class contributes a clay masterpiece for "the boss's" desk. Like a Washington lobbyist, the teacher is not above "buying" a little friendship in high places.

Educating Principals

Good teachers also set out, quite consciously, to educate their principals. They drop into the office with a book or pamphlet on early childhood education, or with a marked copy of a professional journal in the field. Any number of teachers invite their principals to come with them to a local, state, or national meeting of the Association for Childhood Education International, the National Association for the Education of Young Children, or the Southern Association on Children Under Six. At these conferences, it is not the least bit unusual to hear a principal say, "My teacher made me come." But it is apparent that the principal is not the least bit sorry. Some smart teacher has helped the administrator to feel that the field of early education belongs to both of them.

Full understanding, of course, comes only through talks and discussions, face-to-face, with time to state positions and the reasons why. The teacher of young children should have as one of her theme songs: "I'm Just a Girl Who Can Say 'No.'" Or better still: "No, thank you." How about workbooks in the kindergarten? "No, thank you." Could the children put on a little show for the parents? "No, thank you." And "No, thank you" to films and assemblies in the auditorium, and to a host of other bright ideas that are fine for older children.

"No, thank you . . . and I'll tell you why." Because the "no" cannot stem from isolation, sheer negativism, or whim. The "no" has to be the occasion to make clearer what young children are like; what will benefit them because they are the way they are; what will do them little good or even some harm because of their stage of development.

The response isn't always "no," of course. If something must be done, it must be done. But ways can usually be found of doing it so that young children benefit and are not hurt. The teacher of young children, the good shepherd of her flock, is imaginative in suggesting ways to adjust mass rules, regulations, and school-wide procedures to fit the young. How can the entrance to school be handled so that it isn't a frightening or lonely time for little children? How can hearing tests and other medical exams be done in the most personalized, least traumatic way? How can fire drills be managed so that young children are not terrified? How can young children get the benefit of special teachers without allowing these resources to become an intrusion on a program and a cause of undesirable rigidity?

In these dialogues, the teacher is also the salesperson plugging away for new services and provisions that will especially benefit young children. These boys and girls need an outdoor play yard of their own, with their own special equipment. They need greater freedom than other groups to take field trips. They must have a staggered start to school in September. Report cards that may be right for the upper grades can be very wrong for young children; their teacher must have ample time for conferences with parents. Young children need more than one teacher in their classroom—there has to be one aide at least, either paid or a volunteer.

Young children should eat lunch in their classrooms, not in a crowded, noisy cafeteria. They need first claim on whatever psychological services exist so that problems can be nipped in the bud. They need busing arrangements that are not fatiguing or frightening. They need rooms that are acoustically treated. They need arrangements for dressing, undressing, and for hanging up their clothing that will foster independence—crowded, small, high hallway lockers fit the older ages but not these children.

The needed equipment, supplies, space, and arrangements will never come if the initiative rests with others. Not that others do not care—they simply are uninformed. The teacher must be the idea person, taking the lead in making a large public school right for its very smallest, youngest citizens.

Friends in Seats of Power

Public school principals, incidentally, are not the only ones who must become the targets of a "charm campaign." Ministers of churches that have weekday nursery schools sometimes are less than delighted with the mess, activity, and noise of the group. Little in their theological study is centered around the developmental needs and characteristics of children under six. There is no

reason why they should know what young children are like . . . initially. But they can be helped to learn.

Bus drivers—the driver of the private nursery school or day care center pickup, or the driver of the public school bus—are important targets. If the teacher does not help them to understand, they can do bad things when the children are in their care: yell at them, scare them, be gruff. And they can do bad things to the children when the youngsters are with you. Not understanding, drivers can easily spread wrong impressions about your program: "The children are wild." . . . "There is no discipline." . . . "They don't learn a thing."

Custodians can likewise make or break a program for young children. They can fuss endlessly over spills on the floor. They can disappear when heavy equipment has to be moved. They can turn sour and spread tales when equipment is broken. The same people, charmed, can so easily become scouts who spot cartons and boxes young children can use, and wheels, cans, and wood that would otherwise be thrown away. They can so easily become heroes who delight in making minor repairs and who feel proud because they have helped a program move along. They can become strong advocates of activity because "they know" little children need to work and be busy. They know, because someone helped them to know.

The school secretary can speed newsletters to parents or block them forever. Whoever does the purchasing can make supplies and materials flow or get lost in the bureaucratic jungle. Especially in the day care center, all of the food service people are important. Kitchen workers can warmly welcome young children into their domain or they can be like their refrigerators—cold.

Everyone tends to like little children. We have a lot going for us that can win support, interest, backing, and enthusiasm. The battle is half won before we even begin—but winning the second half depends on our lobbying efforts.

The Teacher as Citizen

A good teacher has to lobby outside the classroom, too, winning friends for children beyond the walls of the school. So many crucial decisions affecting boys and girls are made—*not* in the principal's office, *not* in the faculty meeting, *not* in parent-teacher conferences, and *not* at school board meetings—but in the city council, the state legislature, and in Congress.

Class size ultimately boils down to legislation and appropriations. Your equipment and supplies depend on legislation and appropriations. Whether you have a paid aide, whether you have immediate access to guidance help for every troubled youngster come down to legislation and appropriations. The expansion of basic programs for young children hinges on legislation and appropriations: free public education for four-year-olds, enough excellent child care centers, the growth of compensatory education programs.

In addition to the needed improvements in schooling, how young children live in our communities goes back to legislation and appropriation. Our country has too much bad housing. We have grave shortages in medical care. It is almost

impossible to find parks and play spaces that are right for young children. We have hunger in the United States; we have malnutrition. A teacher who cares about children has to be an active citizen.

Many teachers find "politicking" uncomfortable work. Persuading legislators demands aggressiveness, outspokenness, pushiness—qualities not very useful in our classrooms yet necessary in the public arena. But we each must do all we can because—make no mistake about it!—the legislative councilroom controls the classroom.

Fortunately, there are constructive steps each and every one of us can take, the shyest and the quietest among us as well as the most aggressive. One such step is to vote. We can be sure to know how each candidate stands on school issues *and* on the broader social issues that affect children's lives. We should never miss an election.

Second, we can all write to our representatives. We can become letter-writing supporters of children, corresponding with the mayor, governor, president; with our local representatives, and those in the state capital and in Washington; with the chairmen of key committees and with influential party leaders. There is no need for anyone to keep mum.

Then a third simple step: We can each join a professional organization which has an active legislative committee. Official legislative committees can say, more impressively than individuals can: "On behalf of 300 teachers . . . " Or "On behalf of 1,000 young children . . . " Committee members, charged with the job, can watch the progress of legislation as it inches its way through the law-making channels, alerting all the rest of us when our individual pressure is most needed. Legislative committees, made up of people who do have the energy, courage, and know-how to pound away on the needs of young children in legislative councils, are key arms of professional organizations.

Organizations of Teachers of Young Chidren

Many kindergarten teachers find that in-service meetings they must attend never focus specifically on young children. This lack contributes to their sense of isolation. The complaint is nationwide. "Faculty meetings center around older children; the younger ones are never discussed. I feel all alone." State meetings focus on older children: "Nothing is ever said that relates to the under-six age. I feel all alone."

The lack of organization also contributes to the meekness and silence of teachers of young children. It is difficult for the forgotten minority to speak out.

Some public kindergarten teachers have helped their situation by meeting informally on a citywide basis. Starting this way, a number of groups have managed to achieve an organizational status so that on in-service days they officially meet together. Many have persuaded their state education associations to include kindergarten programs in the annual state meeting.

Similar local moves toward organization have taken place among the teachers in private nursery schools, co-ops, child care centers, and Head Start.

Usually, wisely, these groups draw no line between private school and public school, between child care center and school, between Head Start and kindergarten. They include everyone concerned with young children, involving parents, pediatricians, social workers, and psychologists.

In addition, every teacher of the young should belong to at least one of the major early childhood professional associations: A.C.E.I., the Association for Childhood Education International; N.A.E.Y.C., the National Association for the Education of Young Children; and/or S.A.C.U.S., the Southern Association on Children Under Six. Their journals and meetings give teachers of young children a much needed sense of being a part of a larger force committed to youngsters' well-being.

Organization gives strength to the voice of the individual. The public hears better. But many other virtues emerge from belonging. Fighting the too-prevalent notion that school is school is school—a school makes no special ad-justments because children are young—is a lonely job. We are sure to find com-fort when we join up with fellow-workers. Initially, the sense of solidarity only il-lustrates the old motto that *misery loves company*. Soon, spirits rise and a better slogan takes over: *In unity there is strength*. A teacher goes back to her own school with new ideas that come out of organization meetings. Just as impor-tant, a teacher returns emboldened by knowing that others are also fighting for the same goals—better class size, more aides, less pressure on formal reading and reading readiness, more equipment, outdoor space.

The Primary School

As individuals and as members of organizations, teachers must be ready to react to the many new plans, new arrangements, and new administrative proposals abroad today concerning young children. A time of high interest in a field is also always a time for many faddish approaches. Teachers must help keep their schools off the "bandwagons," while giving their support to those new ideas that mean better schooling for young children.

One sensible administrative arrangement—the *primary school*—is slowly taking hold and deserves support. The primary school is an elementary school set apart, established specifically for the youngest children. Today's primary schools usually serve kindergarten children through second or third grade, and they sometimes include a Head Start group. The day may come when primary schools will extend down to nursery school, and certainly include a child care center.

Primary schools are frequently ungraded. Their teachers often stay with groups for more than one year. But their essence is that they are schools set apart. They are schools specifically for the youngest, whether "youngest" ends at Grade 2 or Grade 3.

Children gain directly by being in a small, separate building. There is less crowding, less herding, less confusion. The little school can be more tolerant of the noise young children make: the noise of their play, their conversation, their music, their carpentry. A separate building is more likely to have the outdoor

space and equipment young children need, not the ball fields, courts, and wide-open empty game spaces that are typical of total elementary schools. The errors of omission and of commission that occur when classes for younger children are added on below a regular elementary school are less likely to occur in the primary school. The younger children are *primary,* not afterthoughts.

The indirect advantages are equally important, however. The faculty is homogeneous—everyone who teaches in the school is an early childhood specialist. Everyone thinks and plans for young children. Of course, no law guarantees that the principal will be an early childhood specialist. (Some ex-high school football coaches become principals.) But in a primary school the principal is more apt to be a former kindergarten or primary teacher, and to have taken course work in early childhood education. Such a background does not automatically solve every problem or insure continuous smooth sailing. It does, however, provide an excellent base for discussion, and makes the presence of a sympathetic ear more likely.

The steady interest in year-round Head Start and other compensatory programs for young children may lead to more primary schools. Some of these new programs are housed in temporary quarters—the existing public school does not have the room to take them under its wing. The new programs are found in portable and temporary facilities on a school playground. They are found in rented space in stores and converted residences. Some are in public nonschool buildings: in libraries, recreation buildings, public housing. Some are in churches. These new "isolated" programs may be fortunate, not disadvantaged, because of their separateness. The building they are in is expressly for the children who use it. The program does not have to be toned down or modified to meet the varying needs of many ages.

We do well to remember that such separateness was one of the reasons for having nursery-kindergarten groups in the first place. The needs of young children conflicted with the needs of the older members who make up a home—older brothers and sisters, mothers and fathers, grandparents, visitors and guests. Sensitive parents sought a place young children could have as their own, a place where they could be themselves. This gain is threatened when programs for young children are housed in a multi-age elementary school, just as it was lost when young children spent all their time in a multi-age home.

Team Teaching and Mixed Age Groups

Two other recent administrative arrangements must be viewed with caution. Both move in the direction of exposing young children to masses and to crowds. Both hold the danger of more impersonalization, less warmth, and less intimacy for children. In our hectic, crowded, contemporary world, we ought to follow one general rule: Beware of *megalopolis.* Size corrupts. In all things, and especially for young children, the smaller, the better.

One of today's "new" ideas is team teaching. In the past, this term has been used to mean two adults, or more, working together within one room and with one group of children of the right class size. This was and is the nursery school

approach, a good one. But team teaching today has a different definition. It is more apt to mean that two or more classes are put together, with forty or fifty or sixty children, a mob rather than a group. The moveable walls are pushed back to create a barn rather than a classroom.

Some teachers like this modern version of team teaching. They enjoy the company of other adults. As class size mounts, they feel a pleasing, stronger sense of management and control. They like the fact that team teaching gives them a chance to teach their "specialty" but by "specialty" they usually mean music, science, reading, math—some subject-matter area, *not* the specialty of teaching young children. Despite the arguments in favor of team teaching, it is hard to believe that any arrangement that piles up the numbers is the right approach for little children.

Another idea being tried widely is that of mixed age groups. Some schools are persuaded that a spread of ages—three- and four-year-olds together; three-, four- and five-year olds; four- and five-year-olds; five-, six-, and seven-year-olds—opens up learning opportunities. The older, more mature, and advanced children have the chance to help the smaller, younger ones. The younger ones look on the "olders" as models; unconsciously, easily, they pick up countless facts, skills, and ways of responding. These schools also feel that the wider spread of abilities makes it more possible for children to "float," finding their own best levels of functioning. A child can work with more mature youngsters in some activities, with less able children in others.

One cannot quarrel with these virtues. Heterogeneity generally is a good thing for children. But the virtues of mixed age grouping are best achieved in the small, intimate class size that is right for young children. The vices soon outweigh the virtues when, as so often happens today, two or three groups are thrown together in a big open space to achieve the desired spread of ages.

Instead of increasing class size, a strong case can be made for *reducing* class size when a group includes a wide spread of ages. Obviously, the range of individual differences has been expanded. The adult's task of teaching each child has become more difficult. Some state laws regulating class size in private under-six groups recognize this fact. They specify that the standards that govern the youngest age included in the group should set the size for the group as a whole. Logic supports this point.

Unfortunately, this is not the common practice. Mixed age grouping is more likely to mean that moveable walls are pushed back. We create our private minimegalopolis within the school. One has to look askance at this way of achieving the values that can come from heterogeneous grouping.

Working With Parents

Pressure from parents is another rough abrasive on programs for young children. Parents are glad their youngsters are going to school, but the "school" they remember best is their own last year of senior high school. Most of today's parents did not go to nursery school or kindergarten. They buy the idea of

school for their young children—they think that school is good—but their reasons are not clear: Good for what? What kind of school? And why? Under what conditions?

Youngsters cannot act as the school's interpreters. Their answer to the old question—What did you do today?—is well known: "Played." Nor can any one-shot interpretation—one hectic PTA evening, one brief Start-to-School booklet—suffice to build understanding. Halfhearted and halfbaked efforts to build understanding are more apt to arouse parents' fears and confusions than to allay them. These efforts seem to indicate that their child was right—they do just play! At least, they certainly move around a lot and there is a lot of noise. "School is not the least bit the way it was when I went to school" . . . in twelfth grade!

Parents are buffeted by a steady stream of glib popular magazine articles about early reading, early math, early science. Their anxieties mount: "Teach them something. Teach them something tangible. Teach them something I can grab hold of." Teachers find themselves on the defensive: "We don't teach reading but we do teach reading readiness." . . . "We are getting them ready for first grade." . . ."We are putting on a show for Valentine's Day" or Easter or Hallowe'en or Mother's Day or Arbor Day!

Without active, continuous interpretation by teachers, the classroom becomes less and less right for the children who come. It takes on a design better fitted to older children—the children of many years ago who are fuzzily in the parents' memories, not the live young children of today.

Some Well-Established Techniques

Fortunately, there are many well-established ways of working with parents. Countless conscientious and committed teachers have broken the ground and shown how it is possible to win the support of parents for good practices.

The first step is always the same: We have to build good personal relationships with parents. Mothers and fathers must know their child's teacher; you must know the parents. Strangers cannot communicate. Strangers seldom feel trust and confidence. Distance does not lend enchantment; it only breeds suspicion.

Nursery school and day care center teachers have an advantage here. The age of their children and the need for the parent to make some arrangement for the child's enrollment generally necessitate an initial relationship. In Head Start, and especially in the public school kindergarten, nothing automatically brings home and school together in the most effective way. We need to build in machinery. The present kindergarten practice of one large meeting for all parents, a spring roundup, is totally inadequate, and much too impersonal. Parents need to meet the specific person who will be teaching their child.

Some teachers, sensing the importance of a personal relationship, come on the job early. They give a week or so of their time so that they can visit every parent at home or invite them to school. Their goal is simply to chat so that there is a chance of becoming friends. Other teachers, not as free to give the time, at

least telephone every parent to say "Hello" and to introduce themselves. This is a simple, good beginning, an easy gesture of friendliness.

Either approach requires that teachers know in advance the names of all of the youngsters who will be in their class. A teacher has a right to insist on this simple administrative service. The start of school for young children cannot be a cold, mechanical, confused, frightening melee: youngsters lined up in the hall, assigned to teachers arbitrarily at the last minute, an impersonal machinelike shuffling of humans.

The beginning days of school are critically important, too. Even some nursery schools, where the need for personal attention and for warmth is so apparent, make all children come at once and then bluntly tell parents: "Go home!" Opening days are exciting, emotion-laden days for parents and children alike. We must find ways of living them as sensitively as possible.

A staggered start to school is one sensitive approach. There is not one "Opening Day" but a series of them. A half, a fourth, a fifth of your group begins at one time; "opening day" for the balance of your class comes later. Nursery and kindergarten children feel much more comfortable and safe with such a staggered start.

Parents feel more welcome, too. They and teachers get a better chance to know each other. Some children need their parents with them for the beginning days or longer. Why anyone would deny a young child this comfort is beyond understanding. But parents need comfort, too. When we tell them to go home, they feel rebuffed. Fortunately, more and more teachers find it easy to say the more friendly words: "Stay!" . . . "Stay as long as your child needs you." . . . "I am glad to have you here." Parent is glad and teacher is glad. The parent has the chance to see a good program in operation. The teacher has the chance to know the parent.

Even good day care centers, where mothers frequently are under financial pressure to stay on a job or to find a job, make it clear to parents that they are completely welcome to stay at the start, if they can find a way of doing so. Sometimes parents delay taking a job for a short while until their child is well settled. Sometimes they can make provisions to arrive at work a little late for a few days to insure that their youngster makes a good beginning.

The telephone is a useful tool, especially at the beginning of the school year. We use it too little. If a mother cannot stay — if she is a working mother, has younger children at home, or if the school's anti-parent rules keep her out — a phone call from the teacher at the end of the day brings the parent information she is delighted to receive. More important, the phone call conveys the feeling-tone teachers of young children must build: *We are in this together* — the two of us, home and school. Friends, partners, we keep in touch; we support each other.

Parent Education

"Parent education" has gone out of style. The words have such a snobbish sound. But "parent education" is exactly the right term to describe what a teacher has to do about the happenings in her classroom, once school is under-

way. The teacher is there day after day; the parent is not. The teacher knows what goes on; the parent does not. The teacher has the information; the parent does not. There is no reason for holding back on educating parents about a school's activities.

We should use every technique. Again, the telephone can play a part. Our room meetings can center on the group's program. Bringing parents into the room as aides and participants so that they can see with their own two eyes is obviously an excellent approach. Still another good technique—a simple one, not used nearly as much as it should be—is a teacher's newsletter, a weekly or biweekly report to parents. The newsletter is the teacher's "State of the Union Message," but delivered more often than the president gives his. It is analogous to the reports to stockholders on which industry spends millions of dollars, but a teacher's newsletter does not have to be on glossy paper or bound or illustrated. It is the simple story of what the children have done and why they did it: the stories they have heard, the songs they have sung, the trips they have taken, the visitors who have come, the discussions that have gone on, the experiments the children have tried.

Parents need full information if they are to make constructive judgments about schools. We need the approval of parents if we are not to be everlastingly on the defensive. We need parents who will reinforce what the school is doing. We need parents who will supplement what the school is doing.

Our past relationships with parents (the lack of them) have been geared to keeping the peace. We have tried to stay clear of problems. We have kept away from parents on the theory that what they don't know won't hurt them. But, in fact, ignorance has hurt parents. It has hurt teachers and it has hurt children. We cannot go on this way.

Closer relationships may lead to temporary disagreements. Full and mutual understanding often comes argumentatively, the product of hard and long discussions. No one can say that life is pleasant and cheerful when differing points of view are expressed. But at least we know that life is healthier when feelings are brought out in the open. We have learned this with chidren; we no longer urge them to hide their emotions. Once we know what displeases or worries someone, we stand a chance of doing something about it. And we know from children, too, that problems seldom disappear simply because they are ignored. They are more likely to smoulder underground and then to explode at some unexpected time. Facing problems may cause headaches, but avoiding them can make us hurt all over.

There is, moreover, one reassuring note we must not lose sight of: Most parents are fully prepared to give wholehearted support to good education, once they have the chance to think and talk about it. What parents want for their youngsters is not different from what a good teacher wants. Our task is not the difficult one of "educating" parents to ideas they basically reject. We have the immensely more pleasurable challenge of helping them to see how their deepest convictions translate into school practice.

Parents are as sold as any teacher on the worth and importance and dignity of the individual. The individual, after all, is their child.

Parents are as sold as any teacher on the wholeness of humans, on the inter-relatedness of social, emotional, physical, and intellectual development. A home, after all, does all of these jobs.

Parents know about readiness and motivation, although they may not use these words. They have lived with their children, and have had to take these ideas into account.

Parents are sold, too, on the idea that experience is the best teacher. They only need help in translating this firmly held belief into "play," and "trips," happenings, and other school practices.

Parents know what young children are like. They know their activity. They know their egocentricity. They know their shyness. They know their noise level and their imagination, their messiness, their sociability. Parents have lived with their children since birth. But parents do not always realize that school can be *for* children instead of a device to reform them.

Parents hold the same broad goals for their children that teachers do. We are not competitors or opponents pulling in opposite directions. In the past we have been strangers. We have not talked together enough to discover our common understandings. Our separation has made it hard for the teacher to be a professional, using all she knows in her classroom. It will take time to close the gap, but it can be done and the effort is worthwhile.

A LOOK AHEAD

In the years ahead, programs for children under six will enlarge and expand. No one can predict the speed of the advance, but *more and more children are certain to come to school. They will come at younger ages. And many will stay in school for longer hours of the day, week, and year.*

School practices will change with this growth. One must hope that there will be new developments based on the steady accumulation of experience, and on leads from careful research replicated over and over again. Inevitably, however, if the past is any guide, some of the future changes will be shaped by less desirable influences.

Inadequate funding, for example, is sure to remain a part of the future scene. Some new practices will simply be accommodations, mere ways of coping with shortages.

Enthusiasms of the moment—fads and gimmicks—will be responsible for some new practices. There will always by the enticing promises: "We will teach your baby to read." . . . "This will give your child a superior IQ." And parents will always be susceptible because their hopes and their love ride so high in these early years. The future is bound to have its ample supply of ambition and greed, ignorance and naivete to insure an abundance of lures.

If the past is any guide, the availability of grants—money from foundations, money from the government—will also account for some practices. Millions of dollars invested in an idea can go a long way toward making it look like a new truth. In the years ahead, it will be difficult to know whether any new direction is a desirable development or an undesirable distortion.

Fundamentals That Must Not Be Lost

One safeguard against distortions is to be crystal clear on basic commitments. These are fundamentals that must not be lost no matter what new programs,

new styles, new names, new approaches come along. One's basic values can serve as a measuring rod for estimating whether new developments are good news or cause to be wary.

A Commitment to Childhood

Any program, new or old, should make manifest in all it does that it is pleased with the early years of life. It must not hold its nose, wishing childhood would end. It must not run scared, afraid that someone will hear childhood.

Conservationists have their societies: Friends of the Sea Otter . . . Friends of the Earth. Childhood also is in some danger of extinction. Young children are an endangered species. A good program will make a bold, defiant claim: *We are friends of little children.*

A good program, no matter what its name or style, will be proud of the youngness of its children. It will be geared to honest, real-life children—the noisy, messy, active, dirty kind. It will not be designed for sweet and sitting angelic, Hummel-like figurines. A good school enjoys youngsters as they are:

Imaginative.

Full of ego.

Animal-lovers, lovers of heights and hideaways, lovers of all cuddlies.

Devotees of sand and mud and water.

Gigglers, fast-riders, wrestlers, talkers.

A good program will thrill to childhood. It will oppose as mean any practice that tends to dry up the early years.

Programs for children should encourage active, imaginative play.

A Commitment to Parents

Any program, today or tomorrow, should be a friend of families, too. In a good school, parents never "drop off" a child the way one might drop off a suit to be cleaned or leave a car to be oiled and greased. Today, tomorrow, parents must know intimately their child's life in school, and they must help shape that life. Then, pleased with it, they can support and extend this life at home.

More than this, however, children need strong and healthy homes. The school that forgets its parents' well-being lets its children down. A country like India, beset by massive problems, could not escape facing this reality:

> Our programs found that they could not simply provide for the children alone, although that was greatly needed. They discovered that they also had to establish informal nutrition classes for the mothers. *And* adult literacy classes for the fathers. *And* sewing classes for the young women. *And* carpentry for the older boys. *And* family planning for the adults. *And* medical consultation and medical treatment. *And* so on and on and on. We found that if we cared only for the children, we would not get the best possible results from our investment in time and money.[1]

This is not wisdom for New Delhi alone. A strong child cannot come from a sick family. The best name we now have for any of our programs is "Parent and Child Center." Every program—ours now and whatever new ones the future may bring—should be in fact a "Parent and Child Center." Then children will have what children need: *a twenty-four hour school*—some of the twenty-four hours spent in a good group; most of the twenty-four hours spent in a strong home; all of the twenty-four hours a wonderfully educative experience from beginning to end, bound together—home and school—by an agreeable consistency.

A Commitment to Basic Human Qualities

Any program, new or old, should be concerned clearly and above all with people. It must not get stuck on trivia: little facts that are soon forgotten, little skills of passing importance, the petty, froufrou. A good school aims at basic human qualities, the attitudes that are a child's fundamental resource for sound living.

Today's children will be only young adults when the twenty-first century begins. Barring personal misfortune, natural catastrophe, barring man's stupidities, many of them will be alive in the year 2080. If the life span continues to lengthen, it is not inconceivable that a few will even see a second new century come, still alive in the year 2100. These are children with tumultuous todays, fated for churning tomorrows.

No matter what else it does, a good school will seek to build inner sturdiness into children. Call it a sense of security. Call it healthy self-concept. Or pride. Or confidence. A good school will teach in such a way that children rightly feel pleased with themselves: strong, able, self-respecting.

---

[1] S. Anandalakshmy, "Early Childhood Education in India," in *Early Childhood Education International*, vol. 1, edited by James L. Hymes, Jr. (Arlington, Virginia: Childhood Resources, 1973).

No matter what else it does, a good school will seek to build great enjoyment of people. It will fill each child's school hours with talking to others, thinking together, working with others—with arguing, listening, compromising, laughing. It will provide the experiences a child needs to live, happily and constructively, on a little planet packed with people.

A good school will seek to build into children a love of learning. It will be a center of richness and variety, full of luscious open invitations. Every day will be a mind-boggling, body-stirring, soul-moving confrontation.

Narrow schools—and we will have some tomorrow—set the three Rs as the limit of their task. Good schools teach the three Rs but do it in such a way that children carry away the three Ls: each child's love of one's self, love for other people, and love of learning.

A Commitment to an Ethical Culture

Any program, today or tomorrow, should be the fairest land of all for a child to live in. The classroom should be a gentle spot of earth: with kindness and understanding, with appreciation, and with forgiveness when that is needed. It should be a beautiful spot—with charm, color, light, fine taste. The classroom should be a busy spot, where useful, constructive, and important work is done, and everyone shares in it.

Good programs will have "climate control." The world outside may get out of bounds, but inside the world of the classroom, no child need know the idleness of a depression, the violence of a war, the driven fury of a rat race. Inside, no child need know the ugliness of pollutions, the hatreds, the putdowns, the hurts, the meanness. Inside a good school, children will feel, through their skin, what the good life can be.

They will feel it, and they will raise it to consciousness, having endless practice in thinking through the puzzling questions of human association: What is fair? What is decent? What is useful and helpful? What is appropriate? What makes life more pleasing for all?

The world has now—and will have even more so in the future—a frightening potential for both pain and pleasure. Life can be beautiful; life can be awful. It can be full of exaltation or mere existence, a source of dreariness or delight. Good classrooms will give children a sense of their power to influence the direction their small society takes, and an ethical sense so they know good ways to go.

Teachers of young children, in good schools today and tomorrow, will find their way to move on out beyond their classrooms to help establish a wider ethical culture. Strong children cannot come from sick homes. Nor can good schools grow in blighted communities. Nor can good homes and schools thrive in torn societies. The sicknesses in our world wage war on children. Teachers can, if they will, exorcise these from classrooms. Teachers can, if they work, help lessen these evils in the world . . . for the sake of children.

SELECTED REFERENCES

Looking Back at the Past

Braun, Samuel J. and Esther P. Edwards, *History and Theory of Early Childhood Education*. Worthington, Ohio: Charles A. Jones Publishing Co., 1972.

Early Childhood Education Living History Interviews. Tape cassettes. Arlington, Virginia: Childhood Resources, Inc., 1972.
        Dittmann, Laura. *Parent Education Over the Years*.
        Eliot, Abigail A. *America's First Nursery Schools*.
        Ginsberg, Sadie. *The Child Care Center Chronicle*.
        Goldsmith, Cornelia. *The New York City Day Care Unit*.
        Heinig, Christine. *The Emergency Nursery Schools and the Wartime Child Care Centers, 1933–1946*.
        Hooper, Laura. *The Professional Organizations*.
        Hostler, Amy. *O.M.E.P.: World Organization for Preschool Education*.
        Horwich, Frances. *Ding Dong School*.
        Osborn, D. Keith. *The Early Days of Project Head Start*.
        Stolz, Lois Meek. *The Kaiser Child Service Centers*.
        Taylor, Katherine Whiteside. *Parent Cooperative Nursery Schools*.
        Redefer, Frederick L. *The Progressive Education Association*.

Early Childhood Education Living History Interviews. Transcripts of the above tapes edited by James L. Hymes, Jr. Van Nuys, California: Hacienda Press/Southern California Association for the Education of Young Children, 1979.
        Book 1, *Beginnings* (Dittmann, Eliot, Taylor); Book 2, *Care of the Children of Working Mothers* (Ginsberg, Goldsmith, Stolz); Book 3, *Reaching Large Numbers of Children* (Heinig, Horwich, Osborn).

Greenberg, Polly. *The Devil Has Slippery Shoes*. The story of the Child Development Group of Mississippi (Head Start). New York: Macmillan, 1969.

Grotberg, Edith H., ed. *200 Years of Children*. DHEW Publication No. (OHD) 77–30103. Washington, D.C.: Government Printing Office, 1977.

Meek, Lois Hayden, ed. *Preschool and Parental Education*. 28th Yearbook of the National Society for the Study of Education. Bloomington, Illinois: Public School Publishing Co.,. 1929.

Nelson, Henry B., ed. *Early Childhood Education*. 46th Yearbook of the National Society for the Study of Education, Part II. Chicago: University of Chicago Press, 1947.

Osborn, D. Keith. *Early Childhood Education in Historical Perspective*. Athens, Georgia: Education Associates, 1975.

Snyder, Agnes. *Dauntless Women in Childhood Education*. Washington, D.C.: Association for Childhood Education International, 1972.

Steinfels, Margaret O'Brien. *Who's Minding the Children: The History and Politics of Day Care in America*. New York: Simon and Schuster, 1973.

Weber, Evelyn. *The Kindergarten: Its Encounter with Educational Thought in America*. New York: Teachers College Press, 1969.

The Present Setting

America's Children 1976: A Bicentennial Assessment. Washington, D.C.: National Council of Organizations for Children and Youth, 1976.

Auerbach, Stevanne. *Confronting the Child Care Crisis.* Boston: Beacon Press, 1979.

Austin, Gilbert R. *Early Childhood Education: An International Perspective.* New York: Academic Press, 1976.

Bardwell, Wilma, and Rose Spicola. *Early Childhood Education: Personalities.* Denton, Texas: Box 22547, TWU Station, 1975.

Consortium for Longitudinal Studies. *Lasting Effects After Preschool.* DHEW Publication No. (OHDS) 79–30178. Washington, D.C.: Government Printing Office, 1978.

Consortium on Developmental Continuity. *The Persistence of Preschool Effects.* DHEW Publication No. (OHDS) 78-30130. Washington, D.C.: Government Printing Office, 1977.

deLone, Richard H. *Small Futures: Children, Inequality, and the Limits of Liberal Reform.* New York: Harcourt, Brace, Jovanovich, 1979.

Evans, Ellis D. *Contemporary Influences in Early Childhood Education.* Rinehart and Winston, Inc., 1975.

Fein, Greta G., and Allison Clarke-Stewart. *Day Care in Context.* New York: John Wiley & Sons, 1973.

Goodlad, John I., et al. *Early Schooling in the United States.* New York: McGraw-Hill Book Co., 1973.

Gordon, Ira J., ed. *Early Childhood Education.* 71st Yearbook of the National Society for the Study of Education, Part II. Chicago: University of Chicago Press, 1972.

Hymes, James L. Jr. *Early Childhood Education: An Introduction to the Profession.* Washington, D.C.: National Association for the Education of Young Children, 1975.

_____. *Early Childhood Education: The Year in Review.* Van Nuys, California: Hacienda Press/Southern California Association for the Education of Young Children. Annually, from 1975.

Kenniston, Kenneth, et al. *All Our Children: The American Family Under Pressure.* A Report of the Carnegie Council on Children. New York: Harcourt, Brace, Jovanovich, 1978.

Keyserling, Mary Dublin, ed. *Windows on Day Care.* New York: National Council of Jewish Women, 1972.

Levine, James A. *Day Care and the Public Schools.* Newton, Massachusetts: EDC Distribution Center, 1978.

National Research Council. *Toward a National Policy for Children and Families.* Washington, D.C.: National Academy of Sciences, 1976.

Prescott, Elizabeth, and Elizabeth Jones. *The "Politics" of Day Care.* Washington, D.C.: National Association for the Education of Young Children, 1972.

Roby, Pamela, ed. *Child Care—Who Cares?* New York: Basic Books, 1973.

Ruopp, Richard, et al. *Children at the Center.* Final Report of the National Day Care Study, Vol. 1, Summary Findings and Their Implications. Cambridge, Massachusetts: Abt. Associates, 1979.

Steiner, Gilbert Y. *The Children's Cause.* Washington, D.C.: The Brookings Institution, 1976.

Weber, Evelyn. *Early Childhood Education: Perspectives on Change.* Worthington, Ohio: Charles A. Jones Publishing Co., 1970.

Zigler, Edward, and Jeanette Valentine, eds. *Project Head Start.* New York: The Free Press, 1979.

Children: Their Nature and Needs, and Their Life in School

Adams, Leah, and Betty Garlick, eds. *Ideas That Work with Young Children,* Vol. 2. Washington, D.C.: National Association for the Education of Young Children, 1979.

Allen, K. Eileen. *Mainstreaming in Early Childhood Education.* Albany, New York: Delmar, 1980.

Almy, Millie. *The Early Childhood Educator at Work.* New York: McGraw-Hill, 1975.

Baker, Katherine Read, ed. *Ideas That Work with Young Children,* Vol. 1. Washington, D.C.: National Association for the Education of Young Children, 1972.

Cohen, Dorothy H., and Marguerita Rudolph. *Kindergarten and Early Schooling.* Englewood Cliffs: Prentice-Hall, 1977.

Comer, James P., and Alvin F. Poussaint. *Black Child Care.* New York: Simon and Schuster, 1975.

Elkind, David. *A Sympathetic Understanding of the Child.* Boston: Allyn and Bacon, 1978.

Elkind, David, and Irving B. Weiner. *Development of the Child.* New York: John Wiley & Sons, 1978.

Feeney, Stephanie, and Dorris Christensen. *Who Am I in the Lives of Children?* Columbus, Ohio: Charles E. Merrill Publishing Co., 1979.

Fraiberg, Selma. *Every Child's Birthright: In Defense of Mothering.* New York: Basic Books, 1977.

_____. *The Magic Years.* New York: Charles Scribner's Sons, 1959.

Gardner, D. Bruce. *Development in Early Childhood.* New York: Harper & Row, 1973.

Greenberg, Selma. *Right from the Start: A Guide to Nonsexist Child Rearing.* Boston: Houghton-Mifflin, 1978.

Hendrick, Joanne. *The Whole Child: New Trends in Early Education.* St. Louis: The C.V. Mosby Company, 1975.

Hess, Robert D., and Doreen Croft. *Teachers of Young Children.* Boston: Houghton-Mifflin, 1972.

Highberger, Ruth, and Carol Owen Schramm. *Child Development for Day Care Workers.* Boston: Houghton-Mifflin, 1976.

Hildebrand, Verna. *Introduction to Early Childhood Education;* New York: Macmillan, 1976.

Hohmann, Mary, Bernard Banet, and David P. Weikart. *Young Children in Action: A Manual for Preschool Educators.* Ypsilanti, Michigan: The High/Scope Press, 1979.

Hymes, James L. Jr. *A Child Development Point of View*. Westport, Connecticut: Greenwood Press, Inc. Reprinted 1978.

_____. *Behavior and Misbehavior*. Westport, Connecticut: Greenwood Press, Inc. Reprinted 1978.

_____. *The Child Under Six*. Englewood Cliffs: Prentice-Hall, 1963.

Landreth, Catherine. *Early Childhood: Behavior and Learning*. New York: Alfred A. Knopf, 1967.

Leeper, Sarah Hammond, et al. *Good Schools for Young Children*. New York: Macmillan, 1974.

Moore, Shirley G., and Sally Kilmer. *Contemporary Preschool Education: A Program for Young Children*. New York: John Wiley & Sons, 1973.

Osborn, D. Keith, and Janie Dyson Osborn. *Discipline and Classroom Management*. Athens, Georgia: Education Associates, 1977.

Papalia, Diane E., and Sally Wendkos Olds. *A Child's World: Infancy Through Adolescence*. New York: McGraw-Hill Book Co., 1979.

Provence, Sally, Audrey Naylor, and June Patterson. *The Challenge of Day Care*. New Haven: Yale University Press, 1977.

Read, Katherine, and June Patterson. *The Nursery School and Kindergarten*. New York: Holt, Rinehart and Winston, 1980.

Robison, Helen F. *Exploring Teaching in Early Childhood Education*. Boston: Allyn and Bacon, 1977.

Rowen, Betty, Joan Byrne, and Lois Winter. *The Learning Match*. Englewood Cliffs: Prentice-Hall, Inc., 1980.

Ruopp, Richard, et al. *A Day Care Guide for Administrators, Teachers, and Parents*. Cambridge, Massachusetts: The MIT Press, 1973.

Seefeldt, Carol. *A Curriculum for Preschools*, 2nd .edition. Columbus, Ohio: Charles E. Merrill Publishing Co., 1980.

_____. *Teaching Young Children*. Englewood Cliffs: Prentice-Hall, Inc., 1980.

Spock, Benjamin. *Baby and Child Care*, rev. ed. New York: Pocket Books, 1977.

Spodek, Bernard. *Teaching in the Early Years*. Englewood Cliffs: Prentice-Hall, Inc., 1978.

Stone, L. Joseph, and Joseph Church. *Childhood and Adolescence*, rev. ed. New York: Random House, 1979.

Taylor, Katharine Whiteside. *Parents and Children Learn Together—Parent Cooperative Nursery Schools*. New York: Teachers College Press, 1967.

Working with Parents

Abraham, Willard. *Parent Talk*. Monthly leaflets. White Plains, New York: Grolier Educational Services.

Brown, Sara L., and Martha S. Moersch, eds. *Parents on the Team*. Ann Arbor, Michigan: University of Michigan Press, 1978.

Coletta, Anthony J. *Working Together: A Guide to Parent Involvement*. Atlanta, Georgia: Humanics, 1976.

Gordon, Ira J., and William F. Breivogel. *Building Effective Home-School Relationships.* Boston: Allyn & Bacon, 1976.

Honig, Alice S. *Parent Involvement in Early Childhood Education.* Washington, D.C.: National Association for the Education of Young Children, 1975.

Hymes, James L. Jr. *Effective Home-School Relations,* rev. ed. Van Nuys, California: Southern California Association for the Education of Young Children, 1974.

_____. *Notes for Parents.* Van Nuys, California: Southern California Association for the Education of Young Children, 1977.

Morrison, George S. *Parent Involvement in the Home, School, and Community.* Columbus, Ohio: Charles E. Merrill Publishing Co., 1978.

Parent Involvement. Five sound and color filmstrip sets, New York: Parents' Magazine Films, 1978.
>   Caldwell, Bettye M. *The Importance of Parent Involvement.*
>   Dumais, Mary Dean. *Viewpoints on Parent Participation.*
>   Gordon, Ira J., Thelma Harms, and Patricia Palmer Olmsted. *Working in the Classroom.*
>   Williams, C. Ray., and Ingrid McCowen Wing. *Parents and Policy Making.*
>   Winters, Wendy Glasgow. *Parent-Teacher Communication.*

Swick, Kevin J., and Eleanor Duff. *Building a Successful Parent/Teacher Partnership.* Atlanta, Georgia: Humanics, 1980.

_____ Organization and Journal Resources

Association for Childhood Education International, 3615 Wisconsin Ave. N.W., Washington, D.C. 20016. Journal: *Childhood Education.*

Bush Programs in Child Development and Social Policy. Five centers: Graduate School of Education, UCLA; University of Michigan; Frank Porter Graham Child Development Center, University of North Carolina; Yale University; Center for Early Education and Development, University of Minnesota. Quarterly newsletter: *The Networker.* Box 11A, Yale Station, New Haven, CT 06520.

Center for Parent Education, Burton L. White, Director. 55 Chapel Street, Newton, MA 02160.

Center for the Study of Public Policies for Young Children. High/Scope Educational Research Foundation, 600 North River Street, Ypsilanti, MI 48197.

Child Care Information Exchange, 70 Oakley Road, Belmont, MA 02178.

Children's Defense Fund, 1520 New Hampshire Ave., N.W., Washington, D.C. 20036. Newsletter: *CDF Reports.*

Day Care Council of America, 711 14th St. N.W., Washington, D.C. 20005. Journal: *Day Care and Early Education;* Newsletter: *Voice for Children.*

ECE Options, 255 North Road #110, Chelmsford, MA 01824. Monthly, for teacher educators.

Home-School Institute. Trinity College, Washington, D.C. 20017.

National Association for the Education of Young Children, 1834 Connecticut Ave. N.W., Washington, D.C. 20009. Journal: *Young Children.*

National Black Child Development Institute, 1463 Rhode Island Ave. N.W., Washington, D.C. 20005.

Parent Cooperative Preschools International, 20551 Lakeshore Road, Baie d'Urfe, Quebec, Canada H9X 1R3. Journal: *PCPI Journal.*

Southern Association on Children Under Six, Box 5403 Brady Station, Little Rock, AR 72215. Journal: *Dimensions.*

Today's Child, School Lane, Roosevelt, NJ 08555. Monthly newsletter.

United States National Committee of the World Organization for Early Education, c/o NAEYC, 1834 Connecticut Avenue N.W., Washington, D.C. 20009. Journal: *International Journal of Early Education.*

The Author

JAMES L. HYMES, Jr. has been active in Early Childhood Education since 1934, when he worked as a Research Assistant in the nursery school of the Child Development Institute at Teachers College, Columbia. Since that time he has been involved in every major program for children under six: in the WPA Nursery Schools of the depression years; as Director of the world's largest child care centers, the Kaiser Child Service Centers in Portland, Oregon during World War II; as a member of the National Planning Committee for Project Head Start.

A graduate of Harvard College, he earned his M.A, and Ed.D. degrees in Child Development and Parent Education at Teachers College, Columbia. He is the author of many books for both parents and teachers, including *The Child Under Six, Behavior and Misbehavior,* and *Effective Home-School Relations.* He has also co-authored with his wife, Lucia, two popular books for young children, *Hooray for Chocolate,* and *Oodles of Noodles.* His most recent publications are *Notes for Parents,* and a booklet produced annually that records the significant events affecting young children, *Early Childhood Education—The Year in Review.* He has been Professor of Education, specializing in Early Childhood Education, at the State University of New York at New Paltz, at George Peabody College for Teachers, and at the University of Maryland where he also directed the University's school for children under six. Dr. Hymes now lives in California and is a lecturer and consultant in Early Childhood Education.

Index

Published by
Charles E. Merrill Publishing Co.
A Bell & Howell Company
Columbus, Ohio 43216

This book was set in Oracle.
Cover Illustrator: Don Robison.
Production Coordination: Lucinda Ann Peck.

Photo Credits

Janice Beaty: page 167; Joan Bergstrom: page 56; CMACAO/Head Start, Columbus, Ohio: page 50; Paul Conklin: page 110; Celia Drake: page 144; Ron Engh: pages 83, 123, and 130; Julie Estadt: page 76; Larry Hamill: page 156; David S. Strickler: pages 1, 20, 65, 186, and 188; Elaine Ward, "Dimensions": page 36

Library of Congress Catalog Card Number: 80-82390
International Standard Book Number: 0-675-08063-0
Printed in the United States of America
1 2 3 4 5 6 7 8 9 10—85 84 83 82 81

Teaching
the Child
Under Six

Third Edition

James L. Hymes, Jr.

Charles E. Merrill Publishing Company
A Bell & Howell Company
Columbus, Ohio 43216